W9-DBO-283

Black Judges on Justice

BLACK JUDGES ON JUSTICE

Perspectives from the Bench

Linn Washington

THE NEW PRESS · NEW YORK

PUBLISHED IN THE UNITED STATES BY THE NEW PRESS, NEW YORK
DISTRIBUTED BY W. W. NORTON & COMPANY, INC., 500 FIFTH AVENUE,
NEW YORK, NY 10110

LIBRARY OF CONGRESS CATALOGING-IN-PUBLICATION DATA
WASHINGTON, LINN.
BLACK JUDGES ON JUSTICE : PERSPECTIVES FROM THE BENCH / LINN WASHINGTON.
P. CM.
ISBN 1-56584-437-8
1. CRIMINAL JUSTICE, ADMINISTRATION OF—UNITED STATES. 2. AFRO-AMERICAN JUDGES—BIOGRAPHY. I. TITLE.
KF9223.W27 1995
345.73'05—DC20
[347.3055] 94-27447

BOOK DESIGN BY CHARLES NIX

ESTABLISHED IN 1990 AS A MAJOR ALTERNATIVE TO THE LARGE, COMMERCIAL PUBLISHING HOUSES, THE NEW PRESS IS THE FIRST FULL-SCALE NONPROFIT AMERICAN BOOK PUBLISHER OUTSIDE OF THE UNIVERSITY PRESSES. THE PRESS IS OPERATED EDITORIALLY IN THE PUBLIC INTEREST, RATHER THAN FOR PRIVATE GAIN; IT IS COMMITTED TO PUBLISHING IN INNOVATIVE WAYS WORKS OF EDUCATIONAL, CULTURAL, AND COMMUNITY VALUE THAT, DESPITE THEIR INTELLECTUAL MERITS, MIGHT NOT NORMALLY BE "COMMERCIALLY" VIABLE. THE NEW PRESS'S EDITORIAL OFFICES ARE LOCATED AT THE CITY UNIVERSITY OF NEW YORK.

PRINTED IN THE UNITED STATES OF AMERICA

9 8 7 6 5 4 3 2 1

To those who have fought for what was right
when they could have turned away

Contents

Acknowledgments

About once a week the manila envelope from the University of Pennsylvania Law Library would come in the mail. The manila envelope would be filled with some new material on Black lawyers and judges. This material was from the files of Penn law librarian Ray Trent, who has compiled one of the nation's largest collections of information on Blacks in the law. Ray is a very low-key person who seeks no recognition. The only thing Ray asks in return for providing information is that the information he provides is used.

The information provided by Ray Trent was indispensable in the preparation of this book. Ray is one of a host of individuals who lent me their time and expertise. I extend my thanks to him and to Philadelphia Common Pleas Court Judge John Braxton, Pennsylvania Supreme Court Justice Robert N. C. Nix Jr., and former federal judge A. Leon Higginbotham Jr. for their counsel and encouragement. Thanks are also due to Temple Law Professor David Kairys, attorney Marci Lattimore, and my wife for reading draft chapters of this book and offering suggestions. Special thanks are extended to my wife and daughters for giving me the mental space to work and putting up with my moodiness. And thanks also to essential elements, like sunshine, for inspiration.

Preface

The Black judge is basically a twentieth-century phenomenon. America did not have its first Black federal district court judge, its first Black female federal judge, its first Black state supreme court chief justice or its first Black U.S. Supreme Court justice until after 1960.

The number of Black judges at the state and federal levels did not increase appreciably until the 1970s. There were 54 Black judges out of 7,000 state and federal judges nationwide in 1961, according to a survey published in the *Congressional Record.* By 1980 the number of Black judges had risen to 255. Today there are about one thousand Blacks among the nation's more than 30,000 judges at all levels of the judiciary.

As late as 1992 "firsts" were still being registered in statewide and local court systems across the country. One of those 1992 "firsts" was the appointment of Leah J. Sears-Collins to the supreme court of Georgia, the first African American female to sit on a supreme court in a former Confederate state. Speakers at the American Bar Association's special program in the summer of 1993 honoring "Women of Color in the Judiciary" decried the fact that only ten of the nation's federal judges were Black females.

By the 1970s the majority of Black jurists were located in the nation's large cities, a distribution pattern that continues today. Across the country few Blacks sit as judges at the appellate court level. The percentage of Black jurists nationwide is disproportionately low whether the standard of measure is the number of Black lawyers qualified for judicial consideration or the percentage of African Americans in the population of a given jurisdiction. The need for more diversity in the judiciary was noted even by the predominantly conservative federal judiciary. The 1990 report of the Federal

Courts Study Committee stressed, "The President and the Senate should endeavor to select the most qualified candidates for federal judicial office, irrespective of party affiliation, but with due regard for the desirability of reflecting the heterogeneity of the American people."

The main impediment to increasing the number of Black judges is not a lack of qualified Black lawyers but a lack of equal opportunity, according to studies on race and ethnic bias in the courts completed by nearly twenty states. "There is a pool of minority applicants for judgeships who were rated as qualified but who were not appointed," noted the 1991 report of the New York State Judicial Commission on Minorities.

Our presidents and governors, who appoint judges, and our political parties, which control the selection of judicial candidates, have failed to fairly increase the number of Black judges. During one year of the Reagan administration, more than a third of his court of appeals nominees received the lowest "qualified" rating from the American Bar Association, the organization that conducts nonbinding competency reviews of federal judicial nominees for Congress. None of these lowly rated nominees was Black.

Black judges account for less than 3 percent of the nation's judiciary although African Americans constitute 12 percent of the nation's population. For example, as of 1992 in the state of New Jersey, of the 925 judges serving the state on the supreme court, superior court, and tax court, only 50 were minorities (38 Blacks, 12 Hispanics, no Asians and no Native Americans). On the opposite end of the nation, in the liberal Northwest, the 1990 report of the Washington State Minority and Justice Task Force noted that racial minorities constituted close to 11 percent of the state's population, but only 4.3 percent of the state's 371 judges were minorities. All but two of the minority judges in Washington state are located in King County, which houses the state's major city, Seattle.

The studies on race bias in the courts are unanimous in the assertion that increased representation of minorities as judges is an important goal for the judicial system. The presence of minority judges can have substantive impact in placing a "chill" on overtly racist behavior. The presence of minority judges has a symbolic importance that inspires minorities to excel and dispels the myth that nonwhites have a place only on the lower rungs of society. "Democracy and representativeness are inextricably intertwined," the Washington state report stressed. "The most common means for ensuring adequate representation is for the composition of the judiciary to constitute a cross-section of the community."

Introduction

Black judges are rarely highlighted, even in books on Black history. For example, the widely circulated Black history book *Before the Mayflower* by Lerone Bennett makes scant mention of pioneering Black judges like Robert Morris, who became the nation's first Black judge when he was appointed to the magistrate's court in Boston, Massachusetts, in 1852 and Jonathan Jasper Wright, who made history in February 1870 when he was elected to the Supreme Court of South Carolina, the first Black to hold such a post.

Historically one of the least-heard voices in our justice system has been that of the Black jurist. The book I embarked on would help fill the void in the literature on Black judges by presenting the experiences and insights of distinguished jurists. It could also aid in the perennial debate about crime in America by presenting the informed insights of Black judges on the front line of the so-called war on crime.

This book is based on fourteen in-depth interviews with Black jurists on the federal and state benches, on both the trial and appellate levels. Those interviewed include liberals and conservatives and men and women from cities large and small; some are new to the bench while others have served for decades. The jurists in this book are known for their innovative approaches to sentencing, for their attempts to deal with the inequality that challenges their courtrooms every day, and for safeguarding the constitutional rights of all Americans irrespective of race. The judges are representative of the Black judicial experience, yet they are individuals, the diversity of whose beliefs proves that no group is monolithic in attitude.

Judges, as a group, seldom speak out publicly on issues such as racism within the court system and flawed anticrime policies, due to a combination of custom and ethical-code restrictions. I had expected the interviewees to be guarded in their remarks but they were surprisingly candid. One of the things I heard frequently while doing the interviews for this book was how glad the jurists were finally to have the opportunity to express their feelings.

Federal appeals court judge Timothy Lewis was one of the few Blacks appointed to the federal judiciary by President George Bush. Bush was second only to his immediate predecessor Ronald Reagan in compiling the most racist federal judicial appointment record since 1949, when Truman named the first black federal judge. Lewis is appreciative of Bush for boosting Lewis' meteoric rise in the federal judiciary, yet he pointedly stated he would not let his "appointment become a defense for the indefensible."

All of those interviewed for this book felt there is a need not only for more Black jurists but for more Blacks in decision-making positions within the justice system. African American and other nonwhite employees are underrepresented at all levels of the justice system nationwide, according to a number of studies on race and ethnic bias in the courts released in recent years. On a more positive note, the jurists contend that the increasing presence of minorities at all levels of the court system has improved the quality of quotidian justice.

George Crockett Jr., a retired Detroit judge and U.S. Congressman, says without equivocation that Black people have never received "equal justice" in America's criminal courts. The "quantity and quality of justice is in direct proportion to the size of one's pocketbook and the color of one's skin," says Crockett, an octogenarian. "And this is so, not because the written law says it shall be so, rather it is so because our judges, by their rulings, make it so."

While critical of the role racism plays in the justice system, none of the judges interviewed in this book—whether liberal or conservative—is soft on crime. Conservative federal district court judge Henry Bramwell bluntly calls for "stricter enforcement of criminal laws" and criticizes Black leaders for "not fully" addressing the problem of crime in the Black community. Yet liberal, former federal appeals court judge A. Leon Higginbotham Jr. also advocates fair and efficient law enforcement. "When you have a system where someone can be arrested for a violent crime and not get to trial for a year, that's not efficiency," Higginbotham states.

These Black judges also expressed a lack of sympathy for Blacks who try to use racism as an excuse for the commission of crimes, though the judges are deeply attuned to the role racism plays in sustaining the conditions that foment crime. "Racism plays a role in crime, yet racism is often used as an excuse for the commission of crime," observes Mississippi State Supreme Court Justice Fred Banks. "An individual can overcome racism."

Many of the judges have served as both public defenders and prosecutors, and respect the need to protect the rights of defendants as well as the rights of victims. They note that the poor and people of color are disproportionately the victims of crime in America, and that these victims are too often treated curtly by the justice system.

The experiences of these jurists provide an intimate, oftentimes disturbing portrait of the American justice system and the judicial process. Memphis trial court judge Joseph Brown says the criminal justice system is not operating in a manner that can correct the crime problem because there is a "total lack of coordination" of resources. Brown places most of the blame for this lack of coordination on judges who place more concern on confining criminals than addressing the causes of crime. Brown has won international acclaim for his innovative sentencing, which requires the offender to finish high school, register to vote, and do community service, such as cleaning up public housing projects.

The jurists detail systemic inequities and abuses that are rarely discussed in public. One of these abuses is prosecutorial misconduct, which manifest itself in subtly biased choices about which cases to bring to trial. This quiet form of brutality is both more pervasive and more damaging than beatings by police. Philadelphia Common Pleas Court Judge Theodore McKee tells of repeated clashes with prosecutors who seek prison for nonviolent Black offenders and probation for violent white offenders on the claim that whites from good neighborhoods and home structures are better candidates for leniency.

McKee and other judges are critical of prosecutors who eschew their mandated duty to "seek justice, not merely to convict." The convict-at-all-costs attitude pervading too many prosecutors' offices subverts ethical standards and the law itself.

Popular anticrime policies such as mandatory sentencing are ridiculed as failures by the jurists, who note that these draconian policies have succeeded in overcrowding prisons but not in cutting crime.

Mandatory sentencing has proven to be incredibly counterproductive, in that violent felons—rapists for example—are released early to make room for nonviolent drug users who are serving mandatory sentences.

Whether liberal or conservative, these jurists say America continues to ignore the connection between poverty and crime, attacking the symptoms of crime and not its causes, thereby imperiling public safety and economic solvency. The nation's politically expedient crime policies waste dollars and don't make sense. The $19,000 average annual cost across the nation to feed, clothe, and house one inmate exceeds the annual salary of a minimum-wage job and tuition at many top universities. "We just don't have enough money to keep using the criminal justice system as our main weapon in fighting crime," says Los Angeles Municipal Court Judge Veronica McBeth. "One of the things I've done is tell people we have to do things a different way."

Washington, D.C., Superior Court Judge Reggie Walton, a hardliner on crime, says his biggest frustration as President Bush's assistant "drug czar" and senior White House crime advisor, was his inability to get that administration to address issues of poverty, unemployment, and poor educational opportunities. Decreasing poverty would cut the crime rate more than increasing penalties for committing crimes, Walton says.

These jurists provide workable solutions to the problems confronting the justice system. Their insights provide the way. The question remains: Does America have the will to implement their solutions?

The Black jurist has a unique vantage from which to critique the quality of the justice in America both in terms of the justice system's daily operations and of the development of the law within the system. Unlike their nonminority counterparts on the bench, most Black jurists have not only battled injustices in society on behalf of their clients as lawyers, but, in order to attain their positions, most have themselves had to confront and conquer racism in the legal system.

For over two decades on the bench, New York City Supreme Court Justice Bruce Wright has paid a dear price for speaking out against instances of overt racism within the judiciary, like class biases which color judicial decision making as much as facts. Long before he published his eye-opening book *Black Robes, White Justice: Why Our Legal System Doesn't Work for Blacks* in 1987, Wright's battles against judicial racism led to administrative slaps such as being buried on night court duty and undergoing retaliatory disciplinary proceedings. He has also had to endure dirty tricks, such as tampering with his mail, and has repeatedly experienced death threats. Wright is an equal opportunity critic, lashing out at racist white jurists and "Afro-Saxons"—Black judges who turn white psychologically when they don the Black judicial robe. A septuagenarian, Wright continues his self-appointed quest of trying to "reform" the court system and "rehabilitate" his fellow jurists—a mission that makes him an "Afro-Greek Sisyphus."

Black judges are subjected to burdens not placed on their white colleagues, including persistent questions impugning their ability to be impartial. Defendants in a Philadelphia union race discrimination case once requested that A. Leon Higginbotham Jr., then a federal district court judge, withdraw from the case on the contention that he could not be fair because of his scholarly writings on racism in American law. Higginbotham, in his opinion rejecting the recusal request, which is now utilized in many legal textbooks, stated that white litigants are now going to have to accept the new day where the judiciary will not be entirely white...Black judges should not be required to disparage Blacks in order to placate whites who would otherwise be fearful of our impartiality."

Due to personal experiences with racism most Black jurists feel a special responsibility for improving the quality of justice in the judicial system, and protecting the constitutional rights of all citizens. Federal appeals judge Damon Keith is one of many Black jurists who steadfastly advocates protecting the rights of all citizens irrespective of color due to his own personal experiences with racism as a U.S. soldier during World War II. In the early seventies Judge Keith ruled in favor of a white radical group that was challenging a wire tap initiated by the Nixon administration. For Keith the issue was simple: everybody has to follow the law, presidents and paupers alike. Because Keith upheld the letter of the law, he was sued by Nixon, becoming one of the few judges ever sued by a sitting president. The wire tap was ruled illegal because it had been initiated without the required judicial approval.

Although frustrated with the flaws in the justice system, all of the fourteen jurists stress their commitment to the system, saying it is the best hope America has for fulfilling the goals articulated in the preamble of the U.S. Constitution. Los Angeles Municipal Court Judge Veronica McBeth says, "The thing that is good about our system is not that it is what it hopes to be, but that it hopes to be something better. That's what makes it important...It's the goal itself of fairness and justice that makes it important."

Part I

OPENING ARGUMENT

A. LEON HIGGINBOTHAM JR.

"Black judges do bear burdens that white judges do not."

Before Leon Higginbotham retired in 1993, even U.S. Supreme Court justices called him the "conscience" of the federal judiciary, in part for his ability to reconcile legal precedent and judicial impartiality with an enormous empathy for the victims of injustice.

His fame, however, extends far beyond the bench. While Higginbotham is best known for his three distinguished decades on the federal bench and for his extraordinary career as a legal scholar, he has also made a name for himself as a dedicated humanitarian committed to an array of causes, from improving the lives of America's homeless children to drafting a constitution for South Africa.

After cofounding Philadelphia's first major Black law firm in 1954, the Yale Law School graduate went on to become the first Black and youngest person ever named a commissioner of the Federal Trade Commission. Higginbotham became the first Black judge of the U.S. District Court for the Eastern District of Pennsylvania when he was appointed by President Johnson in 1964 and the second Black to serve on the U.S. Court of Appeals for the Third Circuit when he was appointed by President Carter in 1978. He served as chief judge for both the Eastern District Court and the Third Circuit.

Lawyer, jurist, law professor, college lecturer, legal scholar, Leon Higginbotham holds over fifty honorary degrees from various institutions of higher learning and has garnered hundreds of other awards and honors. A bibliography of Higginbotham's scholarly writings that was published in 1991 listed over sixty works, including the groundbreaking book In the Matter of Color: Race and the American Legal Process—The Colonial Period.

Ironically, Higginbotham's most widely read work was the letter he wrote in the fall of 1991 to newly appointed Supreme Court Justice Clarence Thomas. The open letter was initially published in the January 1992 issue of the University of Pennsylvania Law Review *and sold nearly twenty thousand copies—more than any other article in the history of the review. Excerpts from the letter, a masterful recounting of the legal racism against Blacks and a counterpoint to Thomas's criticisms of the civil rights movement, were carried by newspapers across the country.*

Leon Higginbotham's retirement from the U.S. Court of Appeals for the Third Circuit in March 1993 was the end of an era, an event that occasioned literary retrospectives and months of celebrating. In retirement, his hectic work pace has not decreased but his focus has shifted from judicial opinions to legal briefs and the preparation of another book.

Higginbotham was interviewed on October 20, 1993, in his office at Paul, Weiss, Rifkind, Wharton & Garrison, a law firm in New York City.

No Black judge should work solely on racial matters. I think that would be a profoundly inappropriate abstention, and I would further argue that there is no special role that a Black jurist should play. But while I do not think there is a special role to be played by Black judges per se, Black judges do bear burdens that white judges do not. This is true in cases involving discrimination, where some people will question a Black judge's impartiality.

There was one case that I heard—a race discrimination case involving Local 542 of the Operating Engineers Union—where the law firm for the union asked me to recuse myself from the case. This recusal was based on their contention that I could not be fair. The claim arose because I had spoken publicly about injustice against Blacks. Through my scholarly research into the history of law, I had become a key advocate for the advancement of civil rights and thus, they argued, I could not be impartial.

I think that is a classic example of the different burden imposed on Black judges. No one would have asked a Jewish judge to recuse himself because one of the litigants was Jewish, or a white judge to recuse himself because one of the litigants was white, but a Black judge who had written as a scholar on race relations—suddenly this law firm argues that he should not be able to sit on cases involving Blacks?

One of the many ironies in that Local 542 case was that I had handled many trials where this law firm was representing Black clients and my rulings, based on the law, resulted in millions of dollars in fees for this firm. But when the case involved a predominantly white union charged with racial discrimination, this firm felt I should instantly disqualify myself. I refused their request.

So, I think that as a Black judge, you have the burden of being continually monitored by people who expect you to not say anything about America having been unfair or unjust. And to the extent that you don't do that, that you don't keep quiet, you become suspect.

A minority judge should be very much concerned about the aspects of the system that work unreasonably and harshly against Blacks and others who have historically been treated unfairly by the system. If minority judges do not speak up about those conditions, it gives an imprimatur of satisfaction and approval.

I think the saddest opinion ever written in the history of this country by an African American judge is an opinion written by Justice Clarence Thomas in a case called *Hudson v. McMillian.*

This was a case of a Black prisoner who was assaulted by two prison guards while he was shackled at the legs and hands. The prisoner's dental plate was cracked during the beating, his teeth were loosened, and his lips were burst. Despite these clear physical injuries, Clarence Thomas says that this unprovoked beating was not cruel and unusual punishment. Cruel and unusual punishment is barred by the Constitution's Eighth Amendment.

Fortunately, Thomas was in the minority on the *Hudson* case and wrote the dissent. Justice O'Connor, writing for a seven-to-two majority in *Hudson,* said that this type of assault is intolerable in a civilized society. How could it be that someone from Pinpoint, Georgia, doesn't know how devastating brutality can be?

A Black judge, like all judges, has to decide matters on the basis of the record. But you would hope that a Black judge could never be as blind to the consequences of sanctioning violence and racism against Blacks by state officials as Clarence Thomas was in the *Hudson* case, and as tragically blind as he has been in several other cases.

Opponents of Thomas's confirmation to the Supreme Court were not questioning the color of his skin. They were questioning the color of his soul, his heart, his concern about the weak, the poor, minorities, and Native Americans.

I suppose my motivation for writing my open letter to Judge Thomas was a product of my background. When I entered Yale Law School in September 1949, there was not one Black federal judge in the entire country. In fact, the first Black federal judge in the United States was not nominated for appointment until October 1949. The appointment of Judge Bill Hastie was an overwhelming victory. That single appointment said that those of you who are talented and care can also have a part in the adjudicating process, not merely in litigation. So, I have always been sensitive to the extra burden that I think comes with the minority judge's territory. What motivated me was the fact that Clarence Thomas had taken some positions which seemed incomprehensible to me.

In October of 1987—I believe it was October 6—Judge Thomas wrote a letter condemning Thurgood Marshall for a speech he had given on how we should celebrate the bicentennial of the U.S. Constitution. Justice Marshall had merely said we should recognize that the greatness of the Constitution lies in its evolution, because in the beginning, when it was originally drafted, Blacks and women were excluded from its protections. Thomas said that Justice Marshall's comments were exasperating and incomprehensible. He said Marshall's comments were an assault on the bicentennial of the Constitution and on the very foundations of the Constitution itself. You wonder how a Black person could say that. My daughter suggested the following. (She has a Ph.D. in clinical psychology.) She says Clarence Thomas must think that if he had been living in 1776 he would have been the confidant of Thomas Jefferson, or if he were living in 1787 he would have been the confidant of James Madison, and therefore, from that perspective, Marshall's comments were an assault. Thomas never considered that in all probability he would have been Jefferson's or Madison's slave. We must always recognize the historic fact that despite all of the other good things Jefferson, Madison, and those others did, Blacks were in a status called slavery when the Constitution was drafted. You have a right to condemn the Constitution for its omission in the beginning.

One of my comments in the open letter to Clarence Thomas is that he fully thought that by condemning Thurgood Marshall he would receive a certain adulation from the right-wing conservative structure, and he succeeded.

Thomas had been very critical of the NAACP [National Association for the Advancement of Colored People] and other civil rights organizations that helped open doors to Blacks, including efforts that overturned Virginia laws that would have prevented Thomas, who lives in Virginia, from living in a predominantly white neighborhood or marrying a member of another race. And in fact Thomas lives in a predominantly white neighborhood and is married to a white woman. He wouldn't have been able to do this legally had it not been for civil rights organizations and their leaders, who he has harshly criticized for, as he phrased it, "bitching, moaning, and whining." Had it not been for the NAACP, isn't it highly probable that Justice Thomas might still be in Pinpoint, Georgia, working, as many of his relatives did for decades, as a laborer? Had it not been for the NAACP picketing, protesting, and politicking for the Civil Rights Act of 1964, would the Monsanto Chemical Company have opened their doors to him in 1977?

I am a person who has experienced the racism that conservatives like Thomas disingenuously contend is no longer a problem, both in its current manifestations and in its legacy. I also know the law can be very, very effective in constraining racist conduct, which again, is something conservatives contend is inappropriate for the law to do.

Take the Civil Rights Act of 1964 as an example. Prior to 1964, when I took my children on a trip throughout the South, there was no hotel or any major motel chain where we could stay, and we couldn't eat in most of the restaurants. When I was president of Philadelphia's NAACP chapter, and the NAACP's national convention in '60 or '61 was held in Atlanta, we had to stay at the all-Black colleges Clark, Spellman, and Morehouse. But if you went back to Atlanta after the passage of the '64 act, you would have found that Blacks now had access to the best hotels in town without any serious problem with public accommodation. It would be foolish to say that within a few years the poison of centuries of racism had been eradicated, but the conduct had changed. The law, the Civil Rights Act of 1964 specifically, made a big difference.

The law's ability to change conduct cuts across the question of race. Look at the number of women who were attending or who were faculty members of the University of Pennsylvania in 1964. It was minuscule. If you look at it now, it has increased manyfold. This increase is not because women have suddenly become brighter. That's not the reason for the increase. The increase came only after a whole series of laws were passed prohibiting discrimination on the basis of gender. These gender discrimination laws were spin-offs of the legislation prohibiting race-based discrimination. These laws have caused many extraordinary changes in this country.

Clarence Thomas was someone who had faced obstacles and was able to overcome them, and that's what American society should be about. But Thomas's position is, "Look, I made it and therefore everyone else can." It is this inference that causes a lot of confusion. Very few people can jump up in the air and stay up and float for as long as Michael Jordan can. You cannot assume that every Black has Michael Jordan's dexterity.

It's a wonderful testament to have persevered and overcome obstacles—whether it's Clarence Thomas or Leon Higginbotham. But it would be a tragedy to assume that everyone else can do it, and to further contend that there are no more systemic impediments blocking a person's ability to overcome obstacles. And that's the tragedy of Clarence Thomas.

Thomas's sister was a hard-working person who was forced to go on welfare for a couple of years. Why would he go and publicly condemn his sister for being on welfare when she never had received any of the benefits that he had? The truth of the matter is, she stayed in Pinpoint, while he had the good fortune of moving to Savannah. It has all of the gender implications of many backgrounds, where the men get the education and the women clean the dishes. So, I think the tragedy of Clarence Thomas is not that he made it—I'm delighted that he made it—but that he besmirches his own sister. I think that is a profound revelation of his character.

These positions Thomas had taken and statements he had made caused me to worry about him. I felt that someone should at least put the American jurisprudential record in perspective. And look at what he's done on the Supreme Court. His record during his first term reveals a judicial philosophy centered around a couple of tenets: narrow interpretation of the Constitution's liberty provisions, surrender to the whims of the executive branch, and an acute aversion to protecting civil and political rights in general.

Some say, let Clarence Thomas be himself—but you can't let him be himself. What if he had joined in on the 1857 *Dred Scott* decision, agreeing with the conservative majority that the Black man had no rights that whites were legally bound to respect? It is worse when a Black joins in opinions that are damaging to Blacks, because it legitimizes the wrongness.

Judged by any standard, I think Clarence Thomas has just been a very, very poor Supreme Court justice. And I think that this whole dialogue that says you can't criticize Blacks—particularly not Black conservatives—is misplaced. There is a profound difference between Thurgood Marshall and Clarence Thomas, and I think that is a fair comment to make, since Clarence Thomas is taking, as he consistently has, positions that are 180-degrees different from those of Justice Marshall.

We have been trying to resolve a very tricky problem in this country: To what extent is it appropriate for one Black to criticize another Black? If one Black criticizes another, does that impugn the whole race?

I think it may have been true at one stage in our development. One had to be leery of that. But now, when Blacks hold such powerful positions, being Black should give you no immunity from anyone's criticism—including Black people's. Of course, you have to make your critique in a responsible way—but if a Black mayor or a Black judge or a Black public administrator acts in a way that is seriously harmful to Black people and harmful to the weak and the poor, no one is obligated to remain silent. You should avoid making purely personal criticisms and try to point out that anyone who takes this position causes real harm.

My letter to Clarence Thomas was a way of saying to him, "You've got an extraordinary opportunity to be a truly great justice, but in order to do that, you have to take these factors into consideration." I didn't write that letter because I think I'm some kind of spokesman for Black Americans. I wrote Justice Thomas as an individual, an individual witness to the frustration that is felt when the rights we won through bitter and often bloody struggle are slowly chipped away by the courts.

I have been accused of sour grapes. Some have contended that I criticized Thomas simply because I thought I should have gotten the Supreme Court nomination. That's not true. I would have advised any president not to appoint anyone over the age of fifty-five to the

Supreme Court. I was older than fifty-five when the Thomas nomination was made, so I never considered myself a viable candidate for that position, on the basis of age alone. It's better to appoint a somewhat younger judge. My commentary on Judge Thomas was not at all related to my being considered a candidate for the Court.

I received only one letter from a Black federal official—he happened to be a retired judge—who criticized me for having written the letter. He said it was a case of sour grapes. That person was Judge Bramwell, one of the other judges in this book. Besides his letter, I think every federal official that I talked to or who wrote to me was 100 percent supportive of my letter to Thomas.

I think in all honesty, if Thomas were white he would not have gotten a scintilla of consideration for the position. Obviously Bush knew that it would be virtually impossible for the Senate to "Bork" a Black nominee, no matter how conservative; hence Thomas's nomination. But I was astonished that someone with Thomas's record, his lack of judicial, legal and scholarly substance, be he Black or white, would have been appointed to the Supreme Court.

Thomas's judicial career should also be put in the context of the Reagan era. Thomas was one of only two Blacks appointed to a federal appeals court from 1980 to 1992, during the terms of Presidents Reagan and Bush. During that twelve-year period, Reagan and Bush appointed 115 judges to the courts of appeals and only two were African Americans. Thomas was one; the other was Larry Pierce, an outstanding federal judge from the Southern District of New York. But when Pierce was appointed to the Second Circuit, he was close to sixty and it was known that he would be retiring in five years. Five years later, he was gone, and he was not replaced by an African American.

Now if only two of 115 judicial appointees are Black, then it's fair to say—as I did in an op-ed article I wrote for the *New York Times*—that Black federal judges are becoming an extinct species. There have only been a handful of Black federal judges. The first Black appeals court judge was Hastie, in 1949, and the first Black district judge was not appointed until 1961.

What are the implications of the Reagan-Bush appointment practices? Well, look at who can now become chief judge of a district or circuit court. That position is based on seniority. I became a chief judge because I was appointed during the sixties and had seniority. Constance Baker Motley became a chief judge in the Southern District of New York because she was appointed during the sixties. The same is true of Damon Keith, who like me, was appointed to the district court during the Johnson administration.

The Blacks who rose to hold major managerial positions as chief judges had been appointed ten to fifteen years before they came into those positions. If for twelve years you deliberately appoint few Black judges, you aren't going to see any Black chief judges ten to twenty years from now. Most of the Black judges on the courts of appeals were Carter appointees, and by 1993 most of them were over sixty-five.

There has been an extraordinary diminution in the number of Blacks in the federal judiciary. I think that Bill Clinton will have an opportunity to do something about it; but if he doesn't, it's clear that Black federal judges will become an extinct species—and I use the term "extinct species" deliberately.

If you look at the Southern District of New York in 1980, when Reagan took office, Constance Baker Motley, Robert Carter, Larry Pierce, and Mary Lowe Johnson were among the active federal judges. All of them now have senior status. [Senior status is a semi-retired category where the judge does not carry a full case load.] In the Southern District of New York, Reagan did not appoint one African American to replace them. Reagan didn't appoint one Black to the largest federal court district in the nation during his eight years in office.

Take a look at the Sixth Circuit, which includes Ohio, Michigan, Tennessee, and Kentucky. Reagan and Bush appointed fifty judges to the district courts and the circuit court in the Sixth Circuit, and not one was Black.

During the Reagan-Bush terms, there was a deliberate effort to diminish the number of Blacks on the federal courts. There was no effort to have pluralism in the courts.

The advantage of pluralism is that it brings a multitude of different experiences to the judicial process. It is not that there is an absolute correlation between being a woman or being Black and casting a particular vote. But I think that, generally, someone who has been a victim of racial injustice has greater sensitivity to the court's making sure that racism is not perpetrated, even inadvertently. There are lots of white judges who fully comprehend this. Some comprehend it more clearly than some Blacks.

Having minorities on the court achieves two things: it proffers an enrichment of experiences that one can use to examine issues, and it gives the public the impression that the process is not exclusionary.

Greater pluralism would help reduce the race and gender bias in our court systems. I think the movement to investigate and correct race, gender, and ethnic biases in the court system is clearly appropriate. Often these biases are inadvertent.

In 1968, when Chief Justice Earl Warren appointed me to work on a task force on representation in the federal jury system, it was an eye-opening experience. The first question I asked was, "How do court clerks identify potential jurors?" Someone said, "Oh, the clerk goes to some of the most distinguished citizens, people beyond reproach, and asks them to send in the names of potential jurors." In other words, if someone belonged to a country club, they would send members of their country club; if someone belonged to the Knights of Columbus, they sent people from the Knights of Columbus. But no one who was being asked was from the NAACP, the Urban League, or the National Baptist Convention. So you were getting juries that were completely unrepresentative.

We put a whole series of requirements in the statute in order to improve the process. For example, we pressed to use voting lists, which tend to provide a more representative group than ad hoc selection by "distinguished citizens," which may be inadvertently discriminatory. But then another problem arises because of the lower proportion of registered voters among minorities, so we had to focus on that also.

Another advantage in having a pluralistic judiciary is that different people are open to input from different quarters. For example, I knew people from country clubs, but I also knew people who were the ministers of the Philadelphia Black ministers group. I knew about people like Leon Sullivan and the senior Bill Gray, the father of former congressman Bill Gray. As a member of the judiciary, I could make sure that there was some input from the African American community.

Racism has been perpetuated by the courts, due in part to the insensitivity of judges, who in the federal system were all white and male prior to this century.

One of the most wretched decisions ever rendered by the Supreme Court against Black people was the 1896 decision in *Plessy v. Ferguson. Plessy* was the decision where the Court upheld the "separate but equal" doctrine of Jim Crow segregation laws. This single decision legitimized the worst forms of race discrimination, which then became the law of our nation for six decades. The majority that issued this decision was composed of four Ivy League alumni and graduates of Harvard and Yale law schools. The tragedy of *Plessy* was not that the justices had had the wrong education or had attended the wrong law schools. The tragedy is that the justices had the wrong values, and those values poisoned this society for decades. In all probability pluralism would not have changed the result of the deliberation, but with a more pluralistic Court, Justice John Harlan would probably not have been the sole dissenter in *Plessy*.

There are those who contend that having more Blacks in the judiciary, more women, Hispanics, or Asians, is affirmative action and is therefore objectionable. I think that affirmative action is an issue about which reasonable people can disagree. However, it seems to me that the people who are so much against affirmative action on race are perfectly willing to tolerate, if not openly embrace, affirmative action in other areas.

Here is the classic example: a man named Dan Quayle. He was vice-president under George Bush. Do you know how former vice-president and former senator Dan Quayle got into the University of Indiana Law School? He got in on affirmative action, on a special admissions program designed for people who did not score well on the LSATs and had substandard grades but had promise. The law school wanted to experiment, and they accepted twenty students under this program, sixteen of whom were white. So, Dan Quayle gets in on a *special admissions* program and nobody's arguing that he shouldn't be a lawyer now.

There's an awful lot of hypocrisy. Some of the people who are arguing most hostilely against affirmative action are the individuals who have benefited from it in other ways. Dan Quayle is a vocal critic of affirmative action. He is perfectly willing to deny others the opportunity that enabled him to advance in life.

There is another example I like to use: When I entered Yale Law School in 1949, there were five minority students enrolled in Ivy League law schools. And the reason why you had only five was not because Black people in '49 were so stupid and whites were so smart. It goes back to a whole level of advantages, opportunities, and access.

Look at the policy of most universities to give admissions preference to the children of alumni. If in 1990 a university announces that, all other things being equal, it will give the benefit of the doubt to children of alumni, that is affirmative action in its most positive fashion. And I have yet to hear any college president announce that they do not have a special interest in recruiting children of alumni.

Now if you start putting this in a greater context, the implications are staggering. Up until the 1950s, there was not one Black student at any major college in the South. This exclusion was statutory. So if you're going to talk in terms of children of alumni, you're really saying that individuals who have been the beneficiaries of past oppression should continue to enjoy their relative advantage.

I just can't believe that all the men who have gotten into the American corporate complex have gotten there because men are so superior to women. I think a lot of them have gotten there because of the "old boy" network, and the only way you can deal effectively with old boy networks is to be concerned about promoting pluralism. You have to be concerned about getting women in.

The critics of affirmative action don't recognize the importance of pluralism in our society. For 180 years no woman sat on the United States District Court for the Eastern District of Pennsylvania. And no woman got on the court until President Carter nominated Judge Norma Shapiro. Is a court better off if it has diversity, if it has women and people from a variety of backgrounds? I submit to you that it is.

Lots of people like to think of barriers and oppression in terms of vigilante groups or individuals who wear hoods like the KKK. But the most devastating, massive oppression that has occurred in America has been perpetuated by individuals who do not openly hate like the KKK but who refuse to open doors they have the opportunity to open. I have learned that the person who is polite can be a more of a barrier to equal access than the one who calls you a nigger.

My wanting to pursue the law and become a lawyer was the result of an encounter with one of these civil, *polite* individuals who refused to open a door. If it wasn't for this individual, I might have become an engineer.

This man's name was Charles Elliott. Elliott was the president of Purdue in 1944, the year I entered as a sixteen-year-old freshman. There were only a dozen Black students when I entered Purdue, which at the time had about six thousand white students. All of the Black students lived in a separate house. We slept in the attic, which had no heat. After two winter months of going to bed every night wearing earmuffs, four pairs of socks, and sometimes a jacket, I decided to go talk with the university's president.

I felt we should at least have heat, and I asked President Elliott if we could have a section—a segregated section—of any dormitory on campus that had heat. Elliott looked me in the eye and told me the law didn't require the university to allow colored students in a dormitory. He told me either to accept things as they were or leave—leave immediately.

As I walked back from the president's office, a thousand thoughts were going through my mind. Why would the law not permit a dozen good Black kids to sleep in a warm dormitory? The law had been very effective in the draft for the war going on at the time. Some of my very best friends had been drafted, went to war, and died for our country. At the moment Elliott was telling me about the law, thousands of Black soldiers were overseas, fighting, putting their lives on the line, to make the world safe for democracy. Yet here at home the legal system that proclaimed equal justice for all wouldn't allow a dozen Black boys who hadn't done anything wrong to sleep in a warm dormitory.

I realized after talking with Elliott that I couldn't go into engineering. I realized that I had to try to challenge the system. That experience with Elliott convinced me that victims of oppression have to be willing to fight their own battles. You have to take the burden of challenging the unfairness and injustice in the system or the system is not going to change.

Because of particular rulings on the law, the Elliotts of our nation have been able to gain refuge in their refusal to open the doors they could have opened. It seems to me that the judges in our nation have taken positions that were not required legally and that worked to the specific disadvantage of Blacks. The law gives a legitimization to prejudice. When it is the law, it has an aspect of moral authority in the eyes of many people, so a person who challenged the law is almost immoral, even though the law is unjust.

The rulings of judges to the specific disadvantage of Blacks is a similarity America shares with South Africa, whose judicial system I studied extensively when I was consulting the South Africans who were drafting their new constitution. I argued that the South African judiciary should have independence and substantial powers to review legislative acts. I also have been working with Nelson Mandela to make sure that the election process is as fair as possible and that the people are as well informed as they can be. That is an extraordinary task because 80 percent of the people in South Africa have never had the right to vote in a national election.

The judicial system under apartheid was a parliamentary supremacy system where no court had the right to find a parliamentary statute unconstitutional. Under that system, the courts of South Africa had no right to exercise the power that the United States Supreme Court has exercised since *Marbury v. Madison*, when Chief Justice John Marshall declared that the court had the inherent power to review legislative acts and declare them unconstitutional.

In South Africa you could have had the most liberal of judges, as liberal as any in the United States, as liberal as a Brennan or a Marshall, but if the parliament passed clear and precise legislation that was discriminatory, then the declaration by parliament could not be overturned.

Even with this profound difference of parliamentary supremacy, both America and South Africa have dealt with the issue of racism, and both have, at times, it seems to me, gone beyond the letter of the law to legitimize racist conduct.

The U.S. Supreme Court's decision in *Plessy* gave a racist construction to the Fourteenth Amendment. Incidentally, *Plessy* is a decision that all Supreme Court justices now say was wrongly decided, including the most conservative, such as Kennedy and Rehnquist. Yet under any comparison, the United States has a grossly superior system because of the constitutional protection. Here we were able to get *Brown*. We were able to get *Miranda*. We were able to get "one man–one vote" through the courts. This is the basic difference in terms of the limited leverage the courts in South Africa have had in contrast to the more liberal leverage we have had. We have to be very careful not to overstate the similarities between South Africa and America.

Three hundred years ago, 90 percent of the Blacks in this country were slaves. As slaves, they were denied the right to marry, denied the right to education, and doomed in futurity to suffer enslavement themselves, as would all their heirs. Now, there is no slavery.

Two hundred years ago, when our Constitution was being written, there were no Blacks in the political process. Now, forty members of the United States Congress—thirty-nine in the House and one in the Senate—are Black and have very significant voices. They don't control the Congress. They don't have a majority. But looking at a whole series of areas, you can see there have been some significant developments and changes.

When I was in law school *Plessy* was viewed by most people to be the law. It hadn't been repudiated. When I was in law school, there were only two Blacks who were members of Congress. They were Dawson of Chicago and Adam Clayton Powell of New York. So, again, I think that I would have to honestly say that there have been some significant changes.

Have we eradicated racism? Far from it. We have got very serious problems, but I think that what we have done by using the rule of law, by not having a second civil war, is instructive of what the law can be utilized for.

Look at the Civil Rights Act of 1964, the Voting Rights Act of 1965, and the Housing Act of 1968: the law has become a potential ally of Black people in the United States in many ways.

I think that in South Africa, the law will be able to deal with many of the issues of patent racist conduct. But there is something that the law will not be able to do in South Africa—something it has not been able to do in the United States either—and that is to find promptly some way to eradicate poverty, to ensure good health care, to ensure adequate housing. It is tragic that one-third of the African Americans in the United States have not been beneficiaries at all of the so-called civil rights revolution. I think that about one-half have been.

In South Africa the toughest problem is to come to grips with the pervasive differential in economic options, and it's going to be a long haul. I think that is one of the reasons why Nelson Mandela was talking about investment in South Africa on his last visit here. Nelson Mandela was talking about foreign companies putting money in South Africa because, unless you get a whole industrial infrastructure that is broad enough to support a large number of people, five years from now—I don't care who is in the government—there are going to be very serious problems.

We in America have not learned the importance of attacking poverty and providing economic opportunities. We continue to ignore the connection between poverty and crime. We have problems with crime and violence today in large part because we have not adequately addressed the issues of poverty and economic inequity.

During the late sixties, I was vice-chairman of the National Commission on the Causes and Prevention of Violence. President Johnson had appointed the commission in 1968, after the assassinations of Martin Luther King and Robert Kennedy. President Johnson was very fearful about the future of America. He was concerned about whether we were going to solve all our political differences with a handgun. Were we going to use violence as our main method of resolving disputes, or were there other ways that the problems could be dealt with?

The commission issued its report in 1969. We wrote about fourteen volumes. If you read that report, it seems as if we had a perfect vision of what could happen in America.

To me, one of the most salient passages in the report was the part that reads: "In man's long history, when other great civilizations fell, it was less often from external assault than from internal decay. Our own civilization has shown a remarkable capacity for responding to crisis and for emerging to higher pinnacles of power and achievement, but our most serious challenges to date have been external. While serious external demands and dangers remain, the greater threats today are internal: haphazard urbanization, racial discrimination, disfiguring of the environment, unprecedented interdependence, the dislocation of human identity and motivation created by an affluent society, all resulting in a rising tide of individual and group violence. The greatness and durability of most civilizations has been bound and determined by how they responded to these challenges from within. Ours will be no exception."

We suggested twenty-four years ago that America was at a critical crossroads. All of our predictions have been confirmed. Conditions have in many ways gotten worse. We have failed to come to grips with problems that are solvable.

I think that the Reagan-Bush years were a massive repudiation of all of the thoughtfulness that had gone into the final report of the violence commission and the two other major commissions of the sixties, the Kerner Commission and the Katzenbach Commission. We are now beginning to suffer the consequences of thinking that these problems could be solved by simplistic labels like "volunteerism" or by cutting off funds needed for our cities.

I think that the majority of Americans looked upon these commissions' commentaries as if they addressed the problems of another planet. When you look into the disintegration of cities, you notice as well the vast number of voters who don't live in these hard-core urban centers. Obviously, people in Bryn Mawr, a very affluent area outside of Philadelphia, don't live in the poor Black area of North Philadelphia—and they imagined there to be some kind of curtain that kept these problems that were so malignant, so destructive of our society, from spilling over out of North Philly and into the suburbs.

Look at Florida. I am dreadfully sorry there's been all this violence against tourists down there, but now people in Florida are worried because tourists are being killed. They didn't seem to be worried when this violence was taking place within the Black communities and within the poor communities.

The commission's message was not taken seriously, I think, because of the widespread belief, promoted fundamentally by the Republican Party, that we could build a whole series of iron-curtains and take care of the people of suburbia, take care of the people outside of urban areas, and not worry about what happens in the cities and poor communities. Since the Eisenhower administration we have been willing to spend billions of dollars on interstate highways, airports, sewer systems, and all the other things that made suburbs possible. We have not, however, been willing to spend the equivalent to help our urban communities, and we are now paying a devastating price for that choice.

The commission expressed concern about handguns. (In fact we wrote an entire volume on this issue.) And you have to consider the milieu in which we published this report: It was a time when the John Birch Society and others were willing to portray any critique of America as Communist—or the ranting of the lunatic fringe. Now you see, for example, Governor Florio of New Jersey winning support for the control of certain firearms. Gun control is going to increase significantly. I think we are now beginning to realize that closing our eyes to a problem doesn't solve it. But at this point we've lost two decades in the fight against crime. Every year our chances of success diminish.

Any pathology has to be approached on many levels, and when anyone says you can control crime by doing only *x*, you know their solution is probably too simplistic. President Roosevelt used to say, "We will fight the enemy by land, by sea, and by air." And that was a proclamation of reality: you can't use one type of armed force only and win a war—you need a combination. If you really want to get a handle on crime, you've got to do a whole series of things.

First, you have to have fair and efficient law enforcement. That is as important as any of the components. When I say efficient law enforcement, I mean from the date of arrest to trial to the correction facility.

A system is inefficient when someone can be arrested for a violent crime and not be tried for a year. Suppose that person is out on bail and commits more crimes, so that when he finally does come to court he has, say, three charges of armed robbery against him. His sentence will probably not be three times higher, so, just from a managerial aspect, our court system has not been efficient—particularly in the state justice systems.

When I lived in the Germantown section of Philadelphia, I encouraged a neighbor to go into business. He was a mechanic, and I encouraged him to open an auto repair shop. I said, "Look, if you open your shop, I certainly am going to be pleased to get my gas there and recommend people." I wanted Blacks to get into business. After he had been in business for about two or three years, and he was doing well, someone broke into the station and got caught taking my friend's tools. My friend—I think his name was Keene—went to the police station and identified the suspect. By the time Keene got back to his gas station, the kid was out on the street. A couple of weeks later, the same kid is found in the station again, trying to steal stuff. Now, I can't think of a worse message about the efficiency of the criminal justice system.

So, one of the first things we have to talk about is not merely fairness, although that is important too, but efficiency. We have to have efficient law enforcement administration or else we risk giving the robbers, the rapists, and the murderers more sympathetic treatment than the victims.

We also have to do something about unemployment. Poor people have to have a chance of getting a job. And you have to work on having a quality education system, a quality health system, and adequate housing. Only a combination of all of these factors will help decrease urban violence.

Frederick Douglass said that hungry men will insist on eating and outraged men will seek revenge. Those who oppose an economic system that provides jobs, decent housing, education, health care, and justice are perpetuators of urban and racial violence. And the racism that pervades our society explains in part our failure to implement a multiphase approach to combating crime. My research has convinced me there is a connection between slavery and racial polarization today.

There are some parallels between the decisions of the current conservative majority on the Supreme Court and the Court during Reconstruction and the later part of the last century in terms of the deliberateness in striking down civil rights laws. In 1989, in a dissenting opinion on a case where the Court overturned longstanding employment-discrimination standards, Justice Blackmun wondered whether some of his colleagues still—or ever had—believed that race discrimination against nonwhites was a problem in our society. That same year, Justice Marshall said that thirty-five years after the *Brown* decision, we were back where we had started; we had come full circle.

There has been a retrenchment by the Rehnquist Court concerning civil rights. This Court has become increasingly conservative, and whenever there has been a choice, this Court has not supported the precedents on civil rights matters. The Civil Rights Act of 1991 was passed by Congress because of the narrow rulings of the Rehnquist Court, which has repeatedly overturned settled law. The heartbreaking thing is that a vast number of this Court's decisions have not been redressed by Congress. Still, I don't think the Rehnquist Court is nearly as bad as the Reconstruction Era Court (despite many parallels), but I don't think it is nearly as progressive as the Warren and Burger Courts were.

It's not surprising that many judges and lawyers aren't aware of the extent to which racism has corrupted the law because they have so little knowledge of the cases documenting it. Often these cases are not taught because many law professors are not intimately familiar with them. I wrote an article in 1974 for the *University of Pennsylvania*

Law Review, where I examined all of the American law books that had been written from about 1896 to 1960. I was curious to discover which areas of the law these books ignored, and it became very clear that cases detailing the way racism has influenced the law were excluded. I examined these law books as background for a review I was writing on Derrick Bell's book *Race, Racism, and American Law.* I used those texts to demonstrate how different his book was.

All law students are taught the importance of early Supreme Court cases like *Marbury v. Madison* or *Gibbons v. Ogden,* yet rarely if ever do law students learn anything about the Court's first three major cases involving Blacks.

These cases were *Negro London* in 1806, *Negress Sally Henry* in 1816, and *The Antelope* in 1825. The common denominator in these cases is that Blacks lost their freedom despite the availability of highly compelling legal arguments to the contrary. In *The Antelope* case, the Court held that the international slave trade did not violate the law of nations. What is interesting about this decision is that its author, Justice Story, had written an opinion two years earlier condemning the international slave trade. Yet in *The Antelope* Justice Story reversed his position.

While law schools do teach the *Dred Scott* decision, there is no mention in law school of what I think is the most racist case in Missouri's history: *State v. Celia. Dred Scott* is the case in which Chief Justice Roger Brooke Taney, in rejecting a Missouri slave's claims that he was legally entitled to his freedom, wrote that under the Constitution a Black man had no rights the white man was bound to respect. *Celia* is a case that touches race and gender. Celia was a slave woman who had been raped repeatedly for years by her master, and one night she decided to fight him off. She hit him on the head and he died. Celia was charged with murder, and although Missouri law permitted a woman to physically resist being raped, the Missouri courts held that this slave woman had no right under the law to defend herself against further sexual molestation. Celia was hanged, but her execution was delayed so she could give birth to yet another child from her master's sexual assaults.

There are many major opinions that are not included in the curricula, and therefore the knowledge of these opinions does not become part of the legal tradition. Generations of students do not pick up any of this information and insight.

I realize it is difficult to teach constitutional law. It may very well be impossible to have a "balanced" course in law and cover the scope of things that I cover in my classes. However, it seems to me that on race and on gender, on Native Americans and so forth, you have to incorporate some of those insights into all of the classes.

Many of the judges in this book have written great opinions. Constance Baker Motley has written great opinions on copyrights, maritime law, complicated procedural problems, criminal law, and civil rights law. I think one of the great tragedies in recent judicial history is that Constance Baker Motley was not appointed to the court of appeals or the United States Supreme Court. She would have been a magnificent justice. Or take Damon Keith. His opinion on the Nixon wiretap case was a great opinion that preserved the freedoms of all Americans, not just Blacks. That case wasn't even about Blacks. A large number of Keith's opinions are now contained in legal textbooks.

We are fortunate in this country because a large number of white judges have had a sensitivity to the level of injustice in America. But, even acknowledging that, Black judges have disproportionately made a greater impact. Proportionally, more Black judges have shown a willingness to confront injustices than white judges. In many ways you cannot truly distinguish William Brennan from Thurgood Marshall. Both of these justices have made profound contributions to improving the quality of justice in this land. But Brennan is a rare exception. He had the capacity to look at his own background. I'm not surprised that Marshall did that.

Part II

THE FRONT LINE

VERONICA S. McBETH

"Everybody believes rich people get better treatment."

Los Angeles Municipal Court Judge Veronica McBeth volunteered to arraign suspects arrested during the riot that followed the acquittal of the four policemen charged in the beating of Rodney King. Smoke from buildings burning in South Central Los Angeles was visible from McBeth's chambers. She volunteered because she wanted to make sure that everybody was being treated fairly, that those who did not deserve to go to jail did not go.

In the late sixties, McBeth's desire for social justice motivated her to sacrifice her lifelong dream of being a doctor to become a lawyer. Her passion for fairness has often led McBeth to take time during voir dires *[questioning] to teach jurors about the justice system or tangle with California's chief justice over the issue of race bias in the court system. A California native who made law review at the UCLA Law School, McBeth worked in the Los Angeles prosecutor's office before being appointed to the municipal court in 1981. McBeth has lectured to fellow jurists nationwide on issues involving racism in the justice system, has headed professional organizations, once chairing the National Bar Association's Judicial Council, and has been active in numerous civic organizations. A* Los Angeles Times Magazine *article described McBeth as a model judge, who is able to maintain a busy professional and community schedule and still find time for her two daughters.*

Judge Veronica Simmons McBeth was interviewed in her chambers in January 1993.

A few years ago I decided a case that involved a slumlord. It was the first time anybody in the country ever sentenced a slumlord to live in his own building. And I did it out of a sense of sheer frustration.

Here were these poor people with no one acting as an advocate for them. Most of them didn't even speak English. I went out to these buildings and had a look: people were paying really high rents for places that didn't have running water but that had vermin, rats, and roaches like you've never seen—all within a few blocks of this courthouse.

I thought maybe I could get the owner's attention if he had to live in one of those buildings himself. Maybe I could get him to change his mind about the people who pay him rent. These were real people who lived in his buildings, while he lived in a palace in Beverly Hills. All of his buildings were paid for, but he wouldn't maintain them. This guy had everything. All this money he was getting from these buildings was just money to him.

All the experts came in and testified that the buildings were not decrepit because of the tenants. They said the buildings were decrepit because they had not been maintained. So I sent him to live in one of the buildings.

My decision was based on what my mother had taught me: a kind of basic justice or fairness. This was something we learned at home, not in law school.

As a result of that decision, a number of state legislatures changed their penal systems. In New York they added that type of sentence as part of their penalty when landlords don't follow court orders in housing cases. The Atlanta City Council made it part of their housing code. Newspapers all over the United States ran editorials about it.

And another good thing happened in that case. The tenants of the buildings got Legal Aid involved on the civil side of the matter, and every one of the tenants got twenty-five thousand dollars when the buildings were sold.

Something came out of that decision. It was just a little something but it had an impact, which was rewarding.

After that slumlord decision I received four hundred letters from all over the country. I was overwhelmed by this because I hadn't thought it was such a big deal—just a novel idea that grabbed everyone's attention. The letters I received said it's about time that somebody rich gets treated fairly. Everybody relates to that. You can't always convince people that there is institutionalized racism, or ethnic bias, or gender bias, but everybody believes rich people get treated better.

We are Americans and in America you are not any better just because you have a lot of money.

I had no intention of being a judge. I looked at it the way many people of my age did—as something you do before retirement, a plum at the end of your career.

My thought was to come here and find a way to bring about change. There are many people skills that have nothing to do with law school but which I think are as important in making for a good jurist. Experience and knowledge of the law are very important, of course; but a strong sense of justice and fairness is also necessary. Temperament is equally important. So is a gut level ability to determine the truth. It's not always easy to tell whether someone is lying to you or not.

The good thing about our system is not that it is what it hopes to be, but that it hopes to be something better. That's what makes it important. The only reason I give my life to this institution is because I say, "No, it's not what it's supposed to be right now. But I do everything I can, and I know many others who are doing everything they can to bring us closer to the goal." It's the goal itself—the goal of fairness and justice—that is important.

I choose to do many jury trials because they provide a way to teach people about the criminal justice system and about themselves. I like to do criminal cases because I happen to be one of those strange people who find criminal law interesting—probably because it is about people, not about money. I'm simply not interested in money, how it works, and who gets it.

We as judges have a tremendous opportunity to teach people how our system ought to be. This is particularly important here in California because, through our initiative process, we can wipe out all of our most important constitutional safeguards. With the voter-referendum process in California, any issue can be put on the ballot. Teaching people about the system is as important as anything else we do. People must understand why they have a right to remain silent, why the burden of proof falls on the prosecution, and how terrible it would be the other way around. You can teach and train through the jury selection process.

When I do jury trials, I always do extensive *voir dire* with them. I talk to the jurors for a long time, making up stories in all kinds of ways to make them consider all of the things they should consider when they start to analyze the facts of the case. This questioning also guides jurors to look at themselves and see the ways in which they are similar, even though they come from all over the county. Our problems are real in spite of race. I don't know any place else that has the intensive, in-your-face ethnic and race problems that we have in Los Angeles. There are forty-seven languages spoken in this county.

I get tons of wonderful mail from jurors saying it was a rewarding and refreshing experience to be in court and see that things can work. They learned that court procedures are not just to get sympathy for defendants. They also say it made them confront their own attitudes. I got somebody from the chamber of commerce here who said, "You made me think about what I wouldn't have wanted to call prejudices that exist in myself and about how important it is to confront those prejudices."

I had a juror here the other day tell me that he never has any contact with anybody Black, and everything he hears on TV and reads in the newspapers convinces him that Blacks are more likely to commit crimes. I try hard to create an atmosphere where jurors feel comfortable saying what they really feel. This guy didn't just come out and tell us he thinks Blacks are more likely to commit crimes. He felt comfortable. This was a fairly decent guy. We were having a nice chat about the system and how it works, and he came out with it. Of course, he was removed from the jury, but I could use what he said to me as an object lesson for everybody else in the courtroom. But it illustrates just how ingrained all this stuff really is.

My view on ingrained racism is very similar to that expressed by Elaine Jones of the NAACP Legal Defense Fund. She says everybody is racist, every single one of us. We look out for our own—that seems to be part of the human condition—but you can be made aware of it, and you can rise above it.

Anybody can have a bias against another group—even a Black judge—and this is what I try to tell my colleagues when I talk about racial and ethnic bias—that any one of us can have bias, so let's not just say this is a white thing, something that only affects white judges.

Every single one of us in the justice system has to make sure that people leave this courthouse feeling that they got a fair shake. And we'd better be sure that we give them a fair shake and don't let any of these ingrained prejudices come out when we are under pressure.

We lawyers and judges think we're so perfect and so smart, we're somehow above everything. If anybody even suggests that we could be guilty of these things, we automatically close off. That's what happens. We say, "It's not us." So, what we need to do, in a way that doesn't offend people or make them feel they are under attack, is to say, "Please take a look at yourself and see you are just like everybody else." And that has to happen before you are going to see changes. People are people regardless of the label we attach to them—judge, lawyer, whatever, they are all men and women first.

In 1991 the University of Chicago conducted a study of the way different groups look at other groups. That study showed that although people thought everybody ought to be treated equally, ought to have equal opportunity for jobs, education, liberty, and the pursuit of happiness, those same people—something like 70 percent of them—thought Blacks would rather be on welfare than work and 58 percent thought Blacks were more violent.

On the one hand, people have all these stereotypically racist beliefs but, on the other, they want things to be OK. Lawyers and judges are no different. So you have to bring lawyers and judges in touch with themselves, and hopefully—because we hope they are committed to ideals of equal justice and fairness—you can get most of them to modify their behavior at least. I think people will modify their behavior once they become aware of it.

When I was practicing law, I had personal encounters with racism and sexism. Here is one example that illustrates just how subtle and institutionalized racism had become in our system.

I was the first Black ever to work in this particular calendar court. It was normal to have some two to three hundred cases to deal with daily in this courtroom, so we had to deal, plea bargain, get pleas. We were working under intense pressure that day.

I had worked with this judge (who has since retired) for several months, and I will tell you I never saw him treat people differently based on race. I never saw him treat a lawyer or a defendant differently based on race. So when this thing happened, I guess that's why it was so devastating to me: it would never have occurred to me that he was like that.

We had this one case, involving assault with a deadly weapon, and we didn't have the case file. All day long we had been searching for the case file and I had kept asking the judge to postpone hearing it because we were trying to find the paperwork. I knew if we didn't find the paperwork, the public defender would ask that the case be dismissed and the judge would rightfully grant that request. So about three in the afternoon the judge called the case again and he said, "Listen, you guys have to fish or cut bait. What's going on?" And I said, "Your Honor, to tell you the truth, we don't even have the case file. We've been trying to find it all day long. But the nature of the charges is so serious, can I at least approach the bench and see your file before I announce that I'm unable to proceed?"

As we approached the bench to get the file, he handed it to me and he said, "I don't know why you're so upset about this case anyway. It happened in the heart of darkest Africa."

When the judge said that, I dropped my head. I know my mouth dropped, because I saw the way he looked at me and quickly said, "Oh, well, I meant that it happened in South Central in a crummy bar that you'd never be caught dead in." I was shocked. I'm not naive. I know about racism, but my voice was shaking when I made the motion to have the case dismissed because we were unable to proceed.

The judge called me in the next day and said he didn't know where that "darkest Africa" statement came from, that it was just an expression, and he was really sorry he said it.

I wanted to tell him it was more than just an expression. It bothered me personally and professionally. It said that something that happens in a particular community isn't important. It said that the case wasn't important and the victims weren't important because everybody in that bar was Black. But I lied a little and said I wasn't really bothered personally by his expression. I did say that, professionally, the remark was insulting because a judge has an obligation to avoid all forms of bias. And I said that the public defender, who was white, should have been as upset as I was.

The judge's response was to tell me that, over the months, we had been working just like one big happy family. I suppose it was a big mistake to tell the judge, "I don't want to be in your family, so just treat me like a lawyer and don't forget who I am."

While this judge's remark was a little thing, it was a big one to me —one of the most memorable of my many personal encounters with racism in the justice system. It reminds you that people may seem to be one way, but when the pressure is on, they often act out of character or reveal an aspect of their character that they normally repress. That is why we have to do these sensitivity classes and once in a while have to have these racial- and ethnic-bias incidents to remind us in the system so we won't just keep saying it's everybody else.

We constantly have to be aware of our diversity and the need to treat everyone fairly. One mile from this courthouse I went to a public school where over thirty different languages are spoken. Over thirty languages in just one school. I had a trial here recently that required interpreters of three different languages spoken by various witnesses.

I don't want to pat myself on the back for being fair. In fact I got in trouble with the prosecutor's office about a year ago, and for a month they wouldn't let me hear any cases involving police officers. Two of the lawyers in that office claimed I had said, on the record, that the police had lied. That's not what happened. The police and prosecutors had refused to comply with orders of the court to produce documents in discovery.

I had been assigned a group of cases that had been going on for years. Nobody really wanted to try them. The main case involved eight defendants from the Revolutionary Communist Party. Every year on May first this group would have a demonstration. It always ended up with a confrontation with the police, and there would be hundreds of arrests.

There had been discovery motions and all kinds of motions going on for years. So finally I said these cases had to go to trial. They were getting stale. Nobody would have remembered anything on the witness stand if any more time were to pass. Certainly that wouldn't have served the interests of justice, so I decided that no one would be allowed any continuances. We would go to trial.

I had reams of transcripts and motions from the preceding years. We couldn't even find all the paperwork. I started reading through this stuff, coming in at nine on Saturdays and Sundays, reading through the case files.

The defense kept asking for discovery, and both the police officers and the prosecutors were saying the things requested by the defense on discovery didn't exist. Then the defense started getting some of the things they had requested in discovery and came into court showing me references made to documents that the police alleged didn't exist.

It happened constantly that they'd say something didn't exist and I'd find out that it did exist. So, after a while, I stopped accepting representations from the prosecutors or even affidavits under penalty of perjury claiming that the things requested on discovery did not exist. Somebody had to come and testify that they couldn't find an item even though it was referenced in their files. That was the first thing that happened.

We'd do the motions on Fridays and hear testimony on the other four days. There were eight defendants, and there must have been seventy witnesses. It took us three weeks just to pick a jury because there were so many peremptory challenges.

Finally, we find out that the police department's political division, the department's antiterrorist division that does the surveillance, had the names of all of the officers who were present on the day of the arrests. I ordered them to turn over certain documents, and they came to court and tried to claim a privilege against my order that I found they didn't have. There had been hundreds of arrests that day. This case involved eight of them, and following it I had three other cases each involving five or six defendants. With the other cases I had been assigned, my court was going to be tied up for at least a year.

I could have dismissed the case based on the failure of the police and prosecution to comply with the discovery orders. I could have done that but I didn't. I said I wasn't going to dismiss the case because there were so many witnesses. I told both sides there were enough people testifying that the jury could decide what had happened without knowing about the information the police department's political division had. However, I told the prosecution that because they refused to comply with the court's orders, I was going to instruct the jury that I had ordered the prosecution to turn over certain documents and the prosecution refused, which they had no legal right to do. The jury could infer from that if the documents were exculpatory.

Well, the prosecutors said, "Case dismissed." They figured they couldn't win.

All of the things that had gone on in this case led to my jury instruction. The police did not provide the documents they were ordered to produce under discovery. I had told the jury two things: either the police had lied or they had no respect for the lawful orders of the court. That's why the prosecutors claimed I had said that the police lie.

So for a month they wouldn't let any cases involving police officers come to my court. The public was pretty well outraged by it. If you talk to anyone in the Hall of Justice, they will say many things about me, but no one will say that you don't get a fair shot in my courtroom. After a month it died, but prosecutors are very—I don't want to say "racist," but it interests me how quickly prosecutors draw conclusions or inferences about Black or female judges that they don't draw about others. They couldn't dispute my jury instruction, and most of them thought it was fair. But you see how they reacted anyway: "We just won't let her hear any cases. She thinks all the police lie." Now I've been asked by one of the police organizations to sit on their advisory board, so at least they don't have that kind of problem with me. They said, "People think you are tough on us, but if we go in there and tell the truth, we don't have any problems with you"—and that's right. That is true for anybody who sets foot in my courtroom.

After the Rodney King incident there were those who thought juries would never again believe the police. We had other cases involving the police and use of force, yet jurors did the right thing. The Rodney King case did have an impact in that it let people know the extremes of what the police can do—even people who refused to believe it. The problem arises when we begin generalizing, which we do because we're lazy. People come here and say that if a cop said it, it must be true because they never lie. Others, who may have had a bad experience, feel that the police lie all the time. Neither one is true.

We want people to be right down the middle, to recognize police and judges and lawyers and everybody else is human and capable, at times, of doing things to people, but capable, too, of rising above it all and doing wonderful things for people regardless of race. We need to get rid of this idea that certain people never do wrong. It is also very important for people to recognize that Black people are victims of racism.

Jurors scrutinize the police more now, but they should have been doing that anyway because that is what the law asks for. The law requires the police to be scrutinized as closely as any other person who testifies.

I've given jurors examples that remove this scrutiny issue from the criminal context. I tell them to pretend they are in an automobile accident with a policeman and each accuses the other of being at fault. This accident can't be resolved—the lawyers can't resolve it, the insurance companies can't resolve it, so it ends up in civil court. Now what would happen if the jury said it couldn't decide based on the evidence, but the cop would never lie. Wouldn't that mean that in certain situations, if a policeman ran into your car, you'd never get any money, you'd never win in court? Jurors laugh, but they think about it.

Then I put it in a criminal context. If we are going to believe everything this officer says, the other guy never has a chance. I'm not saying you should disbelieve the officer. I'm saying you should weigh his words the same as anyone else's.

Judges have a tremendous power to educate because everybody looks up to them, even if they are Black. It is important for people to hear a judge up there telling them it is their obligation to be fair, telling them it's the American way to do things.

I volunteered to do arraignments during the riots after the first verdict in the Rodney King case. I volunteered to do them for the same reason I came here to begin with—to make sure people were being treated fairly.

The city attorney wanted every single person to go to jail, and of course the public defenders were saying that it was all wrong and nobody should go to jail. I did the arraignments to ensure that the hundreds of people who were being processed that night were all treated fairly. I didn't say my colleagues were wrong. I just wanted to make sure that I was part of it. I have always believed if a Black person were found guilty and somebody Black had been involved in the conviction, as a juror, say, or as a prosecutor, the defendant would say, "Maybe my behavior isn't OK. Maybe it isn't just the system." With Blacks involved in the system, it makes it a little more difficult for some defendants to just dismiss their conviction as part of a racist conspiracy.

Also, I wanted to make sure that people who didn't deserve to be in jail weren't sent there. A lot of the people who were arrested were homeless. Not every person who got arrested for being a gang member was in fact a gang member even if the arrest report said they were. Not everybody who wears red or blue—which are gang colors—actually belongs to a gang. A lot of young Blacks wear colors because they are scared. Even having a gun in your car doesn't mean you're a gang member.

I heard all kind of arguments. I listened to them. I wasn't always convinced by them, but at least the accused had an opportunity to be heard. There were many judges and lawyers who did a tremendous job, volunteering to work all night, around the clock if necessary, to make sure those cases got through the system fairly and efficiently.

I knew how badly the community had been let down by the Rodney King verdict, but it isn't okay to burn the city down. The rioters destroyed businesses in their own neighborhoods, and many of those businesses were minority-owned. The proprietors are going to have a hard time getting money to rebuild the businesses that were destroyed. And I know very well that the teenage mothers in that community do not have cars, so when the neighborhood store burns down, how are they going to get milk for the baby? I don't have a problem upholding the law, but I do want to make sure that everybody is treated the same. That's our ideal, right? Our system has to be fair and just. I didn't necessarily feel proud of being a judge after the Simi Valley verdict. But I knew it was important to go forward.

I have been very frustrated in the last year or so. Well, "frustrated" may not be the right word—"disappointed," I suppose, is more accurate. The Rodney King verdict and the verdict in the Korean grocer case devastated the Black community because of the perceived unfairness.

I go into the schools often. I average about three grammar school classrooms a week. I go as a role model, and I teach the students about the court system. I want them to know they can be something other than a drug dealer. I don't lie to them, but I let them know that if they work hard, things can be OK for them.

By going into the schools and talking with students, I'm trying to promote respect for the justice system. But events like the Rodney King decision and the Korean grocer case knock down everything I'm trying to do with the students. Those decisions—whether the jurors thought they were doing the right thing or not—devastated our community and undermined people's respect for the system.

This was devastating to me personally. It made me question what I was doing. I didn't have any illusions that I was changing the world, but I thought I was doing something good and positive—and then to have it wiped away by those decisions. How can kids believe that the system is fair when they see decisions like those?

The very day the decision was rendered in the Korean grocer case,

I was over at Metropolitan High School, which is a high school for girls who have been kicked out of every other school, or have gotten pregnant or have to work. I go over there all the time because the principal is doing such a tremendous job and I want to be supportive of her efforts. I want to go over there and give the students some hope—or at least a different point of view, a different look at life. When I'm there I'm always telling them they don't have to be a judge to succeed. I don't hold up being a judge as the greatest thing. I tell them they could be court reporters and that court reporters make a lot of money.

Anyway, I gave a talk at Metropolitan and we had this long discussion about how the system is stacked against us and the fact that cops are racist and racism is everywhere. I emphasized to the students that not everybody is racist, not all cops are racist. I told them that the community has to be protected against the people who prey on us, and we have to stop preying on each other—and then the Korean grocer decision is announced! The grocer shot a girl in the back of the head. The store's own security videotape recorded the shooting. While the grocer was convicted, she was given a suspended sentence and allowed to walk out of the courtroom without serving a day in jail. What does that say to young people who already think the justice system is stacked against them?

The Sunday after that verdict I had to speak at one of the Baptist churches in the city, and I got up to talk. I was ready to give my regular talk about how we have to keep working to make the system better, but I couldn't do it. Eventually, of course, I got over it. But it is disheartening to have come all this way, from the hopes of the late sixties and early seventies, and then end up in 1993, back at the beginning. It may even be worse now than it was then.

There is a big difference, though, between the situation today and the late sixties. Because law schools have been letting in so many more Blacks, we are better equipped to fight things. For example, Blacks in the legal profession are in a strong enough position today that we can oppose Clarence Thomas if we don't want him. We can find a better, more qualified Black for a position on the Supreme Court. It's not just like there is "just one" anymore. It's no longer a situation where we have to cover for people who are unqualified or malfeasant. We can choose people who are excellent, who reflect the best qualities of our community and are representative of it. We don't have to accept a person picked by whites to be our leader. So, in a sense, we've made progress; but for the greater part of our people, things are worse, and they are in worse shape. We Blacks who have achieved can help to a point; but we don't have enough power to keep the doors of opportunity open so other members of our community can come through the way we did.

The past twelve years have been bad for the Black community because of the policies and attitudes coming out of the White House. But with the change in administrations, I have hope—not just because the new administration is Democratic, but because it's a breath of fresh air. I see people in the streets having hope again. For a while there during the past twelve years, there just wasn't any hope. It was hard for me to gear myself up and generate hope for everybody.

Hope is what drove a lot of us in the late sixties. A lot of us went to law school because we thought it was a way to help make things better. I got interested in the law in the late sixties as a result of all the struggles going on to make this society better.

Growing up, I had never wanted to be a lawyer. I had always wanted to be a doctor, primarily because doctors helped people. Throughout high school and even when I started college, I was in a pre-med curriculum.

I quit college after my first two years. I dropped out to give myself a break and to earn more money to pay for school when, eventually, I did go back. During that time I got married (to a man whom I later divorced while in law school). He was a physician, and watching his life convinced me that being a doctor wasn't what I wanted to do.

This was during the whole civil rights movement, the protests against the Vietnam War, and all the other activities that were going on. Like many people, I became more political during that period. I stayed out of college for two years, and when I went back I switched to political science. During that time I decided to go to law school.

One motivation for studying law arose from looking at the system and seeing the lack of access that poor and Black people had to it. I figured that practicing law was the way to effect change. That's why I decided to go to law school.

When I passed the bar, I became a prosecutor. When I was in my second year at UCLA Law School, a man named Burt Pines, who had recently been elected city attorney for Los Angeles, visited. He was going to law schools all over the country saying he wanted the best and the brightest to work for him in his office—just as the Kennedys wanted the best and brightest at the White House.

I was very impressed that Burt Pines wanted to develop an office that would serve the community and have a humane approach to prosecution. It also helped that he was paying more than the U.S. Attorney's Office and the DA. Of course at that time I was married to a doctor and didn't need to make a lot of money. I guess I have never been motivated by making money.

But in any event I found Burt Pines's goals compelling because I was a Black woman on law review, graduating in 1975, and I could have worked just about any place I wanted. Not everybody had a Black woman, which is what they wanted. In those days, Black women were considered "twofers"—you know, a Black and a woman, a double bonus for an employer trying to meet equal employment mandates. But I went to work for Burt Pines because he said you didn't have to work for him for twenty years to have an impact. And he was true to his word.

I went to work at the city attorney's office with people from the best law schools in the country, and we did exciting things. We set up a domestic violence unit—the second one in the country—because we were all reading about the cycle of violence, about the way women were victimized in their homes. This violence against women wasn't considered a crime. Police officers were injured more often investigating domestic violence than other types of crime, so we knew we could sell the idea of a domestic violence unit to the law enforcement community as something good for them.

We also looked at cases in which minority or poor people were victims. Traditionally these cases were prosecuted as misdemeanors rather than felonies. Looking at the victims and how they were treated was important.

That office was very progressive for its time. The city attorney was very open to change, and his office was looking into things like setting up a victim's unit to help people walk through the process. Exciting things going on there, and that's why I picked that job. Plus, I loved doing trials. I found that you could go into a courtroom and change people's lives.

In those days virtually every prosecutor said you couldn't get convictions from minority juries, and I told them they were crazy, that they obviously didn't grow up in those communities. Twelve little Black ladies will convict their son if he's wrong. They will hold him accountable, but first you've got to convince them that what's happening to the defendant, who is a Black male, is fair—that he is indeed guilty and the police haven't been abusive and haven't lied. You get convictions if you are able to do that. So I made sure I always had lots of Black people on my juries and/or Hispanics if the defendants were Hispanic. In a small way, the good things that were happening kept me in that office until I was appointed to the bench in 1981. I was a prosecutor for five years.

When I was a prosecutor, I was very supportive of determinant sentencing, what is called mandatory sentencing in some jurisdictions. I once thought this was a fair process, a way of dealing with the racial- and ethnic-bias problem, a way of dealing with subtle institutional racism. But now everybody can see that is not the case.

Determinant sentencing has shifted too much power to the prosecutors. They now decide who is charged with felonies or misdemeanors. Prosecutors decide who is going to face the death penalty and who is going to get what term in a plea bargain. We've given the prosecutors the power, and that power is influenced by whatever racial or ethnic bias they may have. Judges have very little power under determinant sentencing. So, I've come full circle on this issue.

Determinant sentencing has not been effective in cutting crime, and it has been subject to the type of abuse it was originally intended to counter. We didn't think the matter through well enough at the outset to recognize that we were shifting power from judges. In many cities prosecutors are elected, so the whole question of enforcement becomes political.

We need to scrutinize what we are teaching judges and lawyers and everybody else, because not everybody guilty of committing a crime should go to jail. We've got to work on the social problems that create crime. We have to educate people; we have to let people know that we are already throwing everybody into jail and it hasn't solved anything. We have to teach them that this is not just a law-and-order problem. But it takes courage to say that, because everybody's afraid. Everybody is sick and tired of crime. I am too.

For the past twelve years in this state all we've done is put people in jail. Politicians have been elected by promising to put people in jail. Judges have been appointed to the bench by promising to throw away the key. And after twelve years of posturing, we haven't dealt with any of the problems underlying crime, the problems everybody knows contribute to drug problems and gang problems. We haven't paid any attention to the root causes. Our approach has been political —political expediency—and it has hurt us. Anybody who spoke out against this was labeled "soft on crime" and "liberal."

The criminal justice system absolutely can't solve all the social problems that lead to overcrowded jails. We spend all our money building jails and putting people away, and, again, it is worse than it was twelve years ago.

If you grow up in a household where no one is working, and somebody comes along and offers you five hundred dollars to sell drugs standing on the corner, you're going to do that. Yes, you are—and it's absurd to think a person won't. And then we send that person to jail for the rest of his life after he has never, at any time, been given a chance. That's fairness and justice? I don't think so.

We don't have enough money to keep using the criminal justice system as our main weapon in fighting crime. When I chaired our countywide judges association I did budgets and administrative work, and I learned more about how money considerations form policy than I ever had before. No one can say we have enough money, because we don't. We have finally run out of resources. We have to rethink the whole system. We have to reprioritize where the money is spent. We can't throw money at problems the way we used to.

I've been trying to tell people we have to do things a different way. Two years ago when I chaired the Judicial Council of the National Bar Association, our entire summer conference was aimed at addressing issues related to Black youth at risk—a first for any judges organization.

At this conference, I brought in not just judges and police officers but psychologists, educators, and people who had put together community programs that seemed to work with young kids. I wanted to present alternatives so that we could all go back and say we need to prioritize our budgets and get these types of programs in place.

It's no mystery. Troubled youth usually become troubled adults. If we get these kids in our dependency court, which is called family court in other places, you usually find that the mother is on drugs or she's a teenager or she's got ten kids and is not working. We know from the day that kid is born he's got a problem, and the way our system is working here in California, I can bet you that in eighteen years that child is going to be in my court for me to send him to jail. And nobody will have intervened to stop this child's descent. We all know it.

The conference went well. It was amazing to me to hear people from different parts of the country talking about new programs where parents go to school with their children. The rationale is, how can parents show their kids how to do their homework if they can't do it themselves. We tried to let people know what was happening in other parts of the country, because we're all facing similar problems. The hope was to present useful alternatives to judges. The judges could say to themselves, "Hey, I could borrow that idea and take it to my city." That's the kind of network we're trying to build, and we're still working on it in the judicial council.

Incredibly, one of the main things troubled children need is so simple and inexpensive: they need somebody who loves them. We can't give every kid someone who loves them, but we can give them a lot more than we are now. We know that by providing these kids with meaningful direction, support, and encouragement, they can achieve. I've seen it work.

The County of Los Angeles Department of Children's Services operates a program for children who have been wards of the court and are about to turn eighteen, when they are emancipated. These kids have been living in foster homes or other places and have been victims of abuse or neglect or other things. This program teaches them how to open a checking account, how to fill out an application and apply for a job, how to find an apartment, and so on.

A number of years ago one of the administrators in our court system found there were kids reaching the age of emancipation who had high school grades good enough to go to college. This administrator had ties to the University of Southern California [USC], so he talked to them; and he asked the college people if we could get a career day for some of these kids, who were amazing. If any kids were set to fail, these kids were; yet quite a number of them were making it, and they set up this program for them. USC, which is a private school, had luncheons and a day on campus for these kids. I was asked to come and speak (people know I always like to speak to children).

It wasn't long before USC gave one of these kids a four-year scholarship worth about $80,000. The first kid to receive this scholarship was Vietnamese. The second year USC gave the kids six scholarships, and the next year seven. Here was an example of the private sector finding money for a useful program. The private sector has to help, and this program is a perfect example of the public and private sectors working together.

We need more partnerships of this kind if we are going to have an impact. Here were kids who were destined from birth to end up on the wayside, but some of them made it through. Every single one of those kids, if you sat down and talked with them, would tell you that somebody in their lives touched them and allowed them to rise above the law of the streets. These are tough, streetwise kids who you cannot bullshit. But they have that something in them, that strength that gave them respect and love for themselves so that they didn't get involved in drugs or get pregnant. What these kids need is family. There's just no doubt about that. They need family the way I wish the Republicans had meant when they talked about "family values."

There is a lady here in South Central Los Angeles who has put twenty-three kids through college. She hugs them; she makes them know they are worth something, and they live up to your expectations when you do that. That's what they need, but in the criminal justice system you can't give them that. We can and should let people know that we can't do our job unless we find programs that give family support to kids. That's what we ought to be funding instead of just building prisons. If we would pay more attention to what these kids need from the outset, we would save money because prisons are very expensive. Saving money should appeal to the self-interest of society. And God knows if we don't do something for these kids, they are going to make your kids and my kids their victims. They are going to overwhelm us. We have to be willing to admit that we've been putting everybody in jail and things aren't better but worse.

There is one thing about Black judges: No matter how far we've moved up the ladder of success, and no matter where we may live now, we always go back at some point to the Black community. We go there for church or our mother lives there, so we never sever our roots. We always know what is going on in these communities, and that's a tremendous asset we bring to the system. You can go to Harvard, but you're still going to visit somebody in South Central. You know the crime that is there. You see the drugs and other stuff. You can bring that awareness into a system that doesn't fully understand the problems it is called upon to resolve.

My feeling about Black judges is this: If we sit here and don't say anything and don't do anything, then we don't need to be here. Really, we don't need to be here because anybody could sit here and do nothing. We have to lead and be part of the leadership that is saying things people don't want to hear.

JOSEPH B. BROWN JR.

"Judges are products of the containment system."

It's not difficult to tell that Judge Joseph Brown is a different type of jurist when you see him sitting on the bench. The stocky, bearded Brown wears his judicial robes trimmed in African kente cloth or in red, Black, and green, the colors of Black liberation. Joe Brown sees himself as more than a mere enforcer of the law. He sees himself as a "village chieftain"—the individual in African societies who was responsible for resolving communal problems. Brown believes the criminal justice system could solve the crime problem but will not. Brown sought election to the bench in 1990 specifically to use judicial clout to combat the crime problem. The razor-wire-ringed roof of the overcrowded jailhouse is visible from his chambers in the Shelby County Courthouse in downtown Memphis.

A streetwise native of the Watts section of Los Angeles who collects guns, this criminal court judge has attracted international attention with his unconventional sentencing, such as "reverse theft," where the victim of a burglary is allowed into the thief's home to snatch an object of his choice. Brown requires literacy training as a condition for bail release, and convicts must perform community service as a part of their sentence.

The tough-talking Judge Joseph B. Brown Jr., who slips with ease from legalese to street language, was interviewed in December 1992, at his chambers in the Shelby County Courthouse.

We have more people locked up in this county—Shelby County—than in any other county in America. There are more people confined in this county than in the entire penitentiary systems of twenty-two states. Memphis, which is in Shelby County, is ranked fifth in the nation in terms of the number of people locked up. The lock-up count goes, from highest to lowest, Los Angeles, New York, Chicago, Dallas, Memphis, Houston, Miami, and Detroit.

African Americans account for 90.67 percent of those confined in Shelby County, according to the latest grand jury report. Thirty-four percent of the African American males in Shelby County between the ages of eighteen and twenty-nine are currently serving prison sentences. They are either in jail, on probation, or on parole. This figure does not include eighteen- to twenty-nine-year-olds who have previously been in jail, on probation, or on parole. This figure does not include eighteen- to twenty-nine-year-olds who have previously been in jail, on probation, or on parole. As far as I'm concerned, when you lose that many males of a particular race in one generation to the so-called criminal justice system, then that's not crime, that's genocide. It's a quiet kind of genocide. Clearly its not mass murder but you're still wiping out most of a generation. Getting a job is hard enough without having a criminal record.

When I became a judge the first thing I learned about the criminal justice system was that there isn't a system. The system is not coordinated. It doesn't function as though it is interested in correcting the so-called crime problem. There is a total lack of coordination of the resources available to combat crime.

This crime problem can be addressed. Something can be done about it. But in order to do something about it, you have to have somebody in place who knows something about the problem. And there is really only one professional who could be in charge of the criminal justice system, and that's the judge.

However, traditionally, historically, and presently, judges do not want to be in charge because it brings them to the level of social workers, and most judges have a problem with that. Traditionally, judges do not see it as their role to solve the crime problem. Their role as they see it is to contain crime by confining criminals. They are "above" trying to address the causes of crime.

Judges are a country-club set. They are encouraged to be members of the elite in order to keep the undesirable elements of society under control. Judges are products of the containment system.

Here in Memphis the majority of the defendants are Black and the majority of the judges are white. Most judges here are not members of the community they most affect. They don't understand the defendants. They don't know anything about the kinds of lives the defendants live. They can't speak the defendants' language. The defendants scare the hell out of them!

I think judges act as though they are above addressing the causes of crime in order to disguise the fact that within the criminal justice system, where so many of the defendants are African American or some other minority, most judges have no real contact with, concept of, connection to or empathy with the majority of the defendants who come through the courts.

The courts are supposed to be representative of "We the people"—*all* of the people. Right now, we have alien entities controlling target populations.

We need more diversity on the bench, but what we really need is a "superjudge," a criminal court judge who is a social worker, who is knowledgeable, who is wise, and who is hard working, because the judge's position is tremendously important in terms of its impact on society.

An enormous number of Black males come through the system. The judge can be the point person who corrects them and inculcates in them values that should have been learned at home, in school, or perhaps in church. A judge can address a lot of things because he or she has coercive powers that nobody else has.

The judge can be the village chieftain. The chieftain resolves disputes, corrects what can be corrected, and gets rid of those who refuse to be corrected. We don't have this village chieftain attitude on the bench right now, but when I became a judge I was determined to be a village chieftain.

Right now, the criminal justice system is dysfunctional, for three reasons: sending nonviolent offenders to jail is a waste of resources, keeping a person in jail is expensive, and, for some people, jail is not really a punishment. Going to jail has become a rite of passage in certain areas of town. It has become a viable option. The individual who gets sent to jail has someplace to stay. He's got structure in his life. He gets fed. He gets a bed. He gets clothes. He gets to hang out with his buddies and play basketball with them in a structured environment.

For many people this is not a bad option when they consider there is no public welfare for males. Jail becomes a viable option when young men can't get a job and don't know how to get a job.

Instead of just putting people in jail for nonviolent crimes, I've created a form of restitution I call "reverse theft," which is more effective punishment than these prisons where people are just being stored, warehoused. "Reverse theft" works like this: When a person is convicted of property theft, burglary generally, I allow the victim to visit the offender's home, accompanied by a court bailiff and a court order. The victim comes in, browses around, and if he sees *anything* that he likes (up to a certain value), he may seize it; he may take a pair of the offender's tennis shoes or maybe a leather jacket. The victim can visit the offender's home as many times as he wishes over the course of the offender's probation. The victim can come, accompanied by the bailiff, unannounced, day or night. The defendant must allow the victim in. If the defendant refuses, I deal with that.

I had one case where the victim came into the offender's house, took a portrait of the offender's girl friend, tore it to pieces and burned it. The convict started crying. Destroying the portrait hurt him because that picture had some value to him. Now, *that* is punishment.

Reverse theft also lets the victim eyeball the criminal, see who this character is up close. The victim has probably had all these fantasies of sitting in his kitchen with the windows open, the doors unlocked, a pistol in his hand, waiting for the burglar to return so he can blow the burglar away, smoke him! But, of course, he never gets the opportunity. So the victim is angry.

When you've got angry people, you have an angry community; and when the community is enraged, that breeds crime, too. So you, as a judge, can do something about that problem. You can reduce the level of rage in the community, and you can do something that causes pain to the perpetrator.

My reverse-theft program was on national television recently, here in America and in Australia.

We need judges who understand the defendants. We need judges who understand the real world beyond the little segregated part they live in. I'm from South Central Los Angeles. I know what it is like to get jacked up on a wall by the police. This Rodney King bullshit—I must have seen that ten or fifteen times with my own eyes when I was growing up. One of the reasons I left Los Angeles and didn't want to go back was because I was tired of that crap. I know what it is like to be victimized by somebody with a badge and gun who's saying, "We're the occupation army. We gonna keep all you niggers down on the bottom, flat and Black."

A judge has to have understanding. A judge has to understand the law. He has to understand a lame line when he hears it. And when you have this kind of understanding, then you can sit there and listen and say, "Wait a minute, what is wrong here?"

A defendant came in my courtroom one time and said, "Your honor, I did this because I was addicted to Mary-Juana, Your Honor." I said, "Wait a minute, man. I'm from Los Angeles, California. Don't tell me you went out and stole that car because you were high on some herb. Get a better line. I already know the punch line to yours. Done heard it in 1964. Stealing that car and wrecking it running from the police was wrong. What you did was wrong. Stealing that car had nothing to do with Mary or Juana." My knowing that marijuana is not addictive like heroin had nothing to do with being a judge; it was just something I had learned growing up in South Central.

Another dude comes in here and says I'm trying to "put a case on him." This guy commits a crime, gets arrested, and comes to court and says *I'm* the one who is putting this case on him. I said, "Man, when in the history of the world have you ever heard of any warriors poisoning the wells in the village where they live? When have you heard of warriors salting the rows of the crops they are supposed to eat or sticking a spear in the belly of a fellow warrior?" I said, "You never hear of any of that, but that's what you're doing. You're doing wrong." See, I can speak their language.

A judge has to understand the law. When I really have to lay it on somebody to get their attention, I don't convict them of the crime they are charged with, I convict them of contempt. The law gives me the option in many cases to issue a conviction for the crime and/or convict them for contempt of court.

I can send somebody to jail for up to six months on a contempt citation. If I convict a defendant of the crime he's been charged with, he can be released within a couple of months because of overcrowding. To reduce overcrowding, persons are eligible for early releases. Criminals want to be formally convicted because they know they will get early release and be through with it. But these early releases mandated by overcrowding only apply to convicts, not to prisoners who are serving contempt sentences. Prison and probation officials control the early releases, but I retain control over the contempt citations. By citing defendants for contempt instead of convicting them, I can review the contempt every six months and keep them locked up until they decide to straighten up.

It's terribly important to have experienced judges. We have judges in this city who had only practiced law for eighteen months before taking the bench. If you don't have any experience with, or wisdom with respect to, human nature, then you can't deal with it. You have to be adroit in using the tools of your trade. You need to know what is going on around the courthouse, where to go to get things done, and you can only acquire that by having extensive experience. You are supposed to be learned and experienced in the practice of law, and you must know something about people.

Frankly, one of the worst things that Reagan and Bush did to the U.S. judicial system was to appoint to federal judgeships hundreds of people who have limited experience dealing with ordinary people and limited experience practicing real law. There was a federal judge here who was thirty-two years old and had no experience practicing law and no experience with people.

Judges can be a factor in social engineering. Judges can make an impact on the crime problem by attacking its roots, not just alleviating its symptoms by sticking folks in jail. Courts can be used to effect social change.

The judge has all kinds of powers he or she can use to correct a criminal.

I sometimes make defendants register to vote. I tell them to bring me a voter's registration card as a condition of bond. I make them bring back a receipt to prove they've been to the polling place. I can't make them vote, but I can make them go to the polling place. Getting them involved in voting develops good citizenship and also helps our community assert control over its affairs through the political process.

I make defendants get their GEDs. I often make that a condition for getting bond. When a defendant comes into my court needing his bond reviewed or his bond set, I ask if he has finished high school; if not, he must get a GED. Without one he is unemployable—and dumb to boot. When young men are unemployable, they have time on their hands and crime on their minds.

I require defendants to get vocational training or some furtherance of their education if they look like they may be college material.

I require random and frequent drug tests. That's key to reducing drug use.

I try to do things to rebuild the individual and the community. This town has many areas that need to be cleaned up. That means these offenders ought to give free labor to the community to make up for some of their transgressions. They should go into communities, pick up debris, clean up vacant lots, and clean out abandoned buildings. They should do something beneficial for the community, like cleaning up.

We need to instill the work ethic in a lot of these defendants, so I go out and network with some of the unions. We've set up three community service work crews for nonviolent offenders. If one of the offenders really impresses the union official who runs the crew, the union will often enroll him in its apprenticeship program. Then he gets a job that pays fourteen dollars an hour instead of minimum wage. But that's only if he's a hard worker. I'll let a guy go after he has performed this service, especially if he has impressed somebody enough to get a job out of it.

The funny thing about community service is that, at first, the offenders hate it. But a lot of them come back after being released; they want to volunteer because the community—*their* community—looks better. The neighborhood is cleaned up a bit. Things have improved. These guys say to themselves that they've done something constructive. They say they've been part of the solution rather than part of the problem.

For many of these offenders, getting a job and fitting in is a mystery. It's like being fourteen years old and looking at the dating game from the bottom up. It's a mystery. Until a teen participates in the dating game, he or she can't possibly understand what it's all about and can't figure out how to break into the game. The same applies to getting a job and fitting in. One has to learn. One has to be taught. So we must come up with a viable alternative to incarceration. At times it may be necessary to shock somebody with jail, maybe give them a taste of it. We can use jail to coerce people, but we also have to address other parts of the problem, the parts that can't be corrected through coercion.

A typical offender in the system was born to a teenage mother. He's got a ninth- or tenth-grade education by the time he drops out at the age of eighteen, when he's already way behind, anyway. He doesn't have an occupation, skill, or profession of any kind. He's never had a job. He's never done anything for eight hours a day except hang out.

Working eight hours a day is something you have to be conditioned to. That is what elementary school, junior high, and high school are all about—trying to condition somebody to be able to work eight hours. It's like running. Fifteen years ago I used to run five miles a day. But if I did it now, with my out-of-shape self, I'd probably fall out with a heart attack. It's just like that with these kids. They have to learn to get back in shape or get in shape to do eight hours on a job.

So you have to get these individuals job training and job preparation. You have to get them psychological and psychiatric counseling if need be. You get them evaluated and get appropriate treatment, counseling, and therapy for substance abuse problems, and maybe they need in-house treatment. We have gotten that set up here now. We have been able to do a lot of things by reaching out beyond the bench.

I didn't want to be a judge until I discovered what could be done with the position theoretically. I majored in political science as an undergraduate, and I put that to work in evaluating where exactly I could interject myself and do what I wanted to do to help improve things.

When I came on the bench, I tried to network in the community and bring the resources of the community together so we could address the problem with the judicial system. My role is to get this whole system together. I don't just sit on the bench. I go out into the community and get people together to set up programs to deal with this problem.

We are now networking with the community college here in Memphis. We are trying to set up a boot camp in some of the buildings on Shelby State's campus. This boot camp would be an alternative to incarceration. Offenders will have to show up every day at 8 A.M. for a couple of years and go through a program until 5 P.M. After a couple of hours of class or vocational training, they get trotted over for counseling on a drug problem and, once or twice a week, they get carted out on a bus, to do the community service. Then, maybe, they go over here to one of the medical centers for psychological counseling or family-planning or family-rearing or anger-management courses. Then you bring them back to campus to finish up their classes.

The boot camp setting gives offenders a coherent, organized situation. They get into it. There are peers of a different type around them. Instead of being around peers who want to cut up, clown, and act the fool, the peers that they are around at boot camp are trying to get somewhere. The pretty young women that they'd like to hit on won't have anything to do with them if they're about nothing, so now there is peer pressure that says, "Do something excellent." They don't have that kind of positive peer pressure in the high schools. We have too many eighteen-year-olds who are in the ninth grade. There is no upward-working peer group in most high schools, no peer pressure to do something positive.

It costs $22,360 a year to confine someone in jail, or at least to provide a jail bed. We spend $3,400 a year per child on the school system.

America has traditionally de-emphasized education. That's where the term "pointy-head intellectual" comes from. Americans have not been very forthright in supporting public education. Now that inner-city schools are attended predominantly by Blacks and other minorities, even less money is put into them. A lot of the money that should be going to public education is now being put into jailing folk. That money needs to be put into the schools so that young people don't end up in a situation that leads to jail.

I know boot camp can work, because over at the community college the concept is perfectly illustrated by a similar program called Mid-College High School. They take problem kids who can't make it in any other high school, and they put them into one that works together with the college. Fifteen-, sixteen-, seventeen-, and eighteen-year-olds are placed around college students, who are somewhat older than these kids but close enough in age to impress them. The younger group has a positive direction, and they get swept along with the peer pressure that comes from being on the bottom trying to work up to the top, trying to win acceptance. But that peer pressure is positive rather than negative.

Everybody is astonished when the kids in this program are no longer discipline problems, when they start making A's and B's instead of D's and F's, when they stop going to the principal's office every other day. So, you can do things with these types of programs.

But there are times when you have to put people in jail. I had this one guy who was cursing out his mother in the back of the courtroom, getting on her because she wouldn't pay his bail. Here was a guy who blamed everybody but himself for his problems. I told him I wasn't going to reduce his bail because I had heard how he talked to his mother. I told him he talks about being a man because he has four children, but he's nineteen and he's living with his girl friend's mama, doesn't have a job, and has his hand out begging. I told him we should all take off our belts and spank him, because he is nothing but a child. I told him he should grow up and be a man. Having bass in his voice didn't make him a man.

One time, I made this one dude write a hundred thousand times that he would not issue any more bad paper. He was a forger; he wrote phony checks. It was supposed to take four hours a night for about three months to write what I ordered him to write. I wanted his carpal tendons to be absorbed. He only gave me six thousand lines. I locked him up. I asked him, "How come the judge wants you free more than you want to be free?" He said he didn't know. I told him to "TCB." He said he didn't know what that was. I said, "Take care of business."

I get a lot of guys who come back and say, "Judge, you locked me up for four and a half months but you were dead right, because I needed that. It worked out. You straightened me up." People will come in and say they appreciate the opportunity I gave them. They tell me that not only did they get themselves straight but they have started doing right to other people. One guy told me he had kicked his baby brother's ass because he was doing wrong and he wanted to straighten the brother out before he got too far gone. Then the guy asks me if I minded that he kicked his brother's ass. I told him he had no problem with that from me. I'm telling you, a judge can change behavior and have a real impact.

Another thing I do is make everybody read Malcolm X. I even have some of the white offenders, few as they are, read Malcolm. I assign essays and I grade them. If I don't like an essay, I'll make the offender redo it.

I also have them watch movies like *Boyz N the Hood* and *X*. It does good when they see somebody that they can identify with and see how what they have become fits into the overall scheme of things. Maybe by seeing things on the movie screen, they can put in their minds a picture of what they are and what they can be. That can be motivational.

You must motivate these young men. You must give them a cause outside of themselves. If they are not part of the solution, they are part of the problem in that they are not doing something active to solve the problem; they are not doing anything at all.

You want the defendant to realize it is not enough just to get a job for himself. You want him to realize he has an affirmative obligation to go out and prevent other people from doing what he's done. You want him to go out and get on the corner and run somebody off of it who is doing something wrong. You want him to tell his hard-headed partner he doesn't need to shoot anybody, because he should be at peace with them.

This message of being positive in the community, being a part of the solution and not the problem, was the message we were spreading in the sixties, when everybody was talking revolution. But now it's officially required by a judge instead of just being something somebody with a big Afro and a dashiki was saying on the street corner. Now it's official. The judge is saying, "Be a part of the solution."

If the judge behaves in a fair fashion so that the defendant is assured he is getting justice, he will respect you and your office. The judge becomes a creature of respect instead of scorn, if he does things the right way. If a judge has earned respect, when he tells them to do something, they do it.

You can see people who have these greasy-drip, jerry-curl hair styles, looking like fools, who have shaved their heads after reading Malcolm X, and gotten the curl out of their hair and are now acting with some self-respect. Many of these people had never read anything in their lives. Now they are going through the dictionary learning each word just like Malcolm did. They are changing their vocabularies. They are starting to speak the rhetoric of revolution and change. And if their speaking revolution is phony, even if they're pimping it, at least they've been exposed to it. Some of them may do what a lot of us did in the sixties when we read *The Autobiography of Malcolm X* and *Soul on Ice.* We had the street-corner dialogues going and we had the neighborhood meetings. People became radicalized and committed to changing things. Maybe we need that right now. I suspect we do.

* * *

We need to develop a different perception of what a judge is. I can't be a village chieftain if I don't act like one. Acting like a village chieftain means that if I ask people to put it on the line, to go out and change things in the community, then I have to be willing to put it on the line myself.

I am at war with the juvenile justice system in this city. A former vice-squad cop who does not even have a college degree was appointed in 1963 as a juvenile-court judge. He can't even hear a case and they pay him a full judge's salary. He runs the juvenile court like he is J. Edgar Hoover. In fact, he looks like Hoover. He's this big spider with a monster web in the middle of the Black community, messing everything up. It's like a kangaroo court when it comes to juvenile adjudications, divorces, and custody matters. I pulled the covers off of it. I said, "He's nothing but a fraud. He needs to be taken off the bench."

I can't sit up here in circuit court and tell somebody they have to put it on the line if I don't. I got hauled before a judicial inquiry committee for my criticism of this juvenile-court mess. I told the committee I didn't care enough about my position to bother with their so-called investigation. But I told them they might wind up with an unanticipated consequence they wouldn't like: This place could go up like L.A. I told the members of that committee to look at all the folks packed into the hearing room. They got twenty-two thousand signatures on a petition saying they don't like this committee investigation. Why don't they like it? Because I'm merely pulling the covers off of a "good ol' boy" network of some wrong-doing mess that you all have been up to. You've been messing over my people, and you have to understand that it is a new day. Some of us put it on our mind that things are going to change.

Because I behave in this fashion, people listen to me when I tell them they need to do something. I go out and say things other folks don't dare say. I say it's wrong, it needs to be changed. I tell the system, "You've got to deal with this."

A judge can address a lot of things. A judge has the power. Now whether or not you've got a judge with the balls to do anything about it is a different matter. Quite frankly, a lot of Blacks in positions of power aren't anything but cop-outs, and this goes for Black judges also. They get in a position and they conveniently forget where they came from. They get in a position and they conveniently stop thinking they have a duty that extends beyond themselves. They get someplace and they conveniently forget that yes, you can save your career, but you may not preserve your manhood. It's that old song that goes, "I'm sorry, I can't afford to be involved. It's not that I'm unappreciative of what has been done on my behalf, but I can't afford to jeopardize my career."

We need to start having male Blacks become Black men who are not incapable of putting it all on the line, Black men who are willing to say, "The cause is justified. We have to fight for it." We can't have any more Clarence Thomas–type cop-outs. We've had all the plantation overseers we need. Clarence Thomas needs to be put in the Smithsonian Institution and transported in a time machine back to that day in antiquity when a slave overseer was a tragic reality. We don't need that now. We have enough problems. If a Black jurist cannot identify with, cannot be a part of the community he affects, then he is no different than a white judge.

Jomo Kenyatta of Kenya said it best. He said, "When we Blacks came to power with the Mau Mau, we first had to kill ten thousand white people. Unfortunately, the first nine thousand of those ten thousand had Black faces." And that's a problem here in America. If you're going to act like a white rather than somebody that ought to deal with the problem, then, for all intents and purposes, you are professionally and culturally white.

My personal philosophy is that a judge should be able to walk the streets of the community he serves, without an armed escort, at all hours of the day and night. If he can't do that, he doesn't have any business sitting as a judge.

We need people to speak up and step forward and lead. Today is a good time for us to speak out. You may lose your job, but you are not likely to lose your life these days. Nobody is going to lynch you for speaking up. Somebody may try to shoot you, but at least you don't have to sit there passively and acquiesce in it.

Something is coming together now. There has been some opportunity over the past thirty years, and we now have a number of Blacks who have come out of the inner city, who ordinarily would not have made it yet who've been through college and who are now coming into positions of authority. Now we can do something.

Demographically, 55 percent of Memphis is African American. We have a Black mayor, we've got a Black police chief, a Black superintendent of schools, a majority Black school board, an elected Black clerk at the criminal courts and one over at general sessions court. We can do things. We have got to cause change.

We need to explore the possibility of filing lawsuits that might force localities to elect judges by district instead of through at-large, citywide elections. The localities would have to divide their geographical areas up into districts, and judges would then be elected by community instead of by the city at large. District elections would allow us to gain control over the judicial election process so that we can put judges on the bench who understand. We can get judges who are knowledgeable, learned in the practice of law, and wise in the ways of the world, including the world that embraces a majority of the people who go through the courts.

You have to take a holistic approach to this so-called crime problem, because the crime problem is inextricably tied up with everything else. If you just treat it as though it is isolated, you'll get nowhere. Crime is a problem that affects the entire community. Crime in and of itself is a reflection of the community. Crime is an abnormality. When you have a high incidence of crime, you have an abnormal condition.

Two types of crime confront our criminal courts: traditional crime and crime that is, frankly, the result of slavery. Yes, slavery is alive and well in America in the inner cities. You can be a slave for your labor or you can be a slave of your inaction.

The labor market in America today is glutted. There is a desire to keep the labor market as the dominant means of ordering our society, but it no longer works if everyone is included. There just aren't enough jobs to go around. So it is in the interest of the system to target an identifiable population and exclude them from the market, whether consciously or unconsciously—it doesn't matter. But the result of that exclusion matters: The criminal courts control labor resources.

Historically, what happened when a slave became surplus to the needs of the plantation? He was sold south. Here today, in addition to preventing him from glutting the labor market, the system makes him a scapegoat based on his restless activity, his lawlessness, his behaving in a fashion that causes society-at-large to fear him. When he gets out of control, he is sold south—but now that means to abandon him to the criminal justice so-called system for an enormous profit.

The criminal justice system makes a lot of money for everybody, from the judge to the bailiff, from the bail bondsmen to the police, the sheriff's deputies, everybody. The neoslave, the young Black male, becomes the fodder, the raw material, for this industry-like profit-making system. The fodder is Black, and the beneficiaries—those who profit from the system—are white.

Profit? Look at these so-called private, for-profit prisons. They are the worst obscenity going. Everybody is caught up in this mythology that the best way to deal with something is through private enterprise. Yet in free-enterprise capitalism you know that if there is a profit to be made, someone's going to make it—and they're not going to stop unless forced to do so. And that's a chastening thought when the source of an industry's profit is the incarceration of young Black men.

These private, for-profit jails are nothing but rank, creating a sort of technical slavery. And when you have private entities that spend public moneys, you tend to see padding for executive privileges like trips and luxury hotels and expense-account entries for entertainment and limousines. In general, these facilities are just a rip-off.

Until somebody gets the picture and starts controlling the criminal justice system, it's not going to heal anything at all. The system is not going to heal itself. It is going to remain part of, and perpetuate, the problem. It is a fraud. It has not functioned as a criminal *justice* system. It has functioned as a profit-making entity.

We have to change the slave into a free man. Paradoxically, we cannot do this for him. We must impel him to do it for himself. No one can free you. You must free yourself. To free yourself, you must have self-confidence and self-respect. This self-respect can only come from within. No one will give you respect if you have none for yourself.

There are many things we could change if we were serious about reducing crime. But we leave things to be taken care of at home, too many families are incapable of living up to the responsibilities of child rearing. There has been a breakdown in the family structure because men no longer have absolute control over the household.

We have a feminine component in the crime problem that has to do with too many males who have been raised by their mamas only, without a man's influence. It's an emotional thing that you wind up with, and it leads to a lot of criminal activity. A lot of the hot-headed killings, a lot of the cold-blooded, vicious killings, have feminine aspects. It's the product of the male kids expressing their emotions physically and violently, as females do, instead of quietly holding them in, the way a man is supposed to do.

We have to address a number of things if we are really going to address the so-called crime problem. We have a drug problem, that is not really a problem but a symptom. We have a problem with violence that is not really a problem but a symptom, and I think the pathology behind the symptom is a mass death wish.

Young Black males can't see daylight at the end of the tunnel. There's no hope for getting a job. There is no perceived purpose in life. There's nothing much they can do to help themselves without violating all of the principles of right and wrong. These males, young males, can't protect their families. They can't protect their neighbors. In other words, deep inside they're asking themselves, "Why am I here?" If they can't answer that question they soon will say, "Well, I'll just take it out the best way I can." And when you get to that point, you start getting suicidal.

People kill themselves for all kinds of reasons. And certainly many of those reasons are particularly relevant to life in the Black community. Suicidal desperation manifests itself in self-destructive, violent, harmful behavior. We have to do something about that.

We need to sit up and realize that the criminal justice system, the police, and the courts are not going to solve these problems. These problems have to be solved by the communities themselves. We in the system can give communities a little breathing room, a little daylight in which to work. We can give them a little opportunity to take it back.

To make our communities communities again, males are going to have to act like men. We are going to have to go down into our areas, walk door to door and get young folk off the street corners. We are going to have to start putting these young folk into the whole panoply of things that go on in a healthy community. These young bucks need direction, and the community elders, who have the wisdom, have to provide a nurturing environment.

We must establish a community again. We have to know something about our heritage. We have to be inspired by this knowledge of our heritage. We have to have the bravery to go out and do what we must do. We have to understand our need for self-respect in order to have the personal motivation to go out and win our freedom. We have to understand that nobody is going to give us that freedom.

One of the worst things that happened in the Black community was our reliance on so-called non-violence in fighting for our freedom. When I was growing up I was embarrassed to see Black folk down on their knees with someone whipping their heads, the idea being that if you whip my behind long enough, maybe you will feel guilty and give me what ought to be mine. To hell with that. You need to take it. You have no business appealing to somebody to give you your rights. There is no need to appeal to somebody to let you be a man.

We have to impose our will on the system by being too expensive to keep down. If necessary, we need to imitate two-day-long RAF-USAF air raids and burn down the inner city, if it takes that. This is a strange statement coming from a judge, I know. But that's the consequence. Some people don't look at it this way, but what happened in Los Angeles was equivalent to dropping an atomic bomb in the middle of the city, to destroy property. The economic system of this country can't afford too much of that. Property damage alarms them.

In the sixties I became interested in the law because I was very concerned about what was going on in California. I had never wanted to be a lawyer, and of course I never even thought about being a judge. Some people were saying that the law should be used to effect real social change. That made a little bit of sense. I had majored in political science as an undergrad at UCLA, and when I finished I knew I didn't want to teach that nonsense, so I decided to go to law school. I was so unknowledgeable about law school that I thought I hadn't done very well on the LSAT until someone told me my scores were good. I ended up getting admitted to Stanford, UCLA, USC, Loyola, and Yale. I decided to stay at UCLA.

We helped open UCLA's law school to Blacks in 1967. Only two Blacks had been admitted in the fifty-year history of the law school. We talked to some folks, intimidated a few folks, some folks got jacked up, a few cars were damaged, and then they decided that there was some wisdom in the idea of admitting Blacks to UCLA Law School.

We told them we didn't want reverse discrimination. We didn't want a situation where Blacks who didn't meet the aptitude and grade-point requirements would be admitted. We wanted Blacks who were fully qualified according to the catalog: competitive assessment of grade-point average, aptitude test, and four other factors that indicate an ability to succeed. We told them that because white folks don't understand how to apply fair standards to those "other factors," we wanted a Black committee (eventually to be composed of Black students) that would assist with admissions. We also got a blind grading system in place, so only a computer would be able to associate the names with the grades. And we got them to agree they would no longer compute a student's class standing unless he or she chose it as an option.

Between 1968 and 1973, when I graduated from the Law School, more than 150 Blacks were admitted. We lost only two of them because of academic difficulties, and two others withdrew for financial reasons.

I lived through the 1965 riots in Watts. When I watched TV earlier this year and saw the riot after the Rodney King verdict, it scared me to death. There is still this pent-up violence. No one's gotten it out of their system yet, neither the police nor the people.

In '65, after the Watts riots, the crime rate in the Black inner city just stopped. No more Black-on-Black homicides, no rapes, robberies, thefts, whatever. Crime just stopped. People got together and associated peacefully with the people they had been warring with before the riots. Right now, the gangs in Los Angeles are deciding to make a truce with each other.

We had a Black Caucus meeting in Nashville recently, and there were a couple of emissaries from West Coast gangs that came out to Nashville to see what politics was all about—which is a good sign. One of them told me, "You know, we've gotten the vague sense that what we've been doing is wrong. Killing each other off doesn't seem quite right. Maybe there is another move for us to make, and we're gonna look into it. Maybe we can understand what power is, political power." That's the type of understanding that needs to be developed. So, maybe something will come out of that riot.

In the late sixties we had an opportunity to get somewhere as a country. We were dealing with problems like racism and poverty, and then they elected Richard Milhous Nixon. Instead of the positive signals that were sent by the Kennedy and Johnson White House, under Nixon you had this old-time resurrection of racist nonsense. Blacks are getting too much. They ain't worth a goddam. And then the money flowing into the inner city started tapering off. The national attitude got funky. We lost an opportunity.

And then we got Reagan and his mess. He callously relegitimized all that racist nonsense, playing off the fears of the inept and unable, telling them they need to be racists once again. There had been a psychological clamp on that racist mess until Reagan came along. That fool needs to burn in hell.

THEODORE A. McKEE

"Mandatory sentencing has not been a deterrent to crime."

The 1968 assassination of Dr. Martin Luther King Jr. almost killed Ted McKee's dream of becoming a lawyer. McKee didn't want to be a part of a system he perceived to be unfair. But he pursued his dream, graduated magna cum laude from Syracuse Law School, and served as a federal prosecutor and deputy city solicitor before being elected to Philadelphia's common pleas court in 1983. A decade of presiding over trials ranging from rape to murder to real estate trusts has taught McKee two clear lessons: first, drugs are involved in most of the cases that come to court; and, second, class and color are key determinants in the quality of justice an individual receives. McKee sees himself as a product of the sixties, a person imbued with a desire to help out.

Outside of the courtroom the tall, bearded jurist volunteers his time by serving on the Pennsylvania Sentencing Commission, which writes the sentencing guidelines used by all judges in the state, visiting prisons to talk with inmates, and working with youth mentoring programs. McKee is no softie on crime. He believes that the bad guys should be in jail, but he opposes mandatory sentencing and thinks that the legalization of drugs may be the most viable means of bringing drug-spawned crime under control.

McKee, who was interviewed in his Philadelphia City Hall chambers in April 1992, was elevated to the federal Third Circuit Court of Appeals in 1994. He was appointed by President Clinton.

In the ten years that I've been on the bench the nature of crime has changed. It absolutely has. The best way I can describe this change is to say crime has gotten much more animalistic. These young guys who are committing most of the crimes today are devoid of thought about the consequences of their actions. They don't seem to care about hurting people.

The best description I've heard of the way that criminals have changed came from an inmate I talked to inside Graterford Prison a few years ago. This guy had been in prison for fifteen or twenty years, I forget for what, but he said the young guys coming in there seemed to get some inner pleasure out of inflicting pain and suffering. He said life was like a comic book to them. When they pulled the trigger on somebody, it was just like Daffy Duck blowing somebody away on television. There is no thought of the consequences, and no grasp of the reality, of what they have done.

This inmate said that totally callous kind of attitude was very different from attitudes when he was running the streets. When he was on the streets committing crimes, he said, he had a reason for robbing someone. He would rob someone to get money to buy heroin. He told me I may not like the reason or I may disagree with the reason, but there was a reason why he would hurt someone. But a lot of these young guys hurt people for no reason. They rob someone. They have a mask on, so they can't be identified. Why do they have to shoot the victim?

A lot of these young guys don't think of the consequences because they have no concept of what a life is all about, their own life or anybody else's. That's scary. It's a total absence of respect for anything and a total absence of fear.

These guys don't even fear the cops. When I was growing up, you didn't even dream of fighting a cop. Now it is no big deal. Here are these cops with guns, mace, and all this artillery at their disposal, and people get into fights with them. It's crazy. Then, the thing that blows my mind, the same guy who throws a punch at a white cop will talk about how racist the system is. That may well be true, but if you think the system is that racist, why are you throwing a punch at a white cop with a gun? If you believe what you are saying about the racism, then don't give this white cop an excuse to blow your brains out. It makes absolutely no sense to me. It's like this inner anger, with no thought of consequences whatsoever.

Drugs have a lot to do with crime today. But I think values, and/or lack of values, also has a lot to do with it. What we as a society are doing to fight crime is not working. Mandatory sentencing, for example, has only overcrowded our prisons. It hasn't been a deterrent to crime.

At least 90 percent of the crime today is tied to drugs. I am now at the point where if I see a case and there isn't some aspect of drugs involved, I say to myself that I must have missed something. Maybe I ought to check the arrest report or some of the other records again.

In most criminal cases the defendant has a history of drug abuse or the crime itself involves drugs. Homicides, which we see extensively today, are either the result of a drug grudge or something else tied into a relationship that centers around drugs. Even on the domestic side of the court system, divorces and violence in male-female relations, somebody is high and drugs are involved. Drugs are incredibly pervasive.

When I see a defendant who is not involved with drugs, I often find myself in a conundrum: on the one hand he is somebody who is salvageable, who can be worked with; but on the other hand this guy has no excuse. If somebody is committing a crime, robbery or burglary, say, and it is not being done to feed a drug habit, then maybe that criminal is worse than the person who is doing the same thing because of a drug addiction.

I've gone back and forth on the legalization of drugs. On almost any given day you could probably get me to agree with legalization, even though there is a visceral reaction inside me against it. But I can't think of any sensible alternative to legalization. But legalization still doesn't address values. It just makes it easier for me to live my life with my values, and if you want to be an animal ass, you do that over there. You can be an animal ass without interfering with my lifestyle.

The push in different places around the country, including Philadelphia, to have a drug court, a special court just to hear drug cases, is a bad idea. The problem I have with the idea is I don't think there is any way for a judge in that situation to maintain objectivity.

The judges assigned to these drug courts hear case after case after case where young Black or Hispanic males are coming in saying, "I didn't have the drugs on me," or "I don't know anything about the drugs," or "The cops planted drugs on me," just denying any involvement. A lot of the time those guys are lying, but some of the time they are telling the truth. If you hear the same story over and over again, I don't know how you make the distinction.

You are always going to see the same cops coming in, and there is a built-in bias to believe the cop. If you always see policemen who you are familiar with, and you know you have to deal with these guys next week on other cases, it becomes more and more difficult to feel that you have a reasonable doubt. When you believe the defendant, you are basically calling the cop a liar. There is just no way to maintain your objectivity in that context over a long period of time.

A couple of summers ago I sat in on the waiver program [the non-jury trials], and most of those cases were drug cases. They almost always involved the same set of facts. Almost exactly the same testimony. There is a bias there against the defendant. When you see a young Black guy charged with a crime, there's just a prejudgment of what is going on in the urban community, so much of which is based in reality. But this particular young Black kid on trial may not be a part of that. It is hard weeding all of that out.

Drugs are a part of the crime problem, but like I said, I think we have to examine our values as a society. I'm not really sure where this society's values are. I think we would all agree that the values of the society are respect for human life and respect for the dignity of the human being. Yet if we look at the way our culture expresses itself, it is totally inconsistent with those values. Most of the movies coming out are based on taking some high-tech weapon and totally blowing people away. The underlying theme is not just violence but incredibly intense violence. Violence is also a major theme of today's music. And look at the way the overall value of human life was treated in the media coverage of the Gulf War. The focus was on how many American lives were being saved, and little to nothing was said about the enormous number of people who were dying.

We like to think of our values as a communal possession, but I'm not sure that "our" values—shared values as a society—exist anymore. Many of these young criminals are alienated from the mainstream. They don't have respect for other people or for private property. They just don't have those values. It's weird though, because in a sense they do have the values everybody else has. They value money and they value status. They look up to the guys in the neighborhood who have the money. The problem is the way they go about getting the money.

In the inner city status is tied to money the same way it is in the middle-class community. The difference is how you get the money. Although gold jewelry and flashy cars don't have the status appeal in middle-class areas that they do in the inner city, the symbols of wealth are worshiped in the urban enclave just as they are in the upper-middle-class enclave. Yet in the inner city there is no underlying respect for somebody else's symbol of wealth nor any underlying respect for human life.

Mandatory sentencing laws have not deterred crime as they were intended to do. I don't think there are fewer weapons offenses or drug crimes despite having those mandatory sentencing laws. At meetings of the [Pennsylvania] Sentencing Commission I have often asked, "Are there any studies showing that mandatory sentencing has deterred crime?" I never get an affirmative answer. The director of our commission, John Kramer, has done a lot of research in the area of mandatory sentencing, and he is not aware of any studies that show mandatory sentencing has decreased the crime rate.

The only impact mandatory sentencing has had is an incredibly backward effect. Mandatory sentencing has led to the unacceptable overcrowding of our prisons. In reality, mandatory sentencing has put more, not fewer, people on the street, because it has required the release of inmates in nonmandatory categories to make room for prisoners serving mandatory sentences. A rapist is released so we have room for a small-time drug pusher doing a mandatory. Fewer people can be sent to prison because the other folks in these mandatory categories have to serve such long sentences. It's simple math: If you take one guy and jail him for five years, that means one less prison space is available to the state for five years.

The other problem with mandatory sentencing laws is that they undercut the whole system of justice and the concept of individualized justice. No matter what the circumstances, mandatory sentencing requires sentences based only on the class of offense. We want drug dealers, say, to go to prison for *x* number of years, whether or not an individual deserves *x* years based on the circumstances surrounding his crime. Many offenders don't deserve to go to prison, but they must under mandatory sentencing. A guy who sells one joint automatically gets five years under a mandatory, but a rapist who hurts someone gets two to five because rape isn't under mandatory sentencing. You get inequities in there. It doesn't come up a lot, but because of mandatories there are individuals in prison who everybody would agree shouldn't be.

I don't think society stops to think about the consequences of mandatory sentencing laws in terms of individual inequities. Ironically, the run-of-the-mill badass guys these laws are intended to punish end up in prison anyhow. These guys would probably get five to ten years regardless of the mandatory. Mandatory sentencing legislation doesn't solve anything, it just creates problems, all kinds of problems in terms of the quality of justice and the availability of prison space.

Mandatory legislation was supposed to make sentencing more uniform, but you still have inequities based on race. You see this in terms of judges' deviations above or below the sentencing guidelines. [Certain mandatory sentencing statutes permit deviations if a judge writes a report explaining the reason for the deviation.] Kramer has done a study on this. He thinks the inequities show up in terms of who gets sentenced at the lower end of the standard range allowed by the guidelines and who gets sentenced at the upper end.

I think it is easy for a judge to deviate from the standard sentence and give a white middle-class defendant a break by deviating below the sentencing guideline because of all of the subliminal predispositions. But no break will be given to the Black urban youth. The circumstances that the judge would use to justify the lighter sentencing of the middle-class defendant are all what we call racial identifiers: he's from a good family, he is from a good neighborhood, goes to a good school, has the influence of a good community on him, is active in that community. But what about the kid who grows up in a public housing project? What's good about the community influence in the projects?

A better question is who of the two is more salvageable? It may well be the kid in the projects who has committed a first offense at the age of eighteen. He has escaped all that negative stuff for a long time and has never been involved with drugs—but then finally he makes a mistake. He is probably more salvageable than a kid who has had all the opportunity in the world, all the breaks in the world, and is out there screwing up. So I think society is probably giving the breaks to the wrong folks. I am not sure how often this happens, but I know that it happens often enough.

I don't think there is equal justice under the law in this country. A large part of it is class. I'm not always sure how much of it is class and how much of it is caste. In this society those two things—class and caste—are almost the same anyhow. I don't think there are many judges on the bench who are just out and out racist, but we all have these subliminal attitudes. If a lower-class Black commits the same crime as an upper-middle-class white, there is going to be an incredible discrepancy of treatment. Some of this will be class and some of it will be caste. There are just so many stereotypes out there, and so many people are so afraid—with good cause—it is hard to keep those fears in check when you see a young Black male in a courtroom charged with a violent crime.

Now if a lower-class white comes to court charged with a serious crime, he is in deep shit, too. But I think that there is a different set of reactions to a lower-class white than to a middle-class white that go off in both a white and a Black judge. I just don't think that they are as intense in a Black judge. At any rate, class is a problem in our justice system.

Racism is also very deeply ingrained in our society and in our justice system. And this racism is not just white vis-à-vis Black racism. To an extent, it is also Black vis-à-vis Black racism. For example, if I'm walking down a street in Center City Philadelphia at two in the morning and I hear some footsteps behind me and I turn around and there is a couple of young white dudes behind me, I am probably not going to get very uptight. I'm probably not going to have the same reaction if I turn around and there is the proverbial Black urban youth behind me. Now if I can have this reaction—and I'm a Black male who has studied martial arts for twenty some odd years and can defend myself—I can't help but think that the average white judge in the situation will have a reaction that is ten times more intense. I know that these subliminal attitudes come into play in the courtroom in terms of how sentences are meted out, what is done to a defendant after he is found guilty, and how judges determine the credibility of the defendant.

I think that with more Blacks in positions of authority in the justice system, particularly on the bench, it helps even up the score when the defendant gets on the witness stand and testifies. He is not seen as just another Black urban youth. I would hope not, anyhow. The defendant's story will be listened to. It may not be believed—and maybe it shouldn't be believed, because he may be lying through his teeth—but at least he will have his proverbial day in court.

I think it is very easy for that very subtle, subliminal racism to creep in, and when the defendant comes into court you just disregard him and dehumanize him. That subliminal racism—and it is subliminal—that kind of racism is there when the judge thinks of a Black defendant as part of the stereotype of this dangerous mass out there waiting to take over our schools and our streets and break into our homes. I would hope that this doesn't happen to the same degree with Black judges as white judges. I think it still happens with Black judges, but I hope it doesn't happen to the same degree.

You see race-based disparities in other parts of the justice system, too. I see it a lot in what is called "prosecutorial discretion." Under the law the prosecutor has a lot of discretion in deciding who is charged and what to charge them with. Racism in discretion often surfaces in determining whom to recommend for diversionary programs and who to send to trial instead. These kinds of things really worry me.

I had a case involving a Black guy with two kids, who he was raising on his own. He had been charged with running a methamphetamine lab, and the DA's office initially would not certify this guy for a diversionary program [a pretrial probation program where charges are dropped if the probation is successfully served]. They wanted to put this guy in prison for two to four years, which would leave his children on their own. Here was a guy who had really turned his life around. He was doing very well in community college, where he worked as a tutor. All of his professors raved about him, and he really had made a whole new person out of himself since the days when he had been involved with the "meth" lab.

About this same time, I was considering another case. A guy had robbed someone on the street with a gun, and the DA's office wanted to certify this gunman for the diversionary program. The gunman was pleading guilty, and I kept asking myself why this case was being certified for diversion. The only reason I could see was that the gunman was white. I later found out the gunman was a cop's son.

I called the DA in to find out what was going on with these cases. The defense in the drug case had already raised the issue of racial disparity. I called the DA in to justify why the gunman was being certified and the drug guy was not. The DA swore up and down that it had nothing to do with race, and then he went on to talk about all those things that are markers for race. The DA said the gunman was from a good middle-class family, from a good middle-class community, and his father was a police officer. I think the police officer part may have been the clincher, but he was basically telling me that it had nothing to do with race and then he is pointing to the guy's neighborhood, what his parents did for a living, all these things that this culture translates into race. As it turned out, the DA did certify the drug case for diversion. But that experience reinforced my feeling that a lot of this stuff goes down as to who gets diverted and who gets certified for a mandatory sentence.

I once heard a young female DA talk with a group of college students, and she was talking about how fair the prosecutor's office was. She gave as an example a kid who was a first offender and was convicted of a string of burglaries and given a diversionary program because he had no prior problems. My reaction to that was that if this kid had grown up and lived in the projects, the DA wouldn't have begun to consider giving him a diversion. They would have laughed at any attorney who had even mentioned diversion to them.

A kid who grows up in the projects has every reason to rob. They are not justifiable reasons, but from that kid's perspective, his environment and the mindset of the people around him, it is much more understandable for him to rob than for a kid who doesn't share that background. Yet society treats one much more harshly than the other, and society has it backwards.

Bias creeps into the system at less obvious levels, at the level where an individual's discretion determines who gets arrested, who gets prosecuted, how the guilty are sentenced, and who gets these mandatories. When you look at who gets prosecuted and who gets diversion, the judiciary has no say there. It is totally up to the mindset of the prosecutor. This is why it is important to have more Blacks involved in the policy-making levels within the prosecutor's office.

This subliminal racism that is a part of the justice system is what disturbs me the most about the death penalty. My opposition to the death penalty is not necessarily on moralistic or humanistic grounds; everybody who has ever looked at the application of the death penalty has concluded that there is a grossly inequitable application of it. I don't have any confidence in the assertion that a Black defendant is as likely to get the death penalty as a white man in the same situation. The Black man is a lot more likely to end up in the electric chair. And no matter how careful you are during jury selection in trying to weed out people who have these subliminal prejudices, you can't really weed them all out. You just can't do it.

My initial exposure to the criminal justice system was in the federal court system as a federal prosecutor. The mindsets of federal and state prosecutors are so different. When I was with the U.S. Attorney's office we were keenly aware that our job was to do justice. Yes, that meant getting a conviction, but it meant getting a fair conviction by putting forth the government's case and letting the jury decide. Once I got on the bench I got more and more of the feeling that the method of operation for the state prosecutor was to win the case, period. The state prosecutor takes the position that, well, let's put the evidence out there and let the jury or the judge decide whether or not the person did the crime. It is a very dangerous approach to take.

State prosecutors push cases through the system that really shouldn't be tried. State prosecutor is an elected position, and it may be politics that is pushing these prosecutions. I had one case, a rape case, where the DA talked to the complainant, who was a child of about eleven or twelve, and right before trial the DA said she had real doubts about what the complainant was telling her and she was not going to prosecute the case. But her action in that case was very, very rare. I remember this case because it was an exception. Coming into the job I had assumed it was a prosecutor's job to do justice, but I don't have that illusion anymore.

Many judges were formerly prosecutors, but I don't think they end up favoring prosecutors. Some defense lawyers will argue differently, but I don't think so. My friends who are defense lawyers say, for the most part, that former prosecutors who become judges end up leaning the other way to show that they are fair. They are very conscious of their prosecutorial background, and they try not to let that be a bias for them. I heard about one former public defender whose rulings have made public defenders very unhappy because they feel he is going out of his way to show he does not always favor the defense. The public defenders feel their clients are getting screwed in the process.

It's important that justice be done at all levels, particularly at the prosecutorial level, because it is incredibly difficult for a conviction to be wiped away. Even if a judge wants to change his or her mind, it is very, very difficult to do it, because the test for overturning a conviction is so high.

I had a couple of cases where I thought I had blown it by convicting the defendants, and I wound up being able to grant a new trial both times. One was a little burglary case, and nobody really cared, except the defendant, the defense attorney, and myself. The other time I granted a new trial it didn't go up on appeal. This guy was retried and the jury acquitted him.

I'm still not sure if this second guy was guilty or not, but there was not enough evidence to convict him. I became more and more convinced of that after I convicted him initially. But the problem was, I became convinced of it for the wrong reason—not through reassessment of the evidence so much, but because of the defendant's reaction after I found him guilty. In fact, both times I granted new trials I did so based on the defendant's reaction.

Normally, when you find somebody guilty of a crime, it's no big deal to him. The guy sort of says silently, "I did the crime, you found me guilty, the game is over," and he goes about his business and you go about yours. This is very different from what the public expects. They expect for a person to feel bad after being convicted.

Well, anyway, in this case, the guy's father and mother were in the courtroom, and he turned around after I found him guilty and looked at his parents with this expression like, "Do you believe this shit?" He walked out of the courtroom shaking his head.

There was something in this guy's demeanor that really made me think I had made a mistake. The whole case had hinged on the testimony of a jailhouse snitch. I thought the snitch was lying, but I thought he was lying to help the defendant because he was basically saying the defendant had told him that he was in the cab at the time the cab was robbed but he didn't pull the gun, he didn't pull the trigger, and he didn't go through the victim's pocket. In a prior statement, this snitch had said the defendant told him he did pull out the gun and did go through the guy's pocket. At trial, the snitch backed off his prior statement. I really thought he was backing off to help the defendant, not realizing that once he puts the defendant in the conspiracy it doesn't matter who has the gun or who pulls the trigger. He is still guilty of second degree murder under the conspiracy charge.

I began to reassess my position on this case because of something the defense attorney had said about "reasonable doubt" in her closing argument. She used this example: You go to a strange city, you are lost, and you're trying to find a place. You stop somebody and ask them for directions, and the person you ask for directions is the DA's witness. After you talk to him, you're going to stop somebody else and ask them how to get where you are going. Asking that second person, she said, was reasonable doubt.

I don't know why that argument made such an impact on me. After I thought about it more, I said to myself, Boy, that is a good argument. I still went ahead and convicted him, but after I saw the defendant's reaction I thought about the defense attorney's argument. I said to myself, Yeah, in retrospect, I really do have a reasonable doubt about that testimony; and I gave him a new trial. As I said, he was acquitted in the second trial.

From time to time I have real problems assessing the credibility of defendants. When I have these doubts, I start asking myself whether the doubt that I have is reasonable. I ask myself whether I really doubt the defendant's credibility or whether, based on the evidence, I think that I *should* have a reasonable doubt even though I don't have one. I go around in circles with that because the more I ask myself the latter question, the more that seems like reasonable doubt. It is a tortuous way of approaching the matter, but I find myself unable to avoid it in close cases.

You know, it may sound weird, but I think that reading literature is the best on-going training for a judge. I don't have time to read as much as I'd like to, but I think I have gotten more out of reading Dickens, say, than I have out of reading legal textbooks on evidence. As a judge you have to know a lot about men, and reading literature does a good deal to sensitize you, to put you in another man's shoes. That is extremely important for a judge because it is so easy to lose track of the human dynamic that you are dealing with in the courtroom. You can get so wrapped up in the technicalities of legal procedure that the human element gets shoved aside. That's when the system begins to break down. I think the kind of sensitivity you get from reading literature—more than anything else I can think of—helps a judge do his job.

One of the things that most appealed to me about becoming a judge was the fact that it is a position with some social utility. As a judge I wouldn't just be working from day to day for a paycheck—my job would mean something. And being a judge gave me the kind of independence that I wanted; it allowed me to be my own boss. Besides, I couldn't think of anything else to do with a law degree. I felt fairly certain I didn't want to practice law all my life.

Law is an area that has always intrigued me, particularly during high school. In high school I thought seriously about becoming an attorney. I was very active in high school; I was president of the student body, and all that stuff. A lot of people on the faculty were encouraging me to pursue the law. These were teachers, not the guidance counselors who were talking to me about flower arranging as a career. I think I went to college with the idea of becoming a lawyer in the back of my head.

But I almost didn't go into the law. When Martin Luther King was assassinated I got to the point where I just did not want to devote my life to a system that I then thought of as a part of the atmosphere surrounding the assassination. I thought I couldn't do in good faith what one had to do to be a judge. The assassination of Dr. King really soured me on the system in this society. Years earlier, the assassination of Malcolm X had also raised doubts in me about the fairness of the system.

After college I didn't go straight to law school. But after working a few jobs I began to think having a law degree would give me one more arrow in my quiver in terms of options for my career, so I went to Syracuse Law School.

Even when I was in law school I still wasn't sure I wanted to be a lawyer. But at the time I couldn't stop to ask the question, because law school was so demanding. I put the blinders on and studied and took exams and said to myself, I'll do the work and finish this, and some time down the road I can sit back and ask myself, Do I really want to do this forever?

Before I went into private practice I was a federal prosecutor for about three and a half years. I started out with bank robberies. That's how they trained you in that office. You couldn't lose a bank robbery case. My Saint Bernard could have won those cases. You have the surveillance film, the fingerprints, the handwriting tests from the demand notes, and five bank tellers saying that that is the guy who did it. Eventually I began trying public-corruption cases. Trying those cases was rewarding. I didn't feel like I was simply putting one more Black person in prison.

I never really thought seriously about being a judge until I had been practicing law for a number of years and I began thinking the same thing I had in law school: I don't want to practice law all my life. Being a judge seemed like a good thing to do with a law degree. I couldn't think of anything that was more socially useful. This was a position where I could do things to benefit the community. I didn't see many alternatives to being a judge, so I ended up doing it.

I consider myself a product of the sixties, and I hope the legacy of the sixties has not been reversed within me by the lethargy of the eighties and nineties. I do feel there is a need to help out. When I was doing criminal trials, I saw "helping out" as really just making sure that, within my courtroom, whoever came in there got justice. And I participate in things like the sentencing commission because it gives me a chance to have an impact beyond my individual adjudications.

I'm now sitting in orphan's court, the court in Philadelphia County that handles wills, estates, and things like that. Here you can easily forget the realities of the criminal courts because you're examining arcane legal issues most of the time. The good thing about it, though, is that you can help more directly—because you can put something back the way it was. In criminal court you can't right the wrong. With homicides you certainly can't put it back the way it was. But in orphan's court, a lot of times you *can* put it back the way it was before they ripped off their dead mother's estate or dead sister's estate. You can't heal all of the wounds that fester in these situations, but often you can put people back where they were before the injury. I enjoy orphan's court because I see the way people benefit directly from my judgments, even if those decisions are less dramatically beneficial to society than criminal court decisions.

I don't know exactly what we should be doing to control the crime problem, but I know that what we *are* doing isn't working. It's gotten so bad that the public is willing to sacrifice a few rights as a tradeoff for dealing with this problem and that's scary. In one of his dissents—from a drug case involving search and seizure—Justice Marshall points out that there is no drug exception under the Fourth Amendment. In that case the Supreme Court's majority said traditional constitutional safeguards, such as protection against unreasonable searches, can be suspended in waging the "war on drugs." That type of thinking may be reasonable, but it is questionable legally.

The public and, particularly, politicians are always talking about getting tough on criminals, and getting tough with criminals means kicking the shit out of them—and that is totally inconsistent with the Bill of Rights.

But look at our cop shows on TV. I remember this one show that was on when I was growing up called *Starsky and Hutch*. I would sit there and watch this show in amazement. To begin with, these two cops would violate every civil right ever guaranteed by this society. They would shoot at an unarmed criminal who was fleeing. They would rough up some poor suspect, throw him against a wall, punch him in the stomach, and then arrest him without reading him his *Miranda* rights.

During the bicentennial celebration for the U.S. Constitution people like Philadelphia's then district attorney were talking about the greatness of America, but at the same time they were attacking all the principles that are fundamental to this country, like right to counsel, the right to a fair trial, and the presumption of innocence. Nobody really believes in that stuff, or, I should say, it is rare for people to believe in it.

I have this pet peeve. I'm convinced that if we were to draft the U.S. Constitution right now, you probably could not get anyone to introduce it in Congress, and, even if it were to be introduced, it probably wouldn't be approved. Politicians would be afraid to introduce it because it guarantees freedom of speech, for instance. People would start asking whether freedom of speech means that a Communist can speak at a high school—and it does. Politicians would think the protections in the Bill of Rights would cause voters to identify them as soft on crime, and they would be afraid of not being reelected. They have no backbone. No one would introduce the Bill of Rights in Congress now because they would be afraid that their career would be down the tubes. It's incredible.

FRED L. BANKS JR.

"Many of the judges in Mississippi . . . were like the unrobed Klan."

When Fred Banks returned home to Mississippi in 1968 with a degree from Howard University Law School, racially motivated murders by white segregationists were as common as Black lawyers were rare. Not only was the Mississippi judiciary all white in 1968, many of its jurists did not disguise their dislike for Blacks, eschewing their duty to be impartial.

As a civil rights lawyer for the NAACP Legal Defense Fund, president of the Jackson, Mississippi branch of the NAACP, and a state legislator, the soft-spoken Justice Banks was at the forefront of the battles that broke the social and political barriers that made Mississippi the most segregated state in the nation. The civil rights movement paved the way for the integration of Mississippi's judicial system, from police officers to judges. In 1985 Banks became one of the state's first Black trial court judges. He was appointed to the Mississippi Supreme Court in January 1991, the second Black to serve on the state's high court.

His background as a civil rights attorney did not inhibit Judge Banks from imprisoning those who were found guilty in his court. He believes that many Black criminals use racism as an excuse for their misdeeds.

Justice Banks was interviewed at the Carroll Gartin Justice Building in downtown Jackson in December 1992.

There were no Black judges in the state of Mississippi above the office of justice of the peace until 1977, when Rupert Anderson was named a county judge. Rupert was a law partner of mine at the time. There were no Black judges in this state even during Reconstruction. Black involvement in any aspect of the judicial system of Mississippi simply didn't exist prior to the late sixties to any extent. The first Black justices of the peace were not elected until 1967, following massive voter registration brought on by the Voting Rights Act.

Rupert Anderson was, in a manner of speaking, the only Black judge in Mississippi until 1985, with one exception. Cleve McDowell was a part-time youth court judge in Prentiss County, but he only served one day a month. Rupert was the only full-time judge. He served as a county judge from 1977 until 1982, when he was appointed to the circuit court bench. In 1985 Rupert was appointed to the Mississippi Supreme Court. I was appointed to take his place on the circuit bench in 1985 and on this court in 1991, when Rupert left to go back into private practice.

Prior to 1977 Black judges were few in number throughout the South and probably to a large extent in the North. There were a few Black judges in Memphis and Atlanta. The feeling among the Black community in Mississippi and most places in the South at that time was that the judicial system was not favorable to Black people. It wasn't until the late sixties that Blacks began to sit on juries, let alone serve as judges, in any kind of appreciable numbers.

In Mississippi in 1964, less than 2 percent of the eligible Black voters were registered to vote. The number of registered Black voters increased dramatically after the passage of the Voting Rights Act. The Voting Rights Act got Black people to put their lives on the line—and some lost their lives—to secure the right to vote. The Voting Rights Act got people interested in the political process in greater numbers. Law suits were filed to eliminate the overt discrimination in selecting juries, and Blacks began to serve on juries for the first time in Mississippi in the late sixties and early seventies. The civil rights movement brought down great change in this state.

In 1964 there were only four Black lawyers in the whole state of Mississippi. Rupert Anderson was the first Black graduate of the University of Mississippi School of Law, and that was in 1967. As you know, the University of Mississippi didn't have its first Black student until 1962. That student was James Meredith. When I came back to the state in 1968, I think I was the tenth Black lawyer at the time. There wasn't any Black involvement in the judicial system, but beginning in the late sixties there was a push in the Black community to get some diversity in Mississippi's judiciary.

Cliff Trench was the governor who appointed Rupert Anderson to the bench in 1977. Appointing Blacks to the bench was important to the Black community, and he was asked to do it. He said that he would. Vacancies opened up on this court and on the circuit court. Governor Trench appointed a circuit judge from Hinds County to fill the supreme court vacancy, he appointed a county judge to fill the circuit court vacancy, and he appointed Rupert to fill the county court vacancy that had been created. During Trench's four years in office he appointed Blacks to just about every state board and commission that he could. Trench was elected in 1975. His predecessor, Bill Wyler, who was elected in 1971, was the first governor to appoint any Black person to a state board or commission. He appointed three or four Blacks to boards or commissions.

Many of the judges in Mississippi up to the time of Rupert's appointment were like the unrobed Klan—or the Klan in Black robes instead of white sheets. This kind of attitude was found on both state and federal benches. There were people on the bench like Sebe Dale. I'm talking about the senior Sebe Dale. His son, Sebe Jr., is currently a judge—and he is nothing like his father.

Once Sebe Dale was hearing the case of a defendant named Mack Charles Parker. Parker was represented by Jess Brown, and Jess tells this story of being asked pointedly by Sebe Dale whether he was going to stay in Charleston that night or go back to Jackson. It was the night that Mack Charles Parker was taken out of jail and lynched. Rupert tells the story of having called Dale one time about a matter that was pending in his court, and Dale asked him if his office was located on Shire Street. When Rupert said yes, Dale hung up on him. All of the Black lawyers and all of the civil rights lawyers in Jackson had offices on Shire Street.

There are a lot of stories about Sebe Dale, Marshall Peer, and other judges in this state at that time who were hostile to Black lawyers to the point of mistreating them in the courtroom. Judges were part of the establishment and were willing to follow, to a greater or lesser degree depending upon the judge, the dictates of the powers that be.

There wasn't much difference on the federal bench, particularly in the Southern District of Mississippi. The judges on the Southern District Court were viewed as more actively hostile to civil rights cases. These judges were led by Judge Harold Cox, who was world-renowned for his bigotry. If you were trying a case in federal court in the Southern District of Mississippi you knew that no matter how meritorious your case was, you wouldn't win. You'd make your record and then hope to win before the circuit appeals court.

Now, at the same time, in the Northern District of Mississippi the federal judges had the reputation of being fair. Judge Cady and Judge Homer Smith, both of whom took office in '67 or '68, were viewed as fair, and so was Judge Carl Clayton, who served before them. There was a marked contrast between the way the Northern District handled school desegregation efforts and how they were handled in the Southern District federal court.

When I came back to Mississippi in 1968, I worked exclusively on civil rights cases. One of my first tasks was to prepare and present motions for desegregation plans following the decision in *Green v. Newton County*. We had to prepare plans for each individual school district. In the Northern District, Judge Cady and Judge Smith would have a hearing and would order a new plan. In the Southern District, the three judges, Dan Russell, Harold Cox, and Walter Nixon, consolidated all of the hearings, sat as a panel for all the motions for the new plans, and denied them all. We had to go to the fifth circuit appeals court to get things turned around. When the new desegregation plans were developed by the fifth circuit, the Nixon administration decided to delay their implementation for a year. The matter was taken to the U.S. Supreme Court, and in October 1969 that court ordered immediate desegregation.

The federal judges Cady and Smith experienced a great deal of hostility for their rulings. They were viewed as being too responsive to the constitutional rights of Black people. They were ostracized by their own community. Considering the scorn Cady and Smith received, it's easy to see why a lot of state judges acted as they did. Mississippi has an elected state judiciary. Trial judges are elected every four years in partisan elections. So there was a great deal of pressure on them not to be viewed as soft on the issue of segregation and white supremacy.

Black judges bring two important assets to the bench. The first thing Black judges bring, depending on how many you have, is new respect for the system itself in the community. When people see that the system is representative of all the segments of the community, they have more respect for the system. Much of this respect, or potential respect, depends on how the Black judges perform. Black judges also bring a perspective that is sorely lacking in their absence. They bring some perspective, some insight from a segment of the community that has simply gone unrepresented. This perspective is born out of an experience that one has had growing up in a Black community as opposed to a white community.

Every judge who takes the bench brings the unique perspective of his or her socialization. Mine is the perspective of having grown up Black in Mississippi in the forties, fifties, and sixties. I grew up mainly in Jackson, and it was absolutely segregated then. There were even separate water fountains. There was no aspect of life that was integrated. My schooling was a little different from most Blacks because I went to parochial school and not to public school. Most of my teachers were white nuns, from both the South and the North, and this experience was different than going to public school, where there were no white teachers. My decision to go into the law was, to some extent, related to a desire to contribute to change in Mississippi. I can't say contributing to change was uppermost on my mind. I was like a lot of people in college who didn't know what they wanted to do. Somehow I found myself as an accounting major taking business law courses and income tax courses that were taught by lawyers, and I found out that the law interested me and that I could do well in it. By the time I got around to graduating from college, going to law school had become my number one choice.

When I graduated from law school, I came back to Mississippi to work as an attorney with the NAACP Legal Defense and Education Fund. Marion Wright had been sent into Mississippi in 1964 to establish a civil rights law office for the fund. Marion stayed from '64 until '68. I had met Marion when I was working with Lawyer Legal Services. As a law student I had come on a Legal Services mission to try to get a legal services program started in Mississippi. She recruited me to come to the Mississippi office of the NAACP Defense Fund.

I actually had two options when I graduated from law school: I could have gone with Legal Services in Oxford, Mississippi, or come to Jackson with the Legal Defense Fund. I decided on the Defense Fund, which involved civil rights work primarily in school desegregation but also in the full range of civil rights litigation. In 1970 we converted the office to a private firm, but we still got a retainer from the Legal Defense Fund to do civil rights cases.

When I first started practicing law in Mississippi in 1968, things were still pretty dangerous. When I was traveling to Jackson on July 1, 1968, I passed through Meridian. Three hours after I passed through that city, there was a bombing. I think the home of a Jewish businessman was bombed. Mississippi had a history of fire bombings and murders. NAACP leader Medgar Evers was murdered in 1963. Vernon Dalmer was firebombed in his home in 1965. Some of this was described in the movie *Mississippi Burning*.

Things were dangerous. You had to be careful where you stayed and where you stopped. But having grown up here, I was acculturated to these dangers. My wife at the time was probably more concerned about these things than I was. When I got here there were a few funny telephone calls for the first year or two. There was some organized effort to get at civil rights lawyers, but there was no big overt threat.

Some of the civil rights cases we handled were simple. In public accommodations cases, you'd get an injunction against the party that was discriminating against Blacks. Other cases, like school desegregation cases, could go on and on. There would be constant monitoring. You had to develop desegregation plans. In small counties with just two schools, you simply paired the schools. Instead of sending all the whites to one school and all the Blacks to another, you would send all students in certain grades to one school and all other grades to the other school. In larger districts, like in the city of Jackson, you couldn't do that. You would have to deal with schools all over the area. You would have to deal with magnet concepts to achieve what we call a unitary school system. You would have to deal with the effects of white flight and would still have to deal with the misallocation of resources. Achieving equality in educational opportunity is a difficult task.

I had never much thought about being a judge. In 1975 I ran for the state legislature and was elected. In 1976 I was the state campaign manager for Jimmy Carter. When Carter took office in 1977, one of his promises was to appoint Black federal judges in the South. He kept that promise, and my name was prominent as the person who would be appointed a federal judge in Mississippi should a vacancy occur; but no vacancy occurred in the Southern District of Mississippi during Carter's tenure. Mississippi was excluded from the bill that increased the number of federal judges throughout the nation.

But in any event, I had some ambivalence about becoming a judge then. I was in my mid-thirties and I really didn't know whether I wanted to be a judge of any kind. At the time I was active in civil rights, not just as a lawyer but as a leader, too. I was president of the Jackson branch of the NAACP from 1971 to 1982. I was not the kind of person who could get elected, so I never had any aspirations for a state court judgeship at that time.

In 1985, when Rupert was appointed to the state supreme court, I guess I was a bit older, in my mid-forties by that time. I didn't think we should take a step backwards and not have any Black person sitting as a trial judge in the state. The most likely person to get appointed was me, so I offered my services.

I was not the governor's first choice. The people responded with a massive effort to persuade the governor to appoint me. I was recommended by the Judicial Nominating Commission, and I was appointed. It was with mixed emotions that I then left private practice and the legislature to become a judge.

I really had no problems making the transition from the bar to the bench. Yes, my background as a lawyer was in civil rights work where I was trying to vindicate rights, but it wasn't hard for me when I became a judge to put someone in jail. Quite frankly, some people deserve to go to jail. Basically, I didn't find it terribly difficult to sit as a judge in criminal cases.

However, being a judge was different from private practice, in that most of my experience as a lawyer had been in the civil arena and in federal court as opposed to the state court system. A few years before my appointment to the bench, our state courts had adopted the federal rules, so I was very equipped to handle the federal rules of civil procedure. Some of the judges who had been on the bench for a while didn't have much experience in federal court. I didn't do an awful lot of criminal cases, but I did do major criminal cases. I had a perspective on criminal procedure. I knew that a judge's job, especially in the criminal process, was to make sure that the accused is accorded all of his constitutional rights, and I didn't find any problem doing that.

Most of the criminal cases I heard originated in the rural county where I sat. The bulk of the criminal work in the judicial district where I sat was handled by another judge. Our district included Hinds and Yazoo Counties. Yazoo County had about 25,000 people, while Hinds County, which includes Jackson, had close to 300,000 people. I handled the civil docket in Hinds County and all of Yazoo County. I would get some of the criminal docket overflow from Hinds County, but I handled most of the criminal work for Yazoo County.

Most of the criminal work I had in Yazoo County involved petty crimes. I once sentenced a guy in Yazoo County to twenty-five years for rape, and I think I had maybe one or two life sentences, but I had no problems handing out those long sentences. The sentences I gave were appropriate to the crime and the individual.

The drug problem is widespread in Mississippi, from the smallest town to Jackson, which is our largest city. This drug problem is something I'd say has come about within the last decade. As far as I knew we never had a heroin problem in this state. We didn't have the drug problems that the large northern cities had in the fifties and sixties. Marijuana wasn't even heard of here in the fifties and sixties. Drinking was about it in Mississippi when I was growing up. We began to encounter marijuana in the late sixties, and that was pretty much it until the late seventies when we started getting pills and then cocaine. We never had much of a heroin problem, because it wasn't a drug of choice anywhere in the late seventies. But we have had some problems with "crack" cocaine.

The crack cocaine problem, especially the aspect of selling crack openly on street corners, involves the Black community. There are whites who are using crack cocaine, but crack isn't sold openly on the streets of white communities as it is in Black communities. White drug offenders who come into the criminal justice system tend to be involved with large amounts of marijuana and drugs other than crack cocaine. With Blacks it's mainly crack cocaine.

Crime has increased in Mississippi during the past decade. Crime is tied to drugs, and the drug problem is a symptom of the breakdown of values and morals in our society. It seems to me at least that the use of drugs and the sale of drugs is directly related to two things: the breakdown of values and the continued economic plight of a large segment of our society.

Racism plays a role in crime, yet we should be aware that racism is often used as an excuse for the commission of crime. Obviously an individual can overcome racism or any other condition of our society which puts that person at an unfair disadvantage. To the extent that racism affects a class of persons and affects that class of persons so that a disproportionate number is affected by poverty, then it is to be expected that there will be a disproportionate number turning to crime. To the extent that racism creates a condition of hopelessness, whether warranted or unwarranted, it creates conditions that breed crime.

Blacks commit a disproportionate amount of crime, but the criminal justice system has a different and disproportionate response to crime committed by Blacks. Black people tend to get arrested more often than anybody else. Some of that is because they are Black. The perception that Black people are involved in crime creates a mindset that causes Black people to come under suspicion more often, so the one thing feeds the other. You arrest more Blacks because they are suspected of committing crimes, and then you suspect them of committing crimes because they are arrested more often than other groups.

There is disproportionate poverty in the Black community. There is a disproportionate incidence of poor mental and physical health in the Black community. These conditions led to, or are related to, the level of criminal activity. Even if you adjust for statistics and eliminate that portion of the statistics that are unfair—arrests that should not have been made and charges that should not have been brought—you would probably still wind up with the conclusion that Blacks commit crimes in proportionately greater numbers than more advantaged racial groups.

I think you have to fight crime on two fronts. You have to eliminate conditions that foment crime. You have to deal with things like poverty, and create better employment opportunities, better educational opportunities, and things like that. You have to make sure people understand that there is some other way out. At the same time, we have to create some deterrent, and, of course, in my view deterrents are making sure that people know that there is a high probability that they will be caught. It doesn't mean they are going to spend the rest of their lives in jail if they do get caught, but they will get caught and they will be punished. That may mean we need more police officers to stem the temptation to engage in criminal activity.

Also, at the same time, we need to reinstill in society as a whole the values that work against the criminal mentality. It is very difficult to preach that crime is wrong, that violence is wrong, in a society that glorifies crime and violence. Our society says stealing is wrong, yet in all of its media the kind of greed exhibited by businessmen, taking unfair advantage of the helpless, is projected as being all right. We're sending a mixed signal. We are sending a signal that everything is OK if you can get away with it. That is a message that is being received by young people to a much greater extent today than it was forty years ago.

We have to address the continuing inequities in our judicial system. There have been numerous studies all over the country documenting these inequities. There are inequities in the number of minority judges and minority employees in the judicial system. There are inequities in the fact that certain persons end up with longer sentences than other persons charged with the same crime. These inequities in the judicial system are symptomatic of society as a whole. There are statistics that show that Black women tend to pay more for automobiles than any other group.

On the sentencing issue, the disparities in sentencing, I don't argue that an element of racism is not involved. But again, look back on how a person comes into the judicial system. If a person comes into the system with support from outside the system in terms of family, friends, employees or what have you, that person is going to be treated differently from a person who comes into the system with no support, even though the two have committed the same crime. In all probability the person who gets the better treatment may have less excuse for having committed the crime than the other one, but the one simply had more support in the system and the sentencer doesn't really know what to do with other one. That explains part of the statistical disparity in how we treat different persons charged with similar crimes.

Black people are underrepresented in most areas where power is wielded. And there are explanations for some of that: racism and discrimination. But whatever the explanations, the situation has to change.

Here in Mississippi during the last twenty years things have improved, because in many ways Blacks have attained positions of power. The quality of justice in this state has definitely improved. I'd say this is due primarily to the presence of Black jurors and Black involvement in the political process. Blacks are heavily involved in the political process in Mississippi now, and they weren't twenty years ago. Twenty years ago you didn't see Blacks in the courthouse at all unless they were defendants. You didn't see Blacks in the courthouse as jurors, clerks, lawyers, and certainly not as judges.

Now there are more Black judges in the state of Mississippi than there were Black lawyers in the state when I began to practice law here. There are now 250 Black lawyers in the state. There were ten when I started in 1968. Black lawyers are making money. They are securing large judgments and settlements for Black clients. That wasn't happening twenty years ago, and that is one of the reasons that you only had four Black lawyers in the state. There was no way to make any money practicing law back then.

I certainly think there is a great deal of improvement. I mean, there were no Black policemen in the city of Jackson until 1963. There were no Black firemen until 1974. Black sheriffs and deputy sheriffs weren't seen in Mississippi twenty years ago. Now we have four or five counties where the sheriff is Black. In most counties in the South today, there are Black deputy sheriffs at the lowest level. There are between forty-five and fifty Black justices of the peace in this state. This is justice at its most basic level. Whether you owe three hundred dollars or not, whether you were or weren't intoxicated when you were driving, the resolution of these issues is now in the hands of Black people who are administering the criminal justice system.

You have to think that the level of fairness in this justice system has increased.

REGGIE B. WALTON

"Not enough people of color aspire to be prosecutors."

Washington, D.C. Superior Court Judge Reggie B. Walton established his credentials as tough on crime, serving as a senior White House adviser for crime and assistant "drug czar" for the Bush administration. Walton believes in punishment, yet he also believes prisons are not the only way to punish the guilty. Walton believes effective efforts to curtail crime and drug abuse must include social programs to address poverty-related problems, a position that frequently put him at odds with fellow Bush administration officials who he said were adverse even to the mention of social programs. But Walton believed in a basic tenet of the administration: part of the crime problem is related to the breakdown of the family, particularly the inner-city, nonwhite family.

Judge Walton has truly seen all sides of the American criminal justice system. Beginning on the receiving end of the criminal justice system as a teen in a small mill town in western Pennsylvania, he has served as a public defender, a prosecutor, a judge, and an official in the Bush administration. Walton has firsthand experience with the injustices that plague the criminal justice system and the viciousness of many of those who pass through that system. Walton's interest in being a judge stemmed from his service as chief justice of the student court at West Virginia State College, where he obtained his undergraduate degree in political science.

Despite his heavy work load since graduation from American University's Washington College of Law in 1974, Walton has found time for a variety of other activities, including teaching law at various institutions, volunteering with civic and professional organizations, and being a Big Brother.

Judge Walton was interviewed in his chambers at the Moultrie Justice Center in October 1993.

I decided to become the assistant "drug czar" in the Bush administration because I felt I had an obligation to my people to do it. Although the drug problem is not just a minority problem or a problem of the poor, it does impact disproportionately on minority populations. But ultimately my experience with the Bush administration, was frustrating.

I think we clearly did some things at the drug office that helped along the already decreasing rate of casual drug use. Clearly the number of casual drug users declined significantly. Where I think we did not have the impact that I would have liked to have seen was on the hard-core user and on the problems related to use among poor people in the inner city. I think we needed different strategies to address the problems of those populations.

I met Bill Bennett through his brother Bob. Bob is a big-time lawyer with a major firm and he had called me along with some other people and asked us if we would be willing to sit down with his brother Bill and give him our candid views on the drug problem and what conceivably could be done about it.

I was the only African American among that group, and I spent a considerable amount of time talking to Bill—about three hours longer than the other people—telling him about the drug problem from my perspective. At the end of the conversation I told him that I didn't want him to take what I was about to say as an indication that I thought the problem was only a problem that affected people of color and poor people. But I said that the drug problem does disproportionately affect those populations, and if you are going to have an impact on the drug problem in America overall, I think that you have got to have respect and credibility in minority and poor communities. I told him I didn't see how you could do that unless you had a person of color in the top echelons of your office who was concerned about those people, and left it at that. I didn't say I was looking for a job. I was very happy here in the D.C. superior court and had no inclination to leave.

About two weeks later I got a call from Bill Bennett and he said,

"You made a challenge to me that I thought about and I think you are right. I have decided I want somebody who is Black at the top of my office, and I decided that person is you."

When Bill Bennett offered me the position I really didn't want to do it. I enjoyed being a judge. Plus it meant taking a $9,000 salary cut, which I really couldn't afford because my wife had quit her job to go to medical school. We are paying a $25,000 tuition per year at Georgetown for her, and economically I just really was not in a position to take the White House job. But after I sat down and thought about how I could borrow some money to hold me over for the time I was there, I decided that it was a sacrifice I just had to make, and I did it.

When I served in the drug office I repeatedly stated my belief that efforts had to be made in the area of social programs. There was an aversion to social programs among the people in the drug office. They felt that you didn't need to address the problems of jobs or housing or education or the host of other social issues that I thought had to be addressed if we were going to have any impact on the most depressed areas in the county. I found this aversion to addressing the social issues very frustrating at times, but I kept knocking on the door. I kept making my recommendations. When I left the drug office and went over to the White House as a senior adviser for crime, I wrote a paper stating that we had to do other things if we were going to affect those communities most devastated by the drug problem.

The "drug war" was disproportionately affecting people of color, and clearly it was having a devastating impact on young Black males. Shortly after I went into the drug office I suggested that the president would do well to convene a group of professionals to look at the reasons why these young Black males were involving themselves in drug activities and the concomitant violence and to come up with special strategies to address the problems confronting them. It was frustrating to know that there were things we obviously had to do, but no one would really listen.

When I was with the drug office our policies were not just to lock everybody up. A lot of our strategies were in the prevention, education, and treatment area, but I don't think they were funded anywhere near the necessary level. A lot of these kids live in an environment that is so unwholesome that you can't expect them to avoid the ills of the society in which they are growing up. You have to do something to try and change that environment. So I did find my experience with the Bush administration frustrating.

Another thing I tried to change was the way we funded the courts. We allocated a lot of our money—something like 70 percent of the funding—to law enforcement, but not enough of that funding went to the courts. If you increase police and prosecutors, you are going to have to expand the courts to handle the increased caseloads or you are going to have bottlenecks, which is what happened. Having been part of the court system, I always fought internally to try and get the administration to do more in that area. I fully understood that you could not allow the increasing number of cases we were bringing into the system to back up at the courthouse door and then expect to make any impact on criminal justice.

I argued vigorously that we had to increase our courts' funding. In fact additional moneys were put into the courts, but I don't know whether or not the percentage of increase for the courts was as significant as it was for the prosecutors, police, and prisons. There were proposals to increase the resources for the federal judiciary and the federal court system to deal with the increased loads that were a result of the increased activity of the police. The federal courts received more than the state courts.

There was always a problem with the administration's theory that local activities were principally the responsibility of local government. Many local governments totally lacked the financial resources to do what they needed to do. If they were not going to get assistance from the federal government to address those deficiencies, there was no way they were going to be able to solve the problems within their jurisdiction. Most of the jurisdictions that needed federal assistance are poor, minority communities.

I remember going to a small, Black community outside of Chicago. The people there were fighting against the odds because they did not have the tax base, they didn't have the money, and there was no way they would ever be able to confront the significant social issues that they had to confront, including drugs, unless they got considerable outside help.

Unfortunately the philosophy at the federal level was that we should not be providing assistance. That type of assistance was the responsibility of state and local governments. But the reality was that if the state was not going to do it and the city didn't have the money to do it, then the situation was going to deteriorate. As far as the drug problem is concerned, we could have had more impact if we had pumped more resources into those areas.

I made it a point to go into minority communities wherever I went—Black communities, Hispanic communities, Indian communities, whatever. I frequently heard concerns about the inequities in the way the drug problem was being handled. I heard a lot of folks in poor communities say that if this problem was happening out in the suburbs, if it was affluent white folks being affected, this country would do something to solve the problem. But because it was only happening in inner-city and poor areas, people didn't care because it was only destroying the lives of Blacks. I also heard from other Blacks that Blacks were being targeted, that the police were abusing their power and doing various things to people in the Black community that they wouldn't do to people who were suspected of involvement in crime in other communities.

When I was a public defender in Philadelphia, I came to appreciate how unjust and unfair the system could be. I also found out that the victims of crime were not treated as they should have been.

When I finally decided I wanted to do something other than be a public defender I was representing a young Black man who was charged with aggravated assault on this eighty-seven-year-old Black woman. This woman had been beaten brutally, causing her severe injury. For whatever reason, in addition to the assault, her dog and cat had been killed. These pets were basically the only living beings that she had contact with at that point of her life. The assailants also stole all of her food. It really was a sad, unfortunate case.

The woman took the stand at the preliminary hearing and I used the skills I had learned to show that she couldn't have made the observations she said she had made in identifying my client. I pointed out that she had been struck immediately, she had started to bleed profusely, the blood had gotten into her eyes and impaired her vision. She finally admitted under cross-examination that she could not really be sure that my client had committed the offense. The judge had to dismiss the case.

Right after that happened, the defendant turned to me and said, "Brother, we beat that one, didn't we?" I realized with that remark that he had committed the offense although he had always denied it.

It gave me a very sickening feeling to know that one Black had done this to another Black person and had no remorse about it. He saw this dismissal as a victory against the system. I found that very troubling.

I enjoyed criminal law, so I decided I would give prosecution a chance. I applied to the U.S. Attorney's office in Washington and fortunately was selected. I served for about six years as an Assistant U.S. Attorney, working my way up to the number three position in the office.

As a public defender I had a lot of opportunity to talk to individuals who had been accused of crimes, so I had the opportunity therefore to examine the mentality of people who were involved in crime. As a result I acquired some appreciation for why people commit crimes. As a prosecutor I had the opportunity to work with the victims of crime. This enabled me to assess the impact that crime has not only on the individual victim but on the community at large. I was able to gain a dual perspective from being a public defender and a prosecutor.

I do think that not enough people of color aspire to be prosecutors. This is because people of color see that the injustices in the system are inflicted disproportionately on people of color. Therefore there is a natural inclination on the part of young lawyers coming out of law school to want to be defense lawyers so they can protect the rights of the downtrodden and the poor. I think that is laudable, but at the same time most of the victims of crime are poor people of color and also they have a right to have their rights protected.

One of the things people don't ever think about is the fact that a prosecutor is sworn not just to get convictions but to do justice, and if justice means dismissing a case when the police have inappropriately arrested somebody or have abused somebody's constitutional rights, that is an appropriate action for the prosecutor to take.

I probably had greater impact on the system as a prosecutor than as a public defender. Once I got into a policy-making position I was able to implement policy that clearly had an impact on whether or not people were charged with crimes, what they were charged with, and whether their cases would end up in some type of pretrial diversion program as opposed to being prosecuted.

As a policymaker, I was the codirector of a drug diversion program. It is no longer in existence. In this program, after an interview with the defendant and his or her lawyer, I assessed whether or not the defendant should be admitted into the pretrial diversion program that we operated for drug offenders at the time.

I was also instrumental in expanding the scope of our pretrial diversion so individuals who were charged with certain minor, nonviolent criminal offenses could go to a diversionary program. They would have to come down to court, watch the court proceedings, and then write an essay or do some other things in order to avoid having their case prosecuted.

Diversion programs do not undercut punishment. I believe in punishment. I believe when people do wrong they should be punished. Unfortunately our system doesn't make people accountable to the extent that it should.

But I think we have gotten too much in the mind-set of believing that the only way to punish is through incarceration. I don't think that is true. A lot of people would rather be incarcerated. The way our prison systems work now, assuming the convicts are able to withstand being in prison, they really don't have to do much. They sleep half the day and watch TV half the day and don't really do anything to improve their situation. It is really just idle time for many. Some people are prepared to do that.

If you place somebody into a diversionary program or probation program, you can force them to do a lot. You can force them to get a job, which is very difficult for some people. You can force them to maintain that job.

You can force them, too, if they have children, to take care of those kids. I think one of the most beneficial things you can do as a judge for a man with children is to make that person come to grips with the fact that taking care of his children financially is his responsibility, not society's. Making child support a condition of probation is constructive because people think more about their children if they have to shell out money for them.

I think it's beneficial for a kid who has never taken education seriously to be forced to enroll in school or in a vocational program to develop a skill. You can force someone to get a skill and/or a job because you have the hammer of going to prison over his head. I think that can be very constructive, and it benefits both society and the individual.

* * *

When I was in Philadelphia I came to appreciate how unjust and unfair the system could be. This was during the era of Mayor Frank Rizzo, the former police commissioner. During the Rizzo era it was not uncommon for the police to engage in transgressions of individuals constitutional rights. I had a large number of individuals who, I would find out when I went to interview them in jail, had been severely beaten. There were tales of coercion on the part of the police department to get confessions. In fact, when I came to the United States Attorney's office in Washington, I had the impression that in virtually every homicide case there was a confession, because in Philadelphia, in virtually every case, there was a confession.

There was a tale I used to hear from many of my clients in Philadelphia about being placed into a room by themselves and they would be there for a period of time and all of a sudden this white bunny rabbit would appear. This was a man dressed up as a white bunny rabbit, and he would come into the room with an orange billy club and beat the hell out of them—and that was why they told the police what they did. The first time I heard that story, I went to court and asked that my client be given a mental examination. But as it turned out, there apparently was this ploy on the part of the police in order to coerce confessions.

In fact, one of my colleagues who was practicing in Washington at the time had heard that same story even though he was down here. He was investigating a case where some Black Muslims from Philadelphia came down here and killed a number of Muslims from a rival sect. So this bunny rabbit story had truth to it. I have heard other stories about improprieties on the part of the Philadelphia police department. In the mid-seventies there were some real problems with the police department.

I also had negative experiences with some members of the judiciary in Philadelphia because at that time there were a number of judges in the Philadelphia court structure who had no legal background and they were really just political cronies. I remember one situation very distinctly where this particular magistrate who was nonlegally trained threatened to put me in jail because I had objected to a clearly illegal ruling he had made.

At that time all of the preliminary hearings in the city were held out in the district police stations, which was a very intimidating environment for a young lawyer in the defender's office who tended to handle the cases at the preliminary level. The few private lawyers who took appointments on indigent cases would generally call their cases first so that they could get out and take care of their business. Our cases would be called last, and in all probability you would end up being the only person there who was there in the interest of the defendant, except for maybe his family. You had all these police standing around watching what you were doing, and like I said, it was a very intimidating environment.

Summary offenses, where a person was facing something like sixty days or less in jail, were held at the district stations. I was representing an individual who had been charged with disorderly conduct, and the government had called their first witness. That witness had been sworn, so double jeopardy had attached to the matter, or at least jeopardy had attached. As the testimony started to come out, it was clear that this individual had been undercharged. He should have been charged with assault, which meant it should have been a municipal court case, but the prosecution had mischarged him, they had already put their first witness on, and that witness had been sworn, so they had to go forward because jeopardy had attached.

This judge said, "I am sending this case up to City Hall, because this case should be a misdemeanor case for assault."

I said, "Your Honor, you can't do that."

"What do you mean?" he said. "You can't tell me what I can and can't do. I can do anything I want to do!"

I said, "Well, Your Honor, there is such a thing as the Constitution, and the Constitution bars a person from being placed in jeopardy twice. My client has already been placed in jeopardy, and there is no way under the circumstances, since the case will be predicated on the same facts, that you can now send this case to City Hall for another charge."

He said, "Don't you cite that Constitution to me again."

I said, "Your Honor, it is the Constitution that governs us all. You are saying that I can't protect the interests of my client."

"If you say that word again, double jeopardy again, you are going to jail."

I said, "Your Honor, with all due respect, you are just going to have to put me in jail, because I am here to represent my client's constitutional rights."

And this judge called the police. He said, "Go stand behind him," and the police came up behind me. He said, "Now mention it again and you go to jail."

I said, "Your Honor, I won't mention it again if you don't threaten my client with being sent up to City Hall."

He said, "Well, I am."

He didn't actually put me back in the cell block, but he had me taken to the side and threatened to have me locked up. I had to get people to come down from my office to deal with this situation. When the front-office people arrived, the judge had backed off putting me in jail.

There were several situations where I had similar experiences with members of the Philadelphia judiciary. I am sure other public defenders and private lawyers had similar experiences. I wanted to believe that a lot of the cases I had read about in law school case books were aberrations. But I found out that was not necessarily the case.

I entered the law because I saw it as a way for social change. I saw it as a way of trying to make an impact on the quality of life for people of color in this country.

I have never aspired to make a tremendous amount of money in the profession. I have had opportunities to go into law firms as a partner and could have made a considerable amount of money, but I have always practiced in the area of public law, initially as a public defender, then as a prosecutor, then as a judge, then with the Bush administration, and finally I came back to the court. I anticipate that all my life will be spent in public office and not in private practice, where I would make a lot more money than what I make now.

I first became interested in the law as a kid, because I was charged with juvenile offenses on several occasions. I grew up in Donora, Pennsylvania, which was a small city of about twelve thousand, located about twenty-three miles south of Pittsburgh. On several occasions when I was growing up I was falsely accused of various things. Admittedly, on a couple of occasions, I wasn't falsely accused.

On one of the occasions when I had been falsely accused, because my parents didn't have money to hire a lawyer and at that time there was no provision in the law for indigent individuals to receive a free lawyer, the local minister ended up representing me. Although he may have been a very good minister he wasn't a very good lawyer, and as a result of that I ended up being convicted of an offense I did not commit.

On another occasion I was on my way to a junior high school dance and had not done anything, but a Kaufmann's Department Store truck had been in Donora making a delivery and somebody stole something off the truck and they said it was a Black male. So I guess they decided to stop every Black male, and they stopped me indiscriminately, no predicate for the stop, and took me so that the driver could look at me. Fortunately the driver didn't identify me and they let me go, but several incidents like that, where I saw that the system wasn't totally fair to me, initiated my interest in the law.

The seed of my interest in the law was planted in Donora, but that interest truly developed when I went to college. I played football in high school and got a scholarship to college. While in college I joined a fraternity in which a number of my frat brothers wanted to be lawyers, and in my senior year I was appointed chief justice of the student court by one of my frat brothers, who was president of the student body. It was at that time that I really started to acquire a passion for law and started to make applications for law school. Fortunately I was able to get into the Council on Legal Education, which was a Great Society program created to try to increase the number of minority lawyers. I participated in that program at Howard University for eight weeks. I ended up number five in that program, and as a result I got a scholarship to American University.

When I was chief justice of the student court in college, I was able to change a policy that had in my opinion really destroyed some lives at West Virginia State College. At that time West Virginia State was a primarily Black college, although it is not now. And I think that Black colleges were way behind a lot of the white colleges when it came to changing some of the old strictures, the outdated rules, that lingered from years past. One of the rules at West Virginia State was that females had curfews but males did not. If females got caught sneaking out of their dorms, or sneaking somebody into their dorm, they would get kicked out of school. The individual who went into the dorm would get kicked out as well.

I understood that you have to have rules and regulations. I did think it was somewhat harsh for a first-time offender to be expelled or suspended, because many times this individual would leave the college and for various reasons might not ever come back into an educational setting. I didn't think that was beneficial to them or to society. I felt that a lesser penalty, at least for the first-time offender, was necessary in order to serve the purposes of both the college and the students.

I went to the president of the student body. (He is now a federal judge down in Miami—the only Black federal judge in Florida, although apparently another one is going to be named soon.) We had been classmates, and during the summer between junior and senior year we asked to rewrite the student code and we did. One of our revisions, which, fortunately, the college president didn't pick up on, changed the language to say that the president would not have the authority to overrule a decision made by the student court in favor of a student. Apparently the president didn't read the student code thoroughly.

The first case that came before the court involved three girls who, I believe, snuck out of a dorm to go to a party. The administration was seeking their suspension. Three other justices and I ruled that that was too harsh a punishment, that these girls should not be suspended. We ruled that they should receive a letter of reprimand that would be sent to them and to their parents.

The president, President Wallace, who had been there a long time and was an institution at West Virginia State College, called me into his office and said he was furious with our ruling.

"What do you mean?" he said. "You can't do this. It is a tradition of this school that if a girl does not follow the code she is out of school. I am going to overrule this."

I said, "But, President Wallace, you can't unless you are going to tell the student body that you are going back on your word. You signed off on this student code—did you read *this?*"

He looked at that part of the code, the part we had revised, and he read it. He said, "God darn it, you got me. You knew I didn't have time to read this whole thing."

I said respectfully, "I assumed you had read it before you signed it."

As a result of that experience, which proved I was able to do something that perhaps saved three girls from having their lives destroyed as far as their education was concerned, it started to make me think that at some point in my career I would like to be a judge.

I was surprised that President Reagan selected me at the age of thirty-two to be a judge, especially since I was a Democrat. I was shocked that I was one of the youngest judges ever appointed to the bench in Washington, D.C.

Reagan didn't have a good record of appointing Blacks to the federal courts, but he appointed a few Blacks to this bench. The Washington, D.C. court is sort of a semifederal bench. We are selected the same way federal judges are selected, by Senate confirmation. Reagan put a few Blacks on the court, but he didn't put many.

There were many adjustments to be made in the transition from lawyer to judge. I had always wanted to be a litigator, from the time I was in college. I think I had the most fun in the legal profession as a lawyer. Being a litigator was like an extension of sports. Having been an athlete I enjoyed winning, obviously, and I think there is no greater feeling for a lawyer than to go into a courtroom with twelve total strangers and convince them that your position is correct. I got a tremendous thrill out of being able to do that, and then I became a judge.

As a judge you are a referee, which isn't as much fun, but that's what you have to do. I think the hardest thing to overcome when I first became a judge was the inclination to insert myself more into the proceedings than I should if I saw one side or the other doing something they shouldn't do or obviously missing something they shouldn't have missed.

From an academic perspective I don't think that there is or should be a special role for the African American judge to play. I think all judges should care about the rights of all people regardless of who they are. I think all judges should go about their responsibility to ensure fair treatment to everybody who walks into their courtroom. However, I do think that race is an integral part of the thinking of too many people in America, and because of this I think lawyers and judges have an obligation to make sure that they do all they can to keep the system fair.

I think we have a very good bench here, but like anywhere in America, race is all-pervasive and too often a factor in decisions when it shouldn't be. I remember when I first came to this bench I overheard a conversation in the lunchroom. I was one of the few Black judges who would go down to the lunch table here, and I happened to hear a couple of white judges discussing a sentencing and agonizing over what the sentence should be in this particular case. They said that because our prison facility, Lorton, was 99 percent Black, prison might not be appropriate for the two defendants, who were white upper-class individuals who had committed a horrible crime. They were seniors in high school, I think, and they had attacked a young homosexual man as he was leaving a Georgetown bar. They took him into Rock Creek Park and they mutilated his genitals. It was a horrendous crime.

As I listened to this discussion between these two judges I wondered why there was even a debate about whether they would go to jail or not. I thought it was just a question of how much time they would get. If they had been two young kids from the poor Black section of Southeast Washington this debate would not have occurred, I'm sure. I felt an obligation to disagree. The issue was whether or not they should go to jail, not what their life would be like if they were incarcerated in a predominately Black environment. Now obviously you don't want them abused, so you issue an order putting them into protective custody or whatever. But it seemed to me that once you start talking about race from that perspective, you end up with unequal results, and as it turned out, these two young men did in fact get probation.

As a Black person in this society and as a Black judge, I know that when you see injustice you at least have to speak out. From the perspective of knowing that the system still is not fair—and probably never will be fair—because of race, you do have an obligation to stand up and speak.

I also think that as a Black professional, whether you are a judge or whatever, you have an obligation to look back and help others. I have been a Big Brother for over seven years now. My "little brother" is now a senior in high school. I took him down to look at Morehouse College last week and down to North Carolina A&T a couple of weeks ago. We have an obligation to look back, to try and help young kids.

I also think it is important for us to make ourselves visible in the community. A lot of judges think that is inappropriate, but not me. It is important, especially for kids, to see that Black folks can make a good living and do constructive things the right way. I think it is imperative for me to accept invitations to visit schools. I am going to a high school this week to talk to a group of kids. I do that frequently because I think it is important for any Black professional to be out in the community as a role model. Probably, from an individual perspective at least, Black jurists have additional obligations to the community as well.

One of the most troubling things taking place in courtrooms today is this overwhelming pursuit of victory. Winning at all costs has become all important in the minds of too many prosecutors and defense lawyers. As I said earlier, a prosecutor's main purpose is seeing that justice is done. Justice is not always achieved by getting a conviction, and this mind-set of winning at all costs often leads to transgressions of the law.

Last week in a case where I thought the defendant was obviously guilty, I had to declare a mistrial after four days of trial because the prosecutor had not told the defense that he had shown a photograph to a witness who had participated in the identification procedure after the robbery. Clearly the defense had a right to know about that so they could file a motion to suppress that suggestive identification procedure. However, the prosecutor did not tell the defense lawyer about it, and upon cross-examination, when the witness was being questioned about the photograph that the prosecutor had shown him, it came out for the first time that the witness had been shown the photograph before he came into court, which obviously would give him an advantage in identifying the defendant. Because it was such an unnecessarily suggestive procedure, I had to declare a mistrial and terminate the procedure.

This win-at-all-costs attitude was spread in this jurisdiction by the head of the United States Attorney's office, and I think his influence tainted many of the people who were trying cases here. In my opinion, it is vitally important that a standard of fairness come from the top and that everybody who works in the prosecutor's office understand that there is this standard. While, yes, we have an obligation to vigorously prosecute people, we don't do it at all costs. The head person has to make it clear that our principle objective is to do justice, and if justice means dismissing, then fine. I think the game has to be played that way, and I think that all too often prosecutors don't play it that way because of their zeal to get a conviction.

After nearly two decades in the criminal justice system I've noticed that crime, unfortunately, has become much more vicious and the offender is generally younger. Another unfortunate change in crime is, and I hate to say it, the young offender commits crime without the same degree of remorse that I used to see. We now have more and more individuals who have a total lack of respect for human life, and as a result of that they don't feel the same remorse about having been responsible for taking a human life. I find that very troubling.

Values and morals have changed. Many of the people involved in drugs and involved in drug-related violence are not themselves addicted. Many of them are nothing other than entrepreneurs who make a lot of money on the backs of other people. Attitudes about life have changed.

The proliferation of guns has a lot to do with drug-related violence. Regardless of what the National Rifle Association says, the increase in the availability of guns means more youth are able to get them. And you've got dynamite when you put a gun in the hands of an impressionable, uncontrolled youth. Plus the fire power of many of these weapons is unbelievable. My wife is a doctor, and when she was doing her rotation over at D.C. General Hospital in surgery, she said that often the first thing they have to decide is which of the multiple bullets is the most life threatening, deal with that one first, then move on to the next. So many victims now have been shot multiple times as a result of the high-powered semi-automatic weapons that are on the streets. Clearly the proliferation of firearms on the streets and the increase in their firepower have contributed tremendously to the problem.

I feel strongly that a part of the crime problem has been caused by the breakdown of the family. So many of our Black youth, especially Black males, don't have fathers in their lives. There is a great need for a strong Black male in the life of a young male who is growing up in a family headed by a female. Statistics indicate that about 70 percent of Black children today grow up in single-family, female-headed homes. In and of itself that may not be the worst thing in the world, but many of these single mothers are ill equipped to raise children. In fact, many of them are teenagers who are too young to appreciate how to raise a child appropriately. I think many parents lack even minimal skills. The only way they know how to discipline is through corporal punishment. I had it. I don't disagree with corporal punishment because I doubt I would have been inclined to listen to my parents if my parents had just talked. I needed that slap every now and then. But at the same time, I don't think that brutalizing kids—which happens too often—is the appropriate way to deal with them.

I also think lack of hope is a significant contributor to many of the problems which we see.

When I was growing up we were relatively poor because the steel mills in my hometown went out of business and there was no work available. I probably grew up a lot poorer than most of these inner-city kids who feel they are poor. Despite growing up poor, there was this feeling of hope that I had about the future. I believed that somehow there would be an opportunity for me to do better than my parents had done. I don't think that is necessarily true for many of the kids who are now coming from our depressed inner cities. They have little or no sense of hope.

Too many of our inner-city youth have no perspective on the future. They live only for today. They have not been taught about deferred gratification and they have to have their needs satisfied immediately. People who lack hope and need to have their desires satisfied immediately are inclined to do anything and everything. Because they don't have any respect for human life and they don't foresee anything better happening for themselves, they are prepared to die. These people see selling drugs in order to have instant cash so they can buy fast cars and fancy clothes. That is as far as they see in the future. And they will do anything and everything to get those things. They will commit crimes to get those things.

I don't think that supporting the rights of victims necessarily conflicts with protecting the rights of defendants. You shouldn't abrogate the rights of a defendant merely because you are trying to protect the victim, but I do think that, for example, victims have a right to know what the outcome of their case is.

All too often victims never find out what happened. They have no idea, even if they know the person, whether the accused is going to be back in their community and pose a threat to them again. They don't know how much time the person got, if any. They don't know when that person, if he was sent to prison, is going to be released. Someone who has been victimized has a right to know that the person against whom he or she testified is back on the streets. The victims should have as much right to speak at the sentencing as the defendants. They are the ones who were victimized. Before sentencing a criminal the judge should be aware of what happened to the victim. Fortunately, a lot of new legislation requires that victims be given the opportunity to express their views about sentencing, and I think that is appropriate.

I have mixed emotions about mandatory sentencing. Admittedly it can bring about some undesirable results, but I don't think mandatory minimum sentencing was done in order to lock up more Black folks, as some Blacks have argued. I really don't think that was the intention.

To a large degree the intention was to try and circumvent the discretion of judges who were inclined to give pats on the wrists to drug dealers. There was a feeling that a lot of judges did not take drug violations as seriously as they should and were not meting out the punishment necessary to protect the community. But, irrespective of the intent, mandatory sentencing has, unfortunately, led to the incarceration of a significant number of people of color for significant periods of time. And any time a social policy has a devastating impact on a particular group of people that policy has to be reevaluated.

While I wouldn't say that we should totally abandon the idea of mandatory sentencing, I do think that, as far as sentencing is concerned on the federal level, we have taken the judging out of being a judge. While I believe that judges should have parameters and guidelines in sentencing, judges should also have the discretion to deviate from those guidelines. That's what judging is supposed to be all about. Without guidelines you have the potential for discriminatory practices.

A lot of people are saying that mandatory minimum sentencing discriminates against poor people and Blacks, but, on the other hand, if you give unfettered discretion to judges, as pervasive as racism is in American society, discrimination can creep in. You may end up with courts where a white and a Black defendant who have been charged with the same offense will receive different sentences because the white defendant and the judge share a similar background.

Another problematic situation is the difference in penalties between crack cocaine and powdered cocaine. Penalties for crack cocaine are much more severe for smaller amounts than is the case with powdered cocaine, and these penalties are falling disproportionately on Blacks because of the economics of the situation: Powdered cocaine is usually the drug that you will find in the possession of someone who is white whereas crack is more likely found in the possession of someone of color.

Again, like mandatory sentences, this different penalty structure was done for laudable reasons. I don't think that the powers that be sat down and said, "Well, primarily Black folks are involved in crack cocaine, so, therefore, in order to lock up more Black folks, we are going to increase the penalty for crack cocaine." I really don't think that was it. But I do hope that the powers that be rethink the distinction between crack and powder, because in the end, cocaine is cocaine.

Despite what the courts have said about the constitutionality of that distinction, I know that people of color have a significant concern about it. They feel it is unfair. If our society is going to address the attitude among people of color that our criminal justice system is unfair, then issues like mandatory sentencing and the crack laws, which arose from the desire for a quick fix for the crime problem, have to be rethought.

It took us a long time to get to the point where we are now. We did not step in and consistently implement ways of addressing the deep-seated social problems that exist in this country. Instead, we have let such problems fester. Now, there are many communities that are out of our control. How can we reverse this? It will be very, very difficult because we have to change people's attitudes if we are going to have any impact on crime.

We have to make people think that crime is wrong. We have to make people believe that crime doesn't pay. For a large number of people, crime is not perceived to be wrong. There is an attitude in this nation that you get it however you can. This attitude is not only in the inner city, it is in some of the major boardrooms. The Michael Milkens of the world feel that any way to get money, whether legal or illegal, is acceptable if it lines your pockets. So this is not just the mind-set of young Black males. It is not. A lot of these young Black males have followed the lead of other folks, who should know better because they don't have the social baggage that these kids have. I think that mind-set is a poison that has permeated all segments of our society, and somehow we have got to start making people believe in right and wrong. People have to learn to play by the rules.

While I truly appreciate the significance of the Constitution's separation of powers doctrine, I believe that as we have moved away from religious dictates the social order has in fact broken down. One of the greatest attributes of religion has been in placing strictures on human conduct. But as you move away from the belief that there is this supreme being and there are ultimate consequences that you are going to have to pay, a lot of people feel they can get away with things. They feel they can fool man, and since they do not believe in a supreme being they will not face any ultimate consequences.

I think that the Black community in particular has suffered as it has moved away from the social strictures that were imposed by religious beliefs. As I said before, if people don't feel that there is a potential for a better life—and religion used to give us that hope—then they will try to get what they can get whenever and however they can get it. And we see what that hopelessness is doing to the African American community.

We have got to do something about it. We have to improve the quality of the education we provide our youth. Many are functionally illiterate when they graduate from high school, and in this day and age if you don't have a good education your prospects for making an adequate living are not very good.

But education isn't enough without opportunity. Studies continually show that Blacks who have the same educational background as whites don't make the same amount of money. There is this feeling among a lot of whites that Blacks are able to get in the door easier than whites are. In some situations that may be the case due to an affirmative effort to try and increase the number of Blacks in order to reverse past and present exclusion. But from an overall perspective, Blacks are not being given the breaks whites think Blacks are getting.

Look at the unemployment rates: we are always at the top. When there is a recession in the country, there is a depression in our community. It is sad when you go into inner-city communities and you see strong, young Black males standing on the corner doing nothing.

When my father was out of work, my parents had to rely on the welfare system in order for us to live. But when he was getting surplus food—there weren't food stamps back then—my father was required to get on a dump truck and go out and work. The work ethic is very important in our society. If you lose that ethic, it is devastating.

We now have a number of generations, maybe two or three, where people living in certain environments have never in their lives seen anybody leave the house and go to work. So how are they going to learn about the process of making a living in this society? We have got to rethink some of the ways that we administer social programs, because giving people who can work something for nothing is not a good idea.

A lot of the offenders who come into my courtroom couldn't even keep a job for a day if you gave them one. They just haven't developed the discipline to get up on a daily basis, go to a job, and stay there and work eight to nine hours a day, day in and day out. That's why the work ethic is so important.

I think role models are important, too. My best role models, in spite of their inability to do everything for us economically that they wanted, were my parents. They were the ones who taught me the importance of the Golden Rule, "Do unto others as you would have them do unto you." They were the ones who taught me the importance of education. They were the ones who taught me about deferred gratification and that good things don't come easy and don't come overnight. They were the ones who taught me how a man is supposed to treat a woman.

All of those lessons were lessons I learned at home. We are now turning to our schools to take responsibility for teaching our kids fundamental lessons, like what is appropriate sexual behavior. That issue, like many others, used to be addressed at home. As the home has deteriorated, families have deteriorated, and we've seen the consequent deterioration of our society. We have seen the level of social problems escalate and extend far beyond anyone's imagination.

It is important to society as a whole to restore a certain level of civility to our communities. Without basic civility you cannot even expect positive change in social behavior. A study was done in Los Angeles a couple of years ago that showed that a significant number of kids were not being sent to school by their parents because the parents feared that violence might be inflicted upon their kids on the way to school or even in the school once they got there. When a social environment is so hostile that people are afraid even to leave their homes and go to school, obviously you could put the best school in place and no one is going to learn anything. Kids can't learn in a violent environment. We have got to bring a certain degree of peace and tranquillity to communities if we expect our social problems ever to be resolved.

* * *

People have to be held accountable for their conduct, but at the same time people have to be persuaded that the system is fair. A lot of people, especially people of color, don't respect the system. Surveys repeatedly show that people of color don't respect our judicial system, our criminal justice system, or our police because of persistent, systemic unfairness. Every time you have a case with clearly racial overtones, it reinforces people's belief that the system is unfair. The Simi Valley verdict in the first Rodney King beating case is a prime example.

A certain insensitivity went into the process of deciding that the King case should be sent to an almost all-white community. That process had racial overtones, obviously, and the verdict was predestined by the decision to send the case to Simi Valley. The system has to be vigilant in making sure that it has the appearance of being fair. To many people, it appears otherwise.

We have to quit playing politics with the crime issue and with social policy. We have to quit making the American public think we can solve these problems overnight. We have to sit down, roll up our sleeves, and come up with a *long-term* strategy that will, maybe in fifteen years, start to have a positive impact. But we have got to be prepared to stay the course. If we are not willing to make that long-term commitment, we are going to keep putting in place bandages that are designed to pacify the American public.

If we continue on our current course, things are never going to get better. We're just going to continue to bleed.

DAMON J. KEITH

"I was taught the law should be an instrument of social change."

The walls in federal appeals judge Damon Keith's chambers are filled with photographs and plaques chronicling a distinguished career as civil rights activist, public servant, and federal jurist. One of Keith's many distinctions is being one of the few federal jurists ever sued by a sitting U.S. president. As a federal district court judge, Keith was sued by then president Richard M. Nixon after he barred the Nixon administration from tapping telephones without the required prior judicial approval. Keith's decision was unanimously upheld by the U.S. Supreme Court in a landmark Fourth Amendment ruling, which was frequently cited during the Watergate hearings that unraveled Nixon's presidency.

While serving in the segregated U.S. Army during World War II, Damon Keith decided to pursue the law as a career after seeing that German POWs were treated better than Black American servicemen. His determination to use the law to change social conditions was sharpened by the "legal giants," such as Thurgood Marshall, he encountered at Howard University Law School. When appointed in 1967 by President Johnson, Keith became the second Black to serve on the federal district court bench in his home state of Michigan, and when President Carter appointed him to the Sixth Circuit in 1978, he was only the sixth Black to ever serve on a federal appellate court. The affable Keith manages to find time for myriad civic activities in addition to carrying a full caseload for his court.

Keith was interviewed in his chambers in downtown Detroit in January 1993.

When I was a federal district court judge I was sued by the President of the United States, Richard Nixon. I had told President Nixon and the attorney general, John Mitchell, that they could not wiretap without prior judicial approval. They felt that claiming they were operating in the interests of national security was a defense for any activity, despite its illegality. They felt they had the authority to do whatever they wanted.

The federal government had wiretapped the White Panthers, which was an alleged revolutionist organization. The lawsuit against me grew out of a ruling in which I had said that the evidence the government had gathered against this group was not admissible in court because it had been obtained through wiretapping conducted without the required judicial approval. In court the Nixon administration had asserted that, when national security was involved, it could wiretap without the judicial approval required by the Fourth Amendment to the U.S. Constitution. I told them they must go to a magistrate to get approval to wiretap. I told them they were not the ones to decide if and when they were going to comply with the dictates of the Constitution, even for national security. And remember, they were the ones deciding if a national security threat existed or not.

My ruling was affirmed by the appeals court in a 2–1 decision. The U.S. Supreme Court upheld the ruling unanimously. The lawsuit became known as the "Keith case." It was the case that broke Watergate wide open. A lot of the things Haldeman and "the plumbers" were doing was wiretapping. During the Watergate hearings Senator Irwin quoted from the case all the time.

I had judges on my court say, "You're just a district court judge, a lowly judge. Why are you second-guessing the president and the attorney general on national security?" I would answer, "the Fourth Amendment." The Fourth Amendment to the Constitution does not provide separate standards for the president. He, too, must go to a magistrate. Everybody has to follow the law. The president is not exempt. Privacy is very important in this country, and the Fourth Amendment protects our privacy.

I went to Howard University Law School, where I had the privilege of working with Thurgood Marshall, William Hastie, and Spotswood Robinson—all giants in the legal field—who taught us that no person is above the law and that the law applies equally to everybody, including the president and the attorney general. They also taught us that tough decisions require good, tough judges. Being sued by the president didn't cause me one sleepless night. You do what you have to do. That's one reason that federal judges are appointed for life.

Here I was, an African American judge, protecting the rights of all Americans in terms of the Fourth Amendment.

I remember my good friend Henry Ford said to me after the wiretap case, "Damon, what is this wiretapping case all about that everybody is talking about?"

I said, "Well, Henry, if you and your wife were having a private conversation, the government would say that Henry Ford and his wife are having a conversation that may be a threat to the national security. Once they declared the conversation a threat to national security they could wiretap your telephone without going before a neutral magistrate and showing probable cause that what you were saying was actually a threat to this country. The government could do it alone. If Nixon and John Mitchell wanted to intercept telephone calls they could do it just by invoking national security. National security would be their defense." I told Henry that the Supreme Court decision in that lawsuit against me prohibited the Nixon administration, the government, from wiretapping without judicial approval. Henry said, "My goodness, I would never have believed it."

One of the many ironic things about the Nixon administration was that they would criticize the courts for protecting constitutional rights, but when they got in trouble they cried for every right the Constitution had. I remember when they captured this guy Manson, the serial killer. Nixon was on Air Force One. He was a lawyer and graduate of Duke Law School, and he was saying it was a waste of money to give Manson a trial, and all this law and order stuff. But when members of his staff were indicted they used the Constitution as it should be used. They demanded every legal right they were entitled to.

They used to criticize "soft-headed" judges, but they wanted judges who would extend them their Sixth Amendment presumption of innocence and their Fifth Amendment right not to testify and not be seen as guilty because they didn't take the witness stand. They wanted all their constitutional safeguards, which was their right. They had publicly said others were not entitled to those rights, but they wanted theirs. Equal justice under the law is the bedrock of our democracy.

The wiretapping case happened twenty years ago, but I'm not sure if we have learned any lessons about being vigilant in protecting our civil liberties from governmental excesses. I would hope that we have, but I don't know. We go from Watergate to Iran-Contragate to the "war on drugs."

When I think of the Taylor case, which I handled, where Blacks were being indiscriminately stopped in airports for drug searches simply because they were Black, I wonder if we've learned anything. Fourth Amendment provisions were at issue in both the Taylor case and in the Nixon case. In both cases the government was defending improper actions by saying it had the authority not to follow the Constitution because of national security in the one case and the drug war in the other.

In my decision in the Taylor case I said it was wrong for the police to stop and search a person simply because of his skin color. The detectives testified that the only person they had stopped getting off that airplane was this guy Taylor, the only Black person getting off the plane. These detectives didn't have a tip from an informant that Taylor had drugs, nor had drugs been detected by a police dog. The detectives said they stopped him because their "profile" said Blacks are more likely to carry drugs than whites. The detectives had no probable cause to stop him, no reasonable suspicion—except he was Black. That's racism, and racism has no place in law enforcement.

The detectives targeted Taylor for a search simply because he was Black. When they surrounded him outside of the terminal one of the detectives snatched his bag, searched it, and found drugs. Then they asked him to sign a form consenting to the search. Settled law says those detectives needed the suspect's consent or a search warrant issued by a judge *before* the search. That's what the Fourth Amendment says.

In one of my opinions in that case I said that although law enforcement officers are doing a valiant job in waging this war on drugs, their efforts cannot be done in total disregard to a person's constitutional rights. The fact that drugs were found is not the issue. The issue is that fighting the war on drugs doesn't license law enforcement officers to disregard the rights guaranteed by the Fourth Amendment or the equal-protection principles embodied in the Fourteenth Amendment.

A panel that I sat on unanimously reversed Taylor's conviction, but the full Sixth Circuit heard an appeal of my ruling and reversed, reinstating the conviction. That ruling stood when the U.S. Supreme Court decided not to accept the case on appeal.

The war on drugs is really doing damage to our civil liberties and constitutional rights. There are elements of it that are racially discriminatory. More emphasis has been placed on drugs in the inner cities of our country than on how the drugs make their way into the inner cities. We are putting emphasis on the end users and not the major suppliers, the major dealers, the people who are making all the money in the drug trade. And Blacks are certainly not the ones making the big money. The higher-level dealers who are making the big profits are almost "The Untouchables." Now that is my own theory.

As a federal judge for twenty-five years I've had all sorts of people come before me who were dealing drugs. Most of them have been minorities: African Americans and Hispanics. But the question that keeps recurring in my mind is, How do these drugs end up in the inner cities of Detroit, Washington, D.C., Chicago, Los Angeles, and Cleveland? How do drugs make their way into the inner city? How much money has been made before it gets to the minorities in the inner city? And why aren't the drug lords being arrested? We got this guy from Panama, Noriega, but how many more Noriegas do we have? They are untouchables.

The public is right to demand action against drugs, but the public should also be concerned about the damage to our constitutional rights that fighting the war on drugs is doing.

These drugs are causing all types of problems. They are in the schools. They are behind Black-on-Black crime. There are more Black men in jail than there are in college. The Black male may become extinct because we are killing so many of these young Black males. When you consider the unemployment of Black males, the drug addiction, the percentage that are in prison, we are in serious trouble. Everybody talks about the drug problem, but the drug problem is not down here in Detroit, or in Chicago, Los Angeles, Cleveland, or New York. The problem is: How are all these drugs coming into the country? And no one has been able to answer that with any specificity.

I was first appointed to the federal bench in 1967. I was recommended by Senator Philip Hart, and President Johnson appointed me to the U.S. District Court for the Eastern District of Michigan. In 1978 President Carter appointed me to the U.S. Court of Appeals for the Sixth Circuit.

I never thought about being a judge. When I finished law school in 1949 I think there was one Black federal judge in the country, and that was Bill Hastie, who had just been appointed by President Truman to the Third Circuit court. In 1949 there were no Black judges in the state of Michigan. Charles W. Jones, the first Black judge (above Justice of the Peace), was appointed by then-governor Mennen G. Williams, and he was appointed as a records court judge, whose jurisdiction was exclusively dealing with crimes committed in the City of Detroit. So that was the first time I had ever seen a Black judge locally.

Of all of the decisions I have rendered during my time on the bench, the Nixon case is the most memorable. But there are three others that stick out in my mind. One very important case dealt with discrimination at the Detroit Edison company. I held that Detroit Edison had discriminated against Blacks, because at the time I heard the case, the highest-ranking Black over there was, I believe, a janitor or a driver or an elevator operator. So I found them guilty of discrimination and fined them four million dollars. Now, even today, I run into people on the street, Black people, who say, "Judge Keith, thank you. Years ago I got five thousand dollars as a result of your decision."

Another case that was very important was the Pontiac school busing case. It was the first case dealing with desegregation in a northern school district. I found that the Pontiac school system had gerrymandered boundary lines so that they would have all-Black schools and all-white schools. All of the system's Black teachers were in the all-Black schools. They didn't have a Black deputy superintendent of schools. I found that there was segregation as a result of the school system's action.

Many of the white people in Pontiac didn't like my ruling, in which I ordered busing to achieve a better racial balance in the schools. Some school buses were firebombed. White parents organized a boycott on the first day of school. Law and order means obeying the court's orders when they are given. After the buses were bombed I had to explain that this court would not tolerate any abuse of its orders. When a judge speaks by means of an order, you have to obey that order. The issue should not be decided on the streets of Pontiac or anyplace else. You must let the legal process work, whether you agree with it or not. Without the kind of law and order where the orders of a court are respected, we won't have a democratic country but a country run by the strongest.

The final case that sticks out in my mind involved the city of Hamtramck, Michigan. The city had an urban renewal plan that was in fact a Negro removal plan. I ruled that it was not coincidence that the majority of residents who were forced to move from areas designated by the city for urban renewal were Black.

All of the cases I have decided during my time on the bench, the Nixon case, Pontiac, Hamtramck, Taylor, all of them have been premised on the position that the Constitution is meant to protect all Americans, Black or white, respected or suspected. I was taught at Howard Law School that the law should be an instrument of social change, and that idea just sparked me. My whole life since law school has been dedicated to that proposition. Those giants at Howard I mentioned earlier—Houston, Marshall, Bob Ming, and Jim Neighbors—did a lot to shape my perception of the law.

I feel that Black judges must take every opportunity to fashion the law in a manner that reflects—that is, that seeks to correct—the three-hundred-year history of discrimination Blacks have suffered in this country. Those of us on the appellate benches must provide guidance through our opinions—guidance not just for *stare decisis*, but guidance for those judicial colleagues who have not shared our oppression. Judges, whatever their color, must be impartial, and they must not prejudge; however, in the final analysis they are also human beings, and as human beings they bring to judicial decision making their own perspectives on what constitutes reality in America. Those perspectives are formed through the life experience of a judge: education, social and economic background, and, yes, the judge's race and sex.

I was born and raised in Detroit. At the time I was growing up Detroit was a segregated city. I went all the way through school, from kindergarten through high school, without having had a Black teacher. The Fisher YMCA, which was right across the street from my high school, was segregated. We had to go to another Y. We couldn't come to downtown hotels. The eating places downtown were segregated. When I wanted to get hot dogs for my mother and myself from Coney Island, right over here on Lafayette Street, I'd have to order them take-out. Racism and segregation were pervasive.

Back then, there was a very negative perception of the police and the judicial system in the Black community. The police department was awful. Black policemen could not ride in patrol cars with whites. There were no Blacks on the motorcycles, no Blacks on the mounted police. We didn't have any Black lieutenants or commanders. The department was completely segregated. It was so bad that if two Black officers were assigned to a patrol car and one got sick, rather than put a white in the car, they would park it and make the remaining Black officer walk a beat. I know these things are true because I handled the police cases that led to the integration of the Detroit police department and this historical record was brought out during the course of those trials.

I didn't have any exposure to Black teachers until I got to West Virginia State College, which was all Black at that time. Dr. John W. Davidson was the president of the college when I got there, and he brought in all these Black intellectuals and people I had never heard of to speak to us students. The historian Carter G. Woodson would come to speak to us. People like Benjamin Mays, Mary McLeod Bethune, and Adam Clayton Powell.

I suppose it was my experience during World War II that really sparked my interest in pursuing the law as a career. My God, my eyes opened up during those three years I spent in a segregated army. I saw German prisoners get better treatment than Blacks in the American army got. The German prisoners didn't have to ride at the back of the buses throughout the South, but we had to. They were allowed to use white rest rooms and could eat in white restaurants in the South, but we couldn't.

When I came back from the war, I was riding at the back of a bus going to Virginia and I couldn't eat at certain places. It made me think that maybe I could help alleviate some of these problems. So, the Black experience and the pain and suffering I went through helped to channel my interests and change my life and attitude. And thank God I was able to get into law school and go to Howard, where I was exposed to those Black legal giants.

There is not a day in my life as an African American that I am not reminded in some way large or small that I am Black and that the color of my skin plays a part in how I am treated. This reminder could be a glance, it could be the way whites talk to me, the way they look at me, the way they place me and my wife in a dining room, right next to other Blacks.

I went to a place to eat about a month ago in Cincinnati. I was by myself and there was one Black eating in a corner of the restaurant and the hostess sat me right next to that Black man. I told her I didn't mind sitting next to that man but that I didn't want her to make that decision for me. I told her I wanted a different seat and she was startled. I don't think it was a policy of that establishment to sit Blacks together, but these are the little things that happen to us daily as African Americans. Here's another example. I was at a recent national convention of the National Bar Association. We were up in this suite, all of us lawyers and judges, and somebody in management decides there are too many Blacks up there, so they send up the police to throw us out, saying we were making too much noise.

I sometimes feel as though we take two steps forward in racial progress and then take ten steps backward, but things are getting better. Certainly we have made progress.

A few days ago I administered the oath of office to Alan Page, the football Hall of Famer. He had been elected statewide in Minnesota to a seat on that state's supreme court. Blacks account for less than 3 percent of that state. That's progress.

On the other hand, when you think of Rodney King, or the incident that happened here in Detroit where detectives beat this guy to death, or the incident in Florida where this young Black man was burned and tortured, you just wonder. A few weeks ago I saw some television program in which a Black reporter in California was questioned by police about why he was sitting outside a certain place, but, in contrast, four whites went to the same place and sat there and the police officers didn't stop them. There is a double standard here.

We just had a judgment in a federal district court case in which Blacks went to rent or lease an apartment in one of the suburbs here and they were told the apartments weren't available for rental or lease. Then a white tester came in shortly thereafter and was showed apartments all over that place. These little things happen every day of our lives. And whites try to camouflage them, so we have to be ever vigilant and assertive.

Look at what President Clinton has done in terms of nominating Blacks to his cabinet. He has put them in positions where traditionally there hadn't been Blacks before—not just at HUD [the Department of Housing and Urban Development]. He has appointed Blacks to the Commerce Department, Veterans Affairs, and Energy. His surgeon general and a deputy secretary of state are Black. This is unheard of. It gives hope.

For the past twelve years no one paid any attention to us. When a president reflects that myopic point of view, it trickles down. People on the courts—I'm speaking of judges, personnel, and staff—CEOs of corporations, and other leaders tend to follow the president's lead. If the president has the attitude that excluding Blacks is acceptable, then it becomes more acceptable to everyone else. We have been devoid of leadership for the last twelve years.

It is absolutely a myth that we now live in a color-blind society. As Justice Blackmun said in his opinion in *Regents v. Bakke,* in order to get beyond race we first have to take race into consideration. It is very important that we recognize that racism is very much a part of our way of life here, and we certainly don't live in a color-blind society. That is a goal, but do you think Reagan and Bush appointed only white judges throughout this circuit because they were the only ones qualified? They didn't look to get any Blacks.

During the last twelve years, eight years of Reagan and four years of Bush, not one African American judge was appointed to the Sixth Circuit. Our circuit comprises Kentucky, Tennessee, Ohio, and Michigan. Every Black judge that we have in this circuit, on the district courts and the court of appeals, was appointed by Carter. This is a tragedy, and it was done by design. Where is the diversity? How could any administration fail for twelve years to appoint an Afro-American to a court that covers four states unless it was by design?

The whites that Reagan and Bush appointed to this court were generally young and very conservative. The president has a right to appoint people who reflect his point of view, but to completely bypass African Americans for twelve years is unbelievable. They said there weren't enough minority lawyers with the training and experience to be considered for judgeships, but I don't buy into that. This was done by design and intended, in my judgment, to reverse the progress that African Americans had made under Lyndon Johnson, Kennedy, and Carter. It is a tragedy that any administration would do this to the judiciary and to Black people.

The effort over the past twelve years to deny racism's impact has its genesis in the lack of recognition that there are barriers that prohibit African Americans from achieving. They say, "Why don't you pull yourself up by your bootstraps?" Well, we don't have any boots or any straps to pull ourselves up with. We don't have boots or straps because systemic discrimination against Blacks in America is rooted so firmly in our institutions and because racism was at one time the official policy of the American government. No group in America has faced and overcome these kinds of obstacles.

I was chairman of the Michigan Civil Rights Commission for a number of years. I have yet to hear a white corporate person or a white landlord or a white person say that they are guilty of racism. Look at the owner of the Cincinnati Reds, Marge Schott. She says, "I'm not a racist." And all of a sudden she finds Blacks to put in the front office. She now finds Blacks who are eligible to be team managers in the minor leagues. And yet she admits that she referred to Parker and to Davis as her "million dollar niggers." That is reflective of an attitude. The point I'm making is this: Schott came out and said publicly that she is not a racist, but her actions and her words defy that. In her heart she doesn't believe that what she is doing is racist, but her actions speak loudly and clearly—and *they* say that everything she does is racist. A lot of white people don't understand that what they are doing is racist.

If everything were equal, if we lived in a color-blind society, there wouldn't be any need for set-aside programs. There wouldn't be any need for affirmative action. There wouldn't be any sudden need for Marge Schott to hire all these Blacks. If she had already been doing it, and if professional baseball, football, and basketball had been doing it all along, we wouldn't be playing catch-up now.

We must continue to look to the courts as the last bastion of our constitutional protections. We should also look to the legislature. All three branches of government, the judicial, the executive, and the legislative, must do more to remedy racism. With the concerted effort of leadership in local, state, and federal governments, the ripple-down effect would even extend to the corporate world. But until that happens and for as long as Blacks are excluded from the mainstream of American life, it will be the duty of the courts to enforce the Constitution's guarantee of equal protection in ways that prevent racial exclusion.

We have to work to improve our judicial system. We certainly need more diversity in our courts. It is just awful when a woman goes into a courtroom and everybody she sees, from the judge down to the clerk, is male. The same is true for Blacks who go into courts and see all whites. It's disheartening. Diversity promotes fairness and the feeling that everybody will be treated fairly.

It is important to have women and minorities in the judiciary because of the point of view they bring. As I said earlier, judges are products of their community, their environment, and the way they were brought up. Sandra Day O'Conner said she would always gain more insight into a case after hearing Thurgood Marshall speak in conference, because he would present a view based on his experience. It is important in judicial conferences to explain to our non-Black colleagues what it is like to be Black in America. We also need to work on changing attitudes in the judicial system. We need law enforcement officers who are sensitive to the plight of all people. We need officers who will adhere to the mandates of the Constitution and protect all of our rights and our civil liberties.

There is a presumption in the law, the Sixth Amendment, that says every person is presumed innocent until proven guilty beyond a reasonable doubt. This is a fundamental right that we as Americans have. And it is a concept that is not useless. It has meaning.

When I was a trial judge I would ask prospective jurors, with the defendant sitting in front of them, how many of them believed that the defendant was guilty? I was amazed at how many hands would go up. I'd say, "Well, ladies and gentlemen, the defendant has only been charged through this indictment, and this indictment is an accusation. This is the defendant's first day in court. He has never had an opportunity to face his accusers. No evidence has been presented against him. As he sits here, he is presumed to be innocent, and this presumption of innocence continues for the course of this trial. Do you understand that?" It is surprisingly hard for jurors to really understand that innocent people could be indicted, because they know that the weight and power of the government stands behind that indictment. There is the feeling that the government would not bring someone to trial who was innocent—and yet that is the whole point of a trial.

We have to continually remind people what our government stands for. I think our government stands for those four words written over the entrance of the Supreme Court: EQUAL JUSTICE UNDER LAW. That's what we have to strive for. Now it can't be perfect, but we can strive for perfection.

Part III

THE PIONEERS

CONSTANCE BAKER MOTLEY

"Being appointed to the federal judiciary is a matter of sheer, unadulterated luck."

As a civil rights lawyer for the NAACP Legal Defense Fund, Constance Baker Motley desegregated many facilities, from the University of Mississippi to public parks in Memphis, yet she could not stay in a downtown hotel while fighting those cases, even in the nation's capital, until Congress passed the Civil Rights Act of 1964. Two years later, when Motley was being formally considered for appointment as America's first Black female federal judge, her gender sparked a level of opposition among some federal jurists that rivaled the race-based resistance of southern senators.

The illustrious career of this native of New Haven, Connecticut, is filled with firsts: first Black female state senator in New York; first female president of the Borough of Manhattan; first Black female federal judge; and first woman to serve as chief judge for the Southern District of New York, the largest federal trial court in the country. Motley's first first, following her graduation from Columbia Law School in 1946, put her on the ground floor of the civil rights movement. Hired by Thurgood Marshall, who became her mentor, she was the first female NAACP Legal Defense Fund attorney. This barrier-breaking lawyer became a jurist whose rulings broke new legal ground. Motley has handled over twenty-five hundred cases as a judge. Although Motley has not carried a full caseload since taking senior status in 1986, it is not unusual for her to be in her chambers after seven in the evening, working on current trials or writing opinions.

Judge Motley was interviewed in her chambers in the U.S. Court House on Foley Square in New York City in November 1992.

In 1966, as a result of my work in the civil rights field, I was appointed to the United States District Court for the Southern District of New York by President Johnson. I was the first woman and the first Black to be appointed to the District Court for the Southern District of New York. I was also the first Black woman ever appointed to the federal judiciary anywhere in the nation.

There was tremendous opposition to my appointment, not only from southern senators but from other federal judges. Some of this opposition was racial, but some of it had to do with my being a woman.

When I was appointed in 1966 there were only four other women serving on the federal bench. At that time women lawyers were a rarity in most courthouses and virtually unheard of outside of New York City. I worked as a lawyer for the NAACP Legal Defense and Education Fund, trying school desegregation and other cases in eleven southern states and the District of Columbia. One of the things I remember about my career in the 1950s and early '60s was being the only woman in the courthouse. In that time I saw only one woman argue a case in the Fifth Circuit.

I was nominated in January 1966 but not confirmed until August 1966, thanks to Senator James O. Eastland of Mississippi. Eastland headed the Judiciary Committee and led the opposition. He held up my nomination as well as the nomination of every other African American appointed to the federal bench during the sixties. Eastland had held up Thurgood Marshall's nomination to the Second Circuit Court of Appeals in 1962, and he held up Marshall's nomination to the U.S. Supreme Court in 1967, even though Marshall was then the solicitor general of the United States.

I used to work for Thurgood Marshall at the NAACP Legal Defense Fund. I had tried a number of major civil rights cases for the Defense Fund. I represented James Meredith in his long fight to enter the University of Mississippi. I argued ten cases before the U.S. Supreme Court and won nine of them.

President Johnson had initially submitted my name for a seat on the Court of Appeals for the Second Circuit, but the opposition to my appointment was so great that Johnson had to withdraw my name. This opposition was largely based on my being a woman. I remember how stunned both Johnson and Marshall were by the intensity of the opposition.

The chief judge of the Second Circuit, a man named J. Edward Lombard, was leading the opposition to my nomination. The opposition was great because I was a woman, I can only guess, since Thurgood had been there and he was Black too. But Lombard and others on the Second Circuit didn't want any women in this milieu. New York was the real power center of the whole circuit, which also includes Connecticut and Vermont, because there you had all the great commercial cases and so forth. Their attitude, pure and simple, was that a woman had no business being there.

At that time they didn't even have women trying criminal cases in the U.S. Attorney's Office for the Southern District of New York. There was one woman on the civil side, but the feeling was that women couldn't handle criminal cases. So if a woman couldn't handle a criminal case, you know that a woman couldn't be appointed as a circuit court judge.

I wasn't aware of any opposition from Lombard when I was nominated for the district court. I think they figured it was all right inasmuch as they controlled the whole judicial system in New York. There were then twenty-four judges on the district court, so I was just one judge of twenty-four. Plus, the circuit judges could reverse me.

When I was appointed by President Johnson I was serving as the president of the Borough of Manhattan. I had been elected to that position about a year before my nomination. When I went to see Johnson in Washington the day I was appointed, he told me he had called every civil rights leader in the country and every one of them was backing my appointment 100 percent. The power of Black voters and the strength of the civil rights lobby helped me win confirmation.

After I was appointed to the district court I remember going out to Berkeley, California, to attend a school for new federal judges. At that meeting the chairman, who was a federal judge, introduced each new judge, and during his introductions the chairman told those assembled about how great each new judge was and what each judge had done to distinguish himself in the law. When it came to introducing me, the judge, whose name I've forgotten, simply said that I had been on the board of United Church Women and on the board of the YMCA, and that was it. The chairman said nothing about my work with the NAACP Legal Defense Fund, nothing about me being the first Black woman to sit in the New York State Senate, and nothing about me being elected president of the Borough of Manhattan.

After this curt introduction, former Supreme Court Justice Tom Clark, who was cochairman of the meeting, took the microphone and said, "Just a minute, Mr. Chairman. I would like to say something about Mrs. Motley. She has appeared in our court and argued twenty cases." I said, "No, its only ten." After this session we had lunch together, and Justice Clark told me of a conversation he had overheard in the locker room. A group of male judges were just disparaging this woman appeals court judge. He asked if any of them knew the woman and, of course, none of them did.

I never encountered any instances of racism or sexism openly in the court. Our court is very formal. Everybody is well behaved. My judicial colleagues were all right. I guess one or two of them would rather not have had me there, but the others just shrugged their shoulders. They were New Yorkers. I mean, Black people were not strange to them. They got on the bench themselves through politics, so they knew that Black people had a little more power. They weren't naive. They didn't wonder how I got here, they knew.

But I did encounter a few instances of what you might call sexism and racism within the system. For example, I was never appointed to any committee by the chief judge of the court of appeals. Men with less seniority than I had were appointed, but that would be the extent of it. Thurgood Marshall pushed unsuccessfully for my appointment to Second Circuit court committees. He was our circuit justice. He had a big smile on his face when I became the chief judge of our district court and thus would appoint the members of all twenty-four court committees at the district court level.

As a judge, I did the same work as anybody else. I went to the cafeterias same as anybody else. I didn't have any problems with that. The main thing I noticed when I became a judge was that there were no Black employees at the federal courthouse. In fact there are very few Black lawyers who have ever even appeared in this court. When Thurgood came here as a circuit judge in 1962, the only Black employee was an elevator operator who said he was a college graduate. Eventually they made him a court clerk. I was here several years before they even hired a second Black employee at the court, and there were no Blacks at all in the Court of Appeals. Today, you can still count the Black employees on one hand.

I have experienced racism and sexism in my lifetime. These experiences have made me a stronger person and strengthened my determination to fight for fairness. For instance, when we were traveling around the country fighting these civil rights cases for the NAACP Legal Defense Fund, we usually ended up staying at a "Negro" hotel, which was no more than a private rooming house in a Negro residential area. This even happened in the nation's capital, which was a racially segregated town. We had to stay in such hotels until 1964, when Congress reenacted the Civil Rights Act of 1875, making it possible for us to stay in white hotels and eat in white restaurants.

I remember the reaction I received when I first went to use the law library at the New York Bar Association. When I joined the Defense Fund as a clerk in 1945, it was a small, public interest firm—very small. The law library in the office consisted of a single set of *Supreme Court Reports*. Marshall suggested that I join the bar association so I could use its library since my main responsibilities included research and writing. The first time I went to use the association's law library I encountered the "gatekeeper" at his desk. He was an elderly white gentleman who appeared to be one year older than God. He was having a conversation with someone else and didn't even look my way. When he did turn to me minutes later, I told him I wanted to use the library, to which he replied that I had to be a member of the association. When I told him I *was* a member, it was as if he had seen a ghost. He shouted in disbelief, "You are a member of this association?" He couldn't believe I was a member. There were only one or two other female members. Female members were so recent, there weren't even restrooms for us. The gatekeeper asked for my name and searched the membership list. When he found my name on the list, he said, "Oh, right this way, *Constance*."

I never entertained the thought that I would be appointed to the federal bench. I didn't think they would ever appoint a Black woman to the federal bench. I didn't think that would happen. Thurgood Marshall was the first Black judge in this courthouse, and when he left to be solicitor general there were no Blacks here. Thurgood knew how lonely I would be on the bench with the double handicap of being a woman and a Black. At the time of my appointment only seven other African Americans had been appointed to the federal bench.

I thought I could get a state court appointment, and I sought one. But I couldn't get anywhere with that because I wasn't involved in city politics and, of course, appointments to the state court bench, especially at the lower-court level, were controlled by the politicians.

You never have a drive to become a federal judge, because being appointed to the federal judiciary is a matter of sheer, unadulterated luck. You have to be in the right place at the right time. There was this article recently in the *New York Law Journal* about a qualified Black woman who had been nominated to this court. She never made it because the White House wouldn't approve it. She was too liberal for the Republicans who decide who gets on the federal bench. Once the Republicans are gone she will probably get an appointment.

I got on the federal bench because Johnson was president at the height of the civil rights movement. I was active in the civil rights movement and was a well-known civil rights lawyer. That's how I got appointed. You don't sit up and dream that you want to be on the federal bench. It never happens that way.

There is a need for more women and more minorities in the federal judiciary, but not because I think they bring something totally different to the bench than white men. I don't think women and minorities have a particular view on contract law that's totally different from white men. Rather, I believe that having more women and minorities in the federal judiciary—and the federal courts are a major part of the national government—builds confidence in the government. It makes people feel that the government is fair, in that it includes people from all segments of the population. It says that the courts are fair, in that women, Blacks, Hispanics, Asians, and other minorities are included among the judges. It says that the court system is not an all-white male institution as it once was. When I first came on the bench, that could have been said of the federal judiciary.

People have to see fairness in terms of the sharing of power. Federal judges have a great deal of power, which most people do not understand because they never come in contact with a federal court. But federal judges have the power of life and death over people, as well as power over their wealth and status in society. One of the hopes and promises of Clinton's election is that the government will become more representative of today's society.

The country has changed dramatically in the last forty years. Women and minorities, meaning Blacks and Hispanics, have come to power, so to speak. We now have two women from California in the U.S. Senate. We have a Black woman from Illinois in the Senate. I think there are six women in the Senate now. When I was growing up and for many years, there was only one woman in the Senate. Prior to this past election we only had one Black in the Senate this century. So at no time in our history have we had more than one Black and one woman in the Senate at the same time, but now we are seeing a dramatic change. That change is necessary if we are going to move forward, if we are going to avoid dividing the country and preventing the government from functioning.

There are now about 68 Black federal judges. Of those, I think only 11 are Black women. There are probably about 60 women in the federal judiciary. That means there are approximately 140 women and minorities out of more than 840 federal judges.

I expect that one of the things that Clinton will do is to again appoint substantial numbers of Blacks, women, and Hispanics to the federal bench. When Carter was president [1976–1980] I think he appointed almost forty Blacks and nearly an equal number of women. Since that time, no more than a dozen women and Blacks have been appointed altogether.

So what I'm really talking about is increasing the representation of new groups in the society who are now politically powerful. That is what makes the country so different today from what it was fifty years ago: In the past women and minorities had little if any political power on the national level. There were pockets around the country, in places like Chicago and New York, where Blacks, Hispanics, and women had some local influence because of their numbers, but nationally they had no political leverage at all. That has changed significantly. We need more federal judges so the federal judiciary can reflect society as it really exists.

When I came out of law school in 1946, Blacks were excluded from society by operation of law in the southern states and as a matter of policy at the national level. The armed forces were segregated. We couldn't eat in restaurants in the District of Columbia or stay in hotels. Even some New York hotels would exclude Blacks. When Joe Louis became the world boxing champion [1937] he couldn't stay in a hotel in downtown New York. He had to stay in the Hotel Theresa in Harlem. There has been dramatic change in that respect. Any day of the week, today, you will see Blacks all over downtown New York hotels having social functions, dinners, fashion shows, and the like. It was absolutely unheard of in 1946 for any Black group to sponsor an affair at a downtown hotel.

Between 1946 and the present all legal barriers to Black advancement have been eliminated. Blacks are now able to go into any restaurant or hotel. Blacks can live where they want. With the fair employment practices laws, Blacks now work in places they could not have in 1946, such as insurance companies, banks, retail establishments, restaurants, you name it. In New York there are Black people in all of those areas.

In fact the most dramatic change has been that New York City itself has turned Black—or at least nonwhite—in the last fifty years, so that you now have a majority of Blacks, Hispanics, and Asians. These groups are the new majority in New York City. We have a Black mayor, and the city council has now changed.

Nationally, we've seen change to the extent that no laws exist restricting the liberty of Blacks, whether it is to travel, to vote, to live where we want, to buy where we want. These legal restrictions do not exist any more, so we have become integrated in that respect. That is, Blacks are as much a part of the community as anyone else.

Of course, we still do have segregation in the sense that whites in cities all over the country have moved out of the central city, creating Black central cities. But that doesn't detract from the fact that the law has changed, that we no longer recognize any legal restriction based solely on race. For example, when Levittown was built way out on Long Island in 1946 or '47 Blacks were barred from buying there. Here in Manhattan in 1945 Metropolitan Life Insurance Company erected a housing development that barred Blacks. Of course, none of that can happen now. We have housing laws which prohibit that. But as a practical matter we know that Blacks are discriminated against when they apply for housing.

Had it not been for Thurgood Marshall, no one would ever have heard of Constance Baker Motley. Thurgood Marshall hired me as a clerk in 1945 at the NAACP Defense Fund. Marshall had a liberal view that women ought to have the same chances to become lawyers as men. Thurgood had no qualms giving equal employment opportunities to women. He would always tell me about the successful Black women he encountered. He grew up at a time when African American males were at the bottom rung of the ladder of every conceivable professional endeavor and African American women were not even on the ladder.

Thanks to Thurgood Marshall I was able to get in on the ground floor of the civil rights revolution. Because we were a small staff and it was not very fashionable in those days to be working in civil rights, I got an opportunity that few lawyers graduating from Columbia Law School with me would ever have—and that was actually to try major cases, take appeals to the courts of appeal, and argue cases in the United States Supreme Court.

I guess what sparked my interest in the law when I was growing up more than anything else was the 1938 Lloyd Gaines case. I was in high school in New Haven at the time, and the U.S. Supreme Court ruled that Missouri could not send Blacks to out-of-state law schools in order to prevent them from attending the all-white University of Missouri Law School. It was a major decision. However, that decision did not knock out segregation; all it did was knock out the program where Blacks were given out-of-state scholarships to study law. But that was my first encounter with the idea that the Supreme Court could be instrumental in changing the status of Black Americans, and so that really sparked my interest in pursuing the law.

Growing up in New Haven I was aware that Black people could become lawyers and judges. New Haven had two Black lawyers when I was growing up. One was George Crawford, who became corporation counsel for the City of New Haven. The other one was a man whose last name was Early. Early practiced in the Black community, and Crawford had an office downtown. We lived near Crawford and I knew him personally. I met Early when I was in high school and became active in Black community affairs. I also knew of a Black female lawyer named Eunice Carter. She is the grandmother of Yale law professor Stephen Carter. She was appointed by [Thomas] Dewey to his staff at one point, so she gained recognition in that respect.

In 1936 James Watson and Charles Toney were elected to the civil court in New York, so naturally I heard about them. My parents knew Watson. I also heard of the appointment of Jane Bolin to New York's family court in 1939. She was the first Black woman to be a judge in New York, perhaps the first in the country.

So growing up, I was aware of Black lawyers and judges, and they were role models for me. I was also fortunate to learn Black history when I was a teen. We had a minister at the church I attended, Saint Luke's Episcopal Church, who was interested in Black history, and he conducted classes for the youth. I would read James Weldon Johnson and Du Bois and things like that. That's how I became aware and inspired to do something about the problems facing Blacks.

In high school I became active in local community affairs and began attending the adult meetings. I was very tall for my age and looked twenty when I was fifteen. When I was fifteen I was president of the New Haven Youth Council and secretary of the New Haven Adult Council.

I was able to go to college through the generous financial assistance of a man named Clarence Blakeslee, a very successful businessman who used his money to help Blacks and others secure an education. Mr. Blakeslee had heard me speak one night and invited me to his office the next day. He asked why I wasn't in college when I had graduated with honors, and I told him I didn't have any money. He said he would be glad to pay for my college education and asked me what I wanted to do. I told him I wanted to study law. He said he didn't know much about women and law, but if that's what I wanted he'd pay for it. When I told my parents that I found money to go to college they didn't much believe it. They never encouraged me to be a lawyer and thought I should be a hairdresser. I even thought about being an interior decorator. But my parents didn't oppose my going to college or becoming a lawyer.

I graduated from New York University in October 1943 with a bachelor's degree in economics. I was admitted to Columbia Law School and began in February 1944. The dean of the Law School had earlier voted against admission of women to the school, so there were few women there; but I survived and graduated.

When I graduated from law school you probably couldn't have found a single person who would bet a quarter that I would be successful in the legal profession. I didn't believe it either.

My first job interview, during my last year in law school, was an accurate sign of the times. I had learned from a classmate that a small midtown firm was looking to hire a recent graduate. When I went to the firm for an interview, a balding middle-aged white man appeared at a door leading to the reception room and closed the door quickly. The receptionist didn't invite me to sit down. We both knew the interview was over before it began.

Another classmate of mine, an African American man named Herman Taylor, told me about a law clerk vacancy at the NAACP Legal

Defense and Education Fund. I quickly went down to the fund's office for an interview, and Thurgood Marshall hired me on the spot. He told me he admired Black women who had the courage to enter the legal profession.

When I finished Columbia Law School in June 1946 Marshall received board approval to hire a woman lawyer. I was a member of the fund staff until 1965. My son was born in 1952 and NAACP policy was to have women take a leave of absence after six months of pregnancy, but Marshall simply ignored the pressure brought on him to make me go on leave after six months. I worked until the week before my son arrived. I was the only professional woman employed by the NAACP or the fund. I set a new standard for women, with Marshall's tacit approval.

Much of the work of the fund in those days entailed creating the legal theories on which we would have to win our cases. We became legal craftsmen in that respect. Our early work in civil rights involved segregation in education, which culminated in the *Brown* decision.

A year or two after I became a full-time attorney with the fund Marshall sent me to Baltimore to sit in on a case that was being tried by his mentor, the man who founded the fund, Charles Hamilton Houston, the great lawyer who was dean of Howard Law School when Marshall was there. Houston was representing a Black woman against the University of Maryland School of Nursing. Marshall wanted me to learn from the master.

I have never seen a better prepared trial lawyer in my life. Houston had a notebook in which every question he was going to ask was written out. Houston's advice to me was: "Never ask a question that you have not previously considered."

One of the cases Marshall accompanied me on involved a contempt hearing against the board of trustees of the University of Alabama. During the course of that hearing we stayed in the Birmingham home of a local attorney named Arthur Shores. His home had been bombed over a dozen times. At night we were guarded by Black men with machine guns, and during the day we were escorted to and from court by men who carried handguns.

One of the earliest cases I appeared in as a trial lawyer was a case in Mississippi involving the equalization of Black teachers' salaries. I think this was in 1949. Marshall had sent me to Mississippi to assist Robert Carter. I remember this case well because the local newspaper had a big story the day when the trial began to the effect that there were two Negro lawyers from New York who were going to try the case and one of them was a woman. The courthouse was packed, not only because this was the first case this century in which Blacks in Mississippi sought to attack the establishment to try and end segregation, but also because, as the newspaper stated, here was this Negro woman lawyer from New York. The whole town turned out to see the "Nigra" lawyers.

I was surprised to find there were some fair judges in the South. The federal judge who handled the salary equalization case was fair. His name was Sydney Mize. He was from the Biloxi–Gulfport area. He came from that part of Mississippi where there weren't very many Black people. And his whole attitude toward Black people was different from, say, a cotton grower in the delta. He didn't have all that hatred for Black people, and so when we appeared in his court he treated us just like other lawyers were treated. He really was a federal judge.

There was a mural that dominated the wall in Judge Mize's courtroom behind his bench. The mural had been painted by WPA workers and depicted Mississippi society by showing Black people on one side helping the white people up into their carriage, and next to a bale of cotton the white ladies were in their pretty dresses. That mural just overtook the courtroom, but Judge Mize didn't say anything about it. I guess his attitude was, I didn't put it up there, the government did.

In his opinion in the equalization case he said he would have ruled with us except that the Court of Appeals for the Fifth Circuit, to which the case would have been appealed, had ruled in an Atlanta school case that we first had to exhaust all administrative remedies. So he had to rule against us.

Now Judge Mize's successor, Harold Cox, was just the opposite. Cox was an uncivilized man whereas Mize was a civilized man. Mize knew that you had to respect people. Cox did not. Cox could not stand the sight of Black people. Cox once called an assistant U.S. attorney general a "nigger lover" in open court. So there was a contrast between these two judges.

I once was in Mississippi handling this case in which Mize had ruled against us. It went up to the court of appeals, and they reversed it and sent it back. It was at this point that Cox came on the court.

I was in Mize's court with my secretary to draw up a motion to hold the governor of Mississippi in contempt of court for interfering with the court's decision. We had to go to Meridian, Mississippi, because that's where Judge Mize was sitting. Medgar Evers drove us over there. My secretary had to do this motion hurriedly, and in doing it, she entitled the document "Order" instead of "Motion" in her haste.

I handed the motion to Judge Mize, and Judge Cox was sitting next to him. Cox had just been appointed to succeed Judge Mize, who was going to take senior status. So, Cox grabbed the document and said, "Look at this. It says 'Order,' " and threw it back at me across the table. Judge Mize put his hand on Judge Cox's hand and said, "Judge Cox, it's all over." (At that point the U.S. Supreme Court had affirmed the decision.) In other words, Mize was saying to Cox, "Look, we fought the thing. We did what we could. They ruled against us. It's over. We've lost. You have to act like a judge. It's not your problem personally. You have to be impartial." But Cox was never impartial in any sense.

I personally tried a number of cases that became famous. I represented James Meredith in his fight to enter the University of Mississippi. We brought the University of Georgia kicking and screaming into the twentieth century through the admission of Charlayne Hunter-Gault and Hamilton Holmes. George Wallace and Alabama finally gave up their massive resistance to desegregation in 1963. And we successfully fought to gain Harvey Gantt's admission to Clemson College in 1962. Now South Carolina brags about Gantt, who became mayor of Charlotte, North Carolina, and almost upset Jesse Helms for the United States Senate.

As I said earlier, out of the ten cases I argued before the U.S. Supreme Court, I won nine. There was one particularly busy day in 1962 when I argued four cases on appeal in the Fifth Circuit.

The work of the NAACP Defense Fund broke down a lot of legal barriers, barriers the current Supreme Court seems intent on trying to erect again. We know there has been a shift in the makeup of the Supreme Court since the days of Earl Warren, when many of the cases I was involved in were heard. I think it reflects a backlash against that Warren Court.

The new judges are conservative, and they apparently believe that it is their mission to reverse a lot of the Warren Court's decisions as unwarranted by the Constitution, not having been intended by the framers of the Constitution. I am sure that they will reverse as many of the Warren Court's decisions as they possibly can. I was involved in a Supreme Court case that succeeded in desegregating recreational facilities in the parks in Memphis. Twenty years later a conservative majority on the Court allowed white residents to erect a barrier closing off a street between their neighborhood and a Black neighborhood. The street that was closed off by that decision was a major route for Blacks to get to the main park that had been desegregated in the previous ruling.

We are not going to get any new breakthroughs in terms of civil rights as long as there is a conservative majority on the Supreme Court. However, that situation is not going to last forever, particularly now that we have a Democratic president who is a liberal. He is bound to make appointments to the Supreme Court which would not have been made by Bush or Reagan.

Clinton is not going to appoint conservatives to the Supreme Court. He is going to appoint judges to the Supreme Court that he feels will support civil rights, freedom of choice, the rights of women, and the rights of other minorities. We can look forward to a halt to the paring down of rights that were won back in the fifties and early sixties. And I think we might even see an expansion of rights if we get a liberal majority once again.

Of course, none of us can foresee the future, but it seems to me we are always going to have problems that are too hot to handle politically. The courts are going to be called upon to resolve them because federal judges are appointed for life, barring misbehavior, and therefore they can't suffer reprisals at the polls if they take unpopular positions. I think we were able to get the decisions that we did get from the Warren Court only because federal judges do not have to stand for election. It was the conscious design of the framers of the Constitution that the courts should be free from political influence.

After the civil rights era, I'd say beginning in the late sixties, there was a tremendous backlash against what the civil rights movement had brought about, which was the desegregation of American society. And the most controversial situation was the desegregation of the public school systems, where people were moved, bussed, and everything else in order to comply with the court decisions. People resented it, and they resented it particularly if their children were small. They wanted to go on with life the way it was, meaning you go to the nearest school, you don't have to encounter people that you feel are hostile to you, and you can control, more or less, your children's friends. And resentment over that caused the backlash.

But I think the backlash is tempered by the realization that Blacks have finally been accepted in the community, legally speaking, and because they now have political power that means something. The election of a Black woman as senator from Illinois means white people now have to deal with a Black woman if they want to accomplish certain things in Illinois. That is going to change a lot of views about Blacks and women.

The same in California. The men who have been reluctant to deal with women, writing them off as not capable of dealing with certain complex problems, will now be faced with the reality that they have to deal with women. Both senators from California are women. There is no escape. This will change a lot of men's attitude toward women.

The backlash will be countered by the fact that Blacks have risen to positions of real power in this country, and that is what makes us hopeful that despite the conservative opinions coming from the Supreme Court and other federal courts there is not going to be as much damage as we initially feared.

Moreover, some of the state courts, in response to a conservative U.S. Supreme Court, have decided under their state constitutions that people have certain rights which they may not even have under the U.S. Constitution. State supreme courts in New York, New Jersey, and California are prime examples of states using their own constitutions to protect additional rights of the individual, despite a more conservative Supreme Court. One of the main struggles under the Constitution has been to secure the rights of the individual against the majority.

I think there is a confusion today between racism and—how should I put it—between racism and Black power. I think much of the resentment we see today in New York City and other places arises not so much from racism but from the emergence of Black power. What is really happening in New York City, for example, is resentment against the emergence of Black power. The New York mayoralty represents power over thirty billion dollars, which is one of the largest government budgets in the United States after the national government. There is no other chief executive in the United States who has the kind of economic power that the mayor of New York City has. New

York politics is all about how that thirty billion dollars is going to be spent, and on whom. That is what it comes down to: How much power can the white community retain for itself in terms of dividing that thirty-billion-dollar pie? There is a Black mayor, and naturally whites think the money is being spent only on Blacks. Consequently, whites want to ensure that the Black mayor doesn't get reelected. [In fact, New York's first Black mayor, David N. Dinkins, lost his bid for re-election in 1993 to his white Republican challenger, Rudolph W. Guiliani, who promised to eliminate Dinkins's minority contractors program, which set aside a fixed percentage of public contracts for minority-owned businesses.]

This is not strictly racism in the way that we used to think of racism, that is, racism backed up by laws and policies that restricted the movement and achievement of Blacks. This is far more subtle and sophisticated than that. You won't hear any of these people saying they don't like Blacks. In fact, they'll tell you how they worked in the civil rights movement, so it is not the same kind of racism. The resentment is an antagonism to the growth of Black power and the increasing power not just of Blacks but of Hispanics and Asians, too. You could say it is just a different form of racism, but it certainly is not the same old racism that we knew.

I had an amusing experience when I first came to the bench. We used to have the judges' dinners for our district at the Century Club in Manhattan, two or three times a year. These were collegial affairs where we could get together and talk. In the courthouse you don't often see your fellow judges. Well, the Century Club didn't allow women to go up to the second floor. In fact, the club didn't have any women members until a few years ago. When I came on the bench my fellow judges wondered how in the world they were going to get me upstairs. So, they got up this ruse: They told the club people I was a secretary and that I had to take the minutes of the meeting. I guess the club people didn't want any trouble, didn't want to buck the judges, so they didn't say anything. I'm sure the maître d' who waited on us and made the arrangements for the dinner knew I wasn't a secretary. And the Black guys who worked in the coat room and opened the door, they were amused. They knew I wasn't supposed to be up there, so they would just laugh and smile every time they saw me.

* * *

I've handled about twenty-five hundred cases since I've been on the bench. I have had many cases that broke new legal ground and have since become law. One area where I broke new legal ground was prisoners' rights. *Sostre v. McGinnis* set the court of appeals on fire. They sat en banc [i.e., the full court]. No one had said for the full court to hear the appeal. They sat en banc on their own. No one had ever heard of giving rights to prisoners before that case. Now that's accepted.

When I first came to bench. I had a big case involving Title VII [of the Civil Rights Act of 1964] discrimination against women in the telephone company. Then I had a case involving discrimination against women in a Wall Street firm. The firm's lawyers asked me to recuse myself because I had been discriminated against. I refused. Fortunately, when it got to the court of appeals I was saved from reversal. One of my law clerks tells me that this case is in some textbook used in law school. I suppose in civil procedures, motions to recuse.

I don't think I can say I have a specific judicial philosophy. I mean, so much of all our work is mundane. You couldn't possibly have a judicial philosophy about seamen's injury. But I share with most judges this general philosophy: to give wherever possible the broadest interpretation to federal laws intended to remedy an injury or a violation of rights.

I am working on a case now involving the Warsaw Convention. The case concerns the shooting down of the Korean Airlines flight 007. I have to write an opinion on what kind of damages would be recoverable under the Warsaw Convention. Surprisingly, this issue has not been dealt with before. I will have to make law in its first impression in many areas where there is a survival action, which can be brought by the estate of the deceased. There are many issues, such as what damages her sister and mother can recover? Can they recover for loss of her love, affection, and companionship? Can they recover for their own grief and suffering as a result of her death? Can they recover loss of support? All these kinds of things. So I have the job of deciding how broad the relief should be.

In a case such as this one you might say I have a judicial philosophy of trying to give the people who are bringing the suit against the airline as broad a construction as possible. Another judge might lean the other way to protect the airline and the insurance company against large judgments in such cases. And there is the problem as to whether you should allow certain damages, because the airlines would not be able to function if they had to pay too much money for insurance. It is not an easy task. All I am saying is that my tendency would be to protect the consumer and to make sure that the survivors of people who had been killed wrongfully are able to get some benefit other than the cost of a casket.

I was the chief judge of our court from June of 1982 until October of 1986. The Southern District of New York is the largest federal trial court in the country. Prior to my serving as chief judge only one other woman had ever served as a federal district court chief judge. I was the only woman on our court until 1978, when President Carter appointed Mary Johnson Lowe, who was African American. I took senior status after stepping down from being chief judge. I am a senior judge now.

A number of the judges on the court then didn't like the idea of my being the chief judge. That burned up a lot of them, for sure. The thing that surprised me, though, was that it was the younger men, not the older men, who were most bothered by it. Basically, there were a couple of younger men who really could not handle it. The older guys knew me over the years, so it wasn't as though I were a stranger. The younger guys didn't know me as well, and a couple of them really resented it. One of them tried to make trouble all the time, but I ignored it. Fortunately the others knew he was just being Peck's bad boy. He's not too highly thought of in terms of legal caliber, so they realized what he was up to. The older ones may not have liked it, but they certainly didn't evidence their displeasure in any way. They just went along. They knew chief judges weren't forever. The court was going to go on.

GEORGE W. CROCKETT JR.

"A Black judge's role is to challenge the status quo."

Now retired, George Crockett spent much of his judicial career in the center of controversy for rulings that clashed with efforts by powerful forces that sought to manipulate the criminal justice system for political purposes. His refusal during Detroit's 1967 riot to use high bails as a scheme to clear the streets of potential rioters drew criticism from the White House. Two years later he faced censure from the Michigan legislature and an impeachment effort when he again refused to accede to requests to abuse the bail process in the mass arrest that followed a fatal shoot-out between police and a Black militant organization. Crockett's stance in both cases was later vindicated in independent reviews by legal experts. Crockett says such controversy made him a better judge, because it made him more independent in his thinking.

Crockett's legal career has encompassed being a lawyer, jurist, and legislator (U.S. congressman). His first impressions of the criminal justice system were formed as a child growing up in then segregated Jacksonville, Florida, where Blacks were barred from walking on the sidewalk in front of the city courthouse. An octogenarian, Crockett was one of the first Black jurists to write extensively on the role of racism in America's judicial system and on the duty of Black judges to confront and correct that racism. He helped found the oldest and largest organization of Black judges, the Judicial Council of the National Bar Association.

Crockett was interviewed in October 1992 at his home in a quiet, almost suburban area in the heart of Washington, D.C.

I first entertained the idea of becoming a judge when I was in prison for four months, serving a contempt-of-court conviction, somewhere around 1953 or 1954. In prison I had a lot of time to think about the power of judges and the power of judicial discretion.

A federal judge in New York City had convicted me and four other defense lawyers of contempt in this case that involved top members of the American Communist Party. Throughout the trial the judge was not fair or impartial. He was more like an extra prosecutor in the case. At the end of the trial the judge decided all of the defense lawyers were in contempt of court. He said our working together in unison to prepare the defense amounted to a conspiracy to bring the administration of justice into disrepute. He then combed the trial record and picked out particular instances where he claimed that each lawyer had violated an order of the court.

That is an example of the judicial discretion I just mentioned. Most people don't realize how much of what we call judicial discretion controls what is and what is not the law in this country.

Judicial discretion basically means that many cases are decided on an individual judge's view of right and wrong. It's that simple. Judges determine what the law is and what the law will be. In my particular case the federal judge in New York decided it was wrong for us to mount a vigorous defense. The power of judicial discretion inherent in the law enabled this judge to say that our effort to do our jobs as lawyers properly on behalf of our clients was a conspiratorial act that required punishment. Appellate courts generally give wide deference to the exercise of judicial discretion. Our contempt case went all the way up to the U.S. Supreme Court and the Court affirmed the convictions.

Few people fully appreciate the fact that the most powerful public official in America is a judge. Judges tell legislatures when they are wrong and when they have to do the job over again. Judges tell presidents what they can and cannot do. As the great French critic of American politics, de Tocqueville, once remarked, in America every social and political issue becomes a question for a judge to decide.

You see the wisdom of that observation all the time. Just recently there was a decision in which the lowest level of federal court judge, a district court judge, told the U.S. Senate that it's wrong when that full body declines to hear an impeachment proceeding and reaches its conclusion to impeach based on a hearing by one of its committees.

Where else in the world will you find that situation? I don't think it would happen in English jurisprudence and I don't think it would happen under civil law in other countries either, but here in America the judiciary ultimately decides what is the law.

Most legal issues in this country are decided on the trial court level. They are not appealed to the appellate courts. That's one reason why the trial court is crucial. Most people, particularly Black people, don't have the money to take their cases to the appellate courts. Therefore, if you're going to get justice, you'd better get it on the trial court level or else you're not going to get it.

I think it was Benjamin Cardozo, in his *Judicial Process*, who emphasized how the judge is the product of his own experiences and his own background. That's why it's important to make sure that judges on the trial court level are not just shot through and through with prejudice based on race, creed, or color. And that's why it becomes important for Black people and other minorities to get judges who have somehow shared their experiences and their backgrounds: those experiences will influence the judicial discretion that the law authorizes a judge to use in certain cases.

In our training as Americans, we are trained to respect judicial orders. Our training says that if it's a court order, you obey it. Our training is such that we don't ask if the judicial order came from a Black person or from a white person.

I have always believed that it was a Black judge's role to challenge the status quo, to see what justice requires and go to the law books to find the right remedies to apply. I felt that way before I went on the bench, but before going on the bench it was more theory than anything else. At that time you really didn't have enough Black judges to talk about the special role of a Black judge. At the same time, you felt sort of put out if you went before a Black judge and he treated the matter routinely, like any other matter, when you knew that there were racial overtones involved in the case and he was electing to overlook them. Going on the bench gave me the opportunity to put my theories into practice.

I once shocked everybody in the state of Michigan by calling for a one-man grand jury to investigate the drug situation in Detroit. At the time I think I was the chief judge of Detroit's recorder's court. This would have been in the mid-seventies. My main concern in this investigation was the effect narcotic cases were having on our docket and the way the justice system was handling these cases. Our dockets were overburdened with cases that involved very small amounts of narcotics. I knew that under Michigan law we had a one-man grand jury system, which meant that any court of record could designate one of its members as a grand juror and the county was obligated to provide whatever facilities that grand juror needed to investigate a criminal situation.

I had the feeling that it was wrong to talk about criminal prosecution in many of those cases. A better approach would have been more in the nature of education, medical treatment, and rehabilitation—not just locking people up in prison. I also felt that if you were to take the money value out of the narcotic trade by making the drugs almost free or at least making them as available as alcohol and cigarettes, then there would be a reduction in the number of arrests for narcotic use and a substantial reduction in the caseload of the court.

I'll always remember getting a call from the attorney general of Michigan asking if I would meet with him to discuss this grand juror matter. I met with him and he asked me to hold off because he had assurances from J. Edgar Hoover of the FBI that they were coming into Detroit and they were going to do something about the drug problem. The attorney general didn't want me to present my proposal for a grand jury investigation to my fellow judges for approval.

Meanwhile, the newspapers had come out with editorials supporting the investigation. And Mayor Coleman Young had indicated his support for it. Finally we brought the matter to a vote by the members of my court and it was defeated. About five members of the bench had been assistant prosecutors. The prosecutor's office was opposed to a one-man grand jury because the grand juror would have had the authority to appoint a special prosecutor to supersede the regular prosecutor. I'll always believe that the district attorney got to the former members of his office who sat on the court and persuaded them to vote against the one-man grand jury.

The drug problem continued, of course. There was a legitimate question in the narcotic cases that were being prosecuted whether there was a sufficient amount of the narcotic to make it a meaningful prosecution. There is this old principle in the law known as *de minimis,* which means, there are matters so insignificant that the law should ignore them.

I recalled there was at least one Michigan supreme court case recognizing the *de minimis* principle in drug prosecutions, so I hit upon this principle as a basis of reducing the number of prosecutions that were overburdening our dockets. When a narcotic case was brought before me I required proof that whatever the defendant had been caught with actually contained traces of heroin or other drugs. Additionally, I wanted to know how much narcotic was in the evidence taken from the defendant, so that I could determine whether or not it was enough to justify prosecution.

Well, I was overruled on that approach. One of the cases that I threw out on the *de minimis* principle was taken up either to the court of appeals or the Supreme Court and I was reversed.

I have always believed that you cannot possibly deal with the narcotic issue simply through criminal prosecution and throwing people in jail. It's not going to work. We've spent billions in the past few years fighting a war on drugs by arresting people and putting them in jail, but drug use has increased and our court dockets are still overburdened. We're still arresting and jailing people for small amounts of drugs.

The evidence of the past few years indicates that I was correct in the approach I wanted to use back in the seventies, when I was a judge. But we still are jailing people instead of treating them. In 1990, shortly before I left Congress, I called for the decriminalization of drugs. I believe I was the first member of that body to publicly call for decriminalization. We have to change our national policy on drugs.

There is not equal justice for Black people in our criminal courts, and there never has been. This is the shame of our whole judicial system. In a country whose Supreme Court is emblazoned with the motto EQUAL JUSTICE UNDER LAW the quantity and quality of justice is in fact in direct proportion to the size of one's pocketbook and the color of one's skin. This is so, not because the written law says it shall be so, rather it is so because our judges, by their rulings, make it so.

Historically, law enforcement has been the most racially segregated and class-oriented area in American life. I think that has changed. I think it has changed for the better. Problems of race and class still exist in the justice system, but they are not as acute as they were just twenty years ago.

One reason why racism is not as acute in the justice system today is the increase in the number of Black judges in the past twenty years. Today there are hundreds of Black judges, and that has made a difference. When I first became a judge it was unusual to see Black jurors. Now there are Black jurors, and in some cities with large Black populations you might find all-Black juries. Having Black jurors has made a difference. Another thing that has made a difference is having more Black employees in the justice system.

Further, the changes in the justice system have brought about a tremendous increase in the number of Black lawyers, and they, in turn have had some impact on the judicial system—not nearly the impact I'd like to have seen, but it's growing.

The situation with racism in the justice system has vastly improved, but we still have a long way to go. When you see the Rodney King debacle, you see the extent to which racism still plays a major role in the criminal justice system. I think racism will eventually be purged from the judicial system. I don't think anything lasts forever.

When I was elected in 1966 I don't think you had fifty Black judges in the entire country. Fifty would be a very high figure. Today, I understand the number of Black judges is somewhere near one thousand. That is an improvement, yet there are more than thirty thousand judges across the country. Whatever the exact number of Black judges is, it's still small compared to the total number.

It wasn't until somewhere around 1912 or 1915 that the first Black was elected to the bench in Michigan, and that was as a circuit court commissioner, a glorified justice of the peace. That was in Detroit. I believe the gentleman's name was Straker. Of course, after him we didn't have another Black judicial officer in the state until, I suppose, the early fifties, when Wade McCree was appointed to the circuit court bench in Michigan. Wade became one of the first Black federal district court judges when he was appointed by President Kennedy. I think he went on the federal bench somewhere around 1961.

When we organized the Judicial Council in 1972, the total number of Black judges was somewhere between eighty-five and ninety and we got about seventy-five to become members of the Judicial Council. The council was the first national organization of Black judges. There weren't that many Black judges in the nation in the early seventies; I know because I published the first directory of Black judges that gave their names and the court they served on.

The Judicial Council remains the largest nationwide organization of Black judges because it includes state and federal judges. I was asked to form an organization of Black judges by Ed Bell, a lawyer from Detroit who was then the president of the National Bar Association. I had been a member of the National Bar Association since I began practicing law in Florida in the thirties. The National Bar Association is the bar group founded by Blacks. For decades the American Bar Association would not accept Blacks, or at least Blacks found it nearly impossible to join the ABA.

I agreed to Bell's request to organize a judicial council. That meant finding out who the Black judges were and meeting with them to see if they were interested in participating in such an organization. So I went to New York, Washington, Baltimore, Los Angeles, Chicago, and other cities to talk with the judges, and in each case there was great enthusiasm.

The judges said, yes, we need to get together and have our own judicial organization, just like the Jews, Italians, and other ethnic groups. Frankly, I don't recall a single Black judge who was opposed to organizing the council. I mean, verbally opposed. There may have been those who were opposed by reason of the fact that they didn't join the council, but very few Black judges didn't join.

The Ford Foundation provided us with several thousand dollars, which enabled us to underwrite the expenses of a convention for the purpose of writing a constitution for the council and actually putting the organization together. A group of judges met with me during a midwinter meeting of the National Bar Association. Some of the judges in that group were Leon Higginbotham from Philadelphia, Damon Keith from Detroit, Joe Howard from Baltimore, and Judge Thompson from Washington. We came up with a constitution and decided we would still affiliate with the National Bar Association so long as we had complete autonomy.

The founding convention of the Judicial Council of the National Bar Association was held in Atlanta in 1973. I believe that more than sixty judges attended that convention. The Ford Foundation had given us additional money, which we used to pay the judges' traveling expenses to the convention. I was elected chairman.

During the council's first year we were concerned primarily with increasing our membership and educating Black judges on a variety of topics. At our first midwinter meeting we concentrated on building sentiment for increasing the number of Black federal judges in the South. Richard Nixon was president at the time, and we sent letters to him, calling attention to the small number of Black federal judges in the South. Of course, this effort was to no avail, and he made no such appointments. Our past two Republican presidents, Reagan and Bush, didn't do a good job appointing Blacks to the federal judiciary, either. I'm hopeful that Clinton will do a better job.

I don't think there is any organized effort to keep Blacks out of the judiciary, but, I hasten to add, I don't see any organized effort to get more Blacks into the judiciary. I think that's what we need to be doing, getting more Blacks into the judiciary.

The increase in the number of Black judges that occurred during the seventies was primarily due to the increase in political influence of the Black vote. Blacks finally realized that a lot of things can be done if you have state power. The power is there. The question is, who is exercising the power?

The New Bethel Church case in 1969 probably did more than anything else to open the eyes of Blacks in Michigan to the political potential that they had. The New Bethel Church case in Detroit involved a shoot-out between the police and a Black nationalist organization. Over 140 people, including women and children, were arrested inside the church.

Suddenly, after the New Bethel Church case, Blacks out there on the streets realized that one way to take care of police brutality was to get themselves some Black judges. So they went to the polls and they elected Black judges. That's why we have the large number of Black judges in Michigan that we have today. I am amazed when I go back to Michigan to see how the number of Blacks on the bench has increased, particularly the number of Black women on the bench in Michigan. It's really outstanding.

In the New Bethel case Blacks discovered that, having gone to the polls and elected a Black judge, all of a sudden they had a Black judge in the position to tell the white authorities in Detroit that they were wrong in their treatment of these 140 Black people. The people had been arrested and were being held in a police garage because there weren't adequate lock-up facilities for that many people. The authorities were deliberately misusing and abusing the system in order to keep them in custody. The Black judge ordered their release because there was nothing in the law that required these people to be held in jail without bail.

The Black judge in the New Bethel case was me.

Serving four months in prison heightened my sensitivity to the abuses that can and do occur in the justice system. My prison experience had an impact on my judicial thinking. I knew what I was doing when I sent someone to prison, because I had had the experience of being there. I also knew from that experience how imprisonment can be abusive.

The case that led to my imprisonment involved the federal Smith Act. In 1948 the federal government decided to indict the top leadership of the U.S. Communist Party under what was commonly known as the Smith Act. The Smith Act was a congressional statute that prohibited teaching and advocating the violent overthrow of the U.S. government. It also prohibited membership in any organization that taught and advocated the violent overthrow of the government. The prosecution's theory in this case was that the Communist Party was an organization whose top leadership constituted a conspiracy for the purpose of teaching and advocating the violent overthrow of the government.

At the time of the indictment there were two Blacks in the top leadership of the Communist Party. One was Benjamin Davis, who was the first Black elected to the city council in New York City, and he was on the city council at the time of his indictment. The Communist Party, true to its general attitude with respect to the question of race, decided it wanted one Black lawyer, at least, included among the lawyers who would defend the party in federal court in New York.

A lawyer with whom I had been associated in Detroit, Maurice Sugar, asked me if I would consider coming to New York as one of the defense lawyers. Sugar had been general counsel of the United Automobile Workers, and I had initially gone to Detroit to work with the UAW. When Maurice and I left the UAW, I worked as an associate in his office. Maurice had retired from the firm and was living in New York when this case came up, but he was very familiar with it. I knew nothing about the case. He had to tell me all of the facts because I had not been following it in the press.

He said it was a First Amendment issue: To what extent do we defend freedom of speech, freedom of expression, and freedom of association even for groups we do not agree with? After hearing the facts I felt the matter was simple. The First Amendment of our Constitution says that Congress shall make no law that abridges the freedom of speech or the right of the people peaceably to assemble. For me this case involved the First Amendment principle. I knew there were risks in getting involved in the case because of the feelings in the country at the time about communism, but I felt it was my duty as a lawyer to see that Benjamin Davis received adequate representation.

A close friend of mine who overheard me talking to Sugar on the telephone about the case told me that taking this case would affect my usefulness in the "Negro Struggle"—that's what the civil rights movement was called then. He said I would be labeled a Communist just for taking the case, and he was right. But I told him if being labeled a Communist was the price I had to pay, then I would have to pay it. The Canon of Ethics for a lawyer requires you to take cases even if you personally don't agree with the parties. Lawyers have to provide defense. I discussed the matter with my wife, and she agreed that it was important for me to take the case, even knowing what the consequences might be.

To make a long story short, after a lot of soul searching I decided to join the defense team. So I went to New York. But my fears about the consequences of participating in that trial proved true when I returned to Detroit after the trial.

This was during the McCarthy era, and people whom I had known for years suddenly found that it was not exactly the right thing to be seen in my company. There were times when I'd see someone coming down the street and as I anticipated greeting them they would cross to the other side to keep from coming in contact with me. One of the Detroit papers, I think it was the *Detroit News*, carried a headline that implied I was a member of the Communist Party. I was not a party member and never have been. The paper later retracted the headline.

As I said earlier, this is the case that landed me in prison. The judge picked out six instances of contempt against me, in addition to the overall charge of conspiracy that he leveled against all of the defense attorneys. He found me guilty of each instance of contempt and sentenced me to four months on each count, to run concurrently. That way I'd have to get all of them reversed in order not to go to prison. On appeal the court of appeals reversed the conspiracy contempt charge, but I still had the other six counts.

A typical example of my alleged violation of an order of this judge involved a birth certificate of the daughter of one of the defendants. The prosecution wanted to put the birth certificate into evidence. I knew the birth certificate would indicate that this little girl was born before her parents had gotten married. Her father didn't want that to be made a matter of public record. So I went up to the bench and explained that to the judge and told him that was our objection. The prosecution wanted to use the birth certificate to establish that the father was living in a certain place in California at a certain time.

So, the judge said, "I'll tell you what I'll do, Mr. Crockett. I will admit it with the exception of the date of birth," and so forth. I said that would be all right. That served my purpose, and the judge said fine. The judge said he would himself read the birth certificate into the record so there would be no mistake about which part of the certificate got admitted into the record. I said fine.

The judge begins to read the certificate and lo and behold he reads the very part that he said he was going to exclude. I objected, and he raised his eyebrows. "You object, Mr. Crockett?"

I said, "Your honor, I thought we had stipulated to this, but Your Honor seemingly, unintentionally, read it into the record."

The judge said, "Seemingly?" I said yes, he had read the very part we had agreed would not be included in the record. The judge said that was contemptuous conduct on my part.

Another one of my alleged acts of contempt occurred when one of the defendants was sent to prison because he declined to answer a question that he said would incriminate him. The Fifth Amendment protects you against being compelled to incriminate yourself in court. This defendant declined to answer the question, and the judge immediately revoked his bail and ordered him to jail. The suddenness of the judge's order was such that all of the defendants stood up, which they never should have done.

I didn't say anything to my client except to tell him to sit down. And my client was telling me I should be on my feet objecting, too. The other lawyers objected, but I didn't move. The judge found us all guilty of contempt for not controlling the conduct of our clients. So, therefore, I was convicted of contempt because my client stood up and I was unable to get my client to sit down.

I went to prison for four months. We served our sentences in the minimum security federal institution in Ashland, Kentucky. Obviously, it was out of the ordinary for lawyers to be in prison. One interesting thing was that this case had attracted nationwide attention and the inmates at Ashland knew about the case. The inmates treated us with deference. They thought that if anybody in the jail didn't deserve to be there it was us.

They showed us this deference in subtle ways. I like to tell the story of the Ping-Pong table. In our dormitory there was one Ping-Pong table and one ball. If the ball got broken or lost you couldn't play Ping-Pong. Well, the inmates in my dorm gave me my very own individual Ping-Pong ball so I could play whenever and with whomever I wanted.

Perhaps the worst thing I suffered from that contempt conviction was the disbarment proceeding that was initiated against me in Michigan, based on the fact that I had been convicted of contempt of court in New York. I had to fight the disbarment. It was finally settled with the understanding that if I went back to New York and apologized on the record to the judge for my conduct, then the Michigan Bar Association would recommend to the court authorities that I get no more than a private reprimand. Initially I was opposed to this option, but a lawyer friend of mine convinced me I was toying with my whole future as a lawyer and I'd better just bow low and go on back and apologize.

I went back and apologized. I was not disbarred, but the bar didn't keep its promise. I received a public reprimand, not a private one, as promised. The difference between a public and a private reprimand is that with a public reprimand you are called before a judge in a regular session of court and the judge tells you in open court what a bad fellow you were and that he hopes you won't do it again. That's what happened in my case. I was lucky. Two of the other defense lawyers were disbarred.

Before I went to prison, between the time I was convicted of contempt and the day the conviction was upheld, we organized in Detroit the first interracial law firm in the country. It was called Goodman, Crockett, Eden & Ross. So when I came out of prison my law firm was still functioning and I continued in private practice. We were handling most of the civil rights litigation in the Michigan area. Obviously you don't make any money handling civil rights cases, so we became very proficient in the handling of personal injury cases and workmen's compensation cases. That's how we made our money.

We were doing well, very successful. I was making more money than I ever had, but I wasn't happy in the way I was making it. I would find myself working out a decent settlement in a personal injury case, a settlement I thought was fair and my client thought was fair, but my partners would say, "Oh, no, that case is worth twice that amount of money." They would tell me not to settle the case for $10,000 when we could easily get $20,000 or $30,000 out of the insurance company. They'd tell me to have the firm's bookkeeper give my client an advance if he needed some money and that I should go on pushing the case for a higher settlement. It got to the point where I tired of it, and I began looking around for something else that I might rather do.

I decided I should run for city council in Detroit. In 1965 I ran for city council and was successful in the primary, but I lost the general election. That same year the Michigan legislature increased the size of the recorder's court in Detroit, adding something like five new judges, and I decided to run for one of those judgeships and was successful. I was elected in 1966.

The law was not an area I wanted to pursue when I was young. I was born in Jacksonville, Florida, on August 10, 1909—which means I'm eighty-three years old now.

There was nothing in Jacksonville even to suggest to a young Black that the law offered a future for him or her. I don't mean to suggest that we didn't have Black lawyers. My recollection is that when I was growing up there were about three active Black lawyers in Jacksonville. You didn't have any Black lawyers in Florida south of Jacksonville.

Jacksonville in those days was, of course, segregated, highly segregated, like every other community in the South. The house in which I was born had no indoor plumbing, no running water, no electricity, and the nearest telephone was at a neighbor's house a block away. That neighbor placed a little receptacle near the telephone, where you would deposit your nickel if you wanted to make a call. The streets in my neighborhood were unpaved. The educational level—not just in the neighborhood where I lived, but among Blacks in Jacksonville generally—was extremely low. Being a high school graduate was outstanding, and being a college graduate was rare.

Law enforcement in Jacksonville, and in fact the entire justice system, was not viewed by Blacks as friendly. It was inconceivable that you would have a Black police officer in Jacksonville. I remember when I was ten years of age a Black man who was accused of killing a white person had a rope tied around his neck and the rope was tied to the back end of an automobile and they dragged his body through the Black neighborhood. My mother made us stay inside the house, with the doors closed and the shades pulled down.

One of my mother's constant admonitions to me whenever I went into town to pay the rent was that I should walk on the side of the street opposite the courthouse. The rental office was close to the courthouse. There was a little park outside the courthouse, and it was a congregating place for white people. I was not supposed to walk on the sidewalk bordering on the courthouse, and I never did. The park area by the courthouse was considered an area for whites only. I had never seen the inside of a courthouse until I was a junior or senior in law school.

When I decided to go off to college it was my intention to become a dentist. This was because the dentist in Jacksonville was riding around in a big, pretty Buick Roadmaster, and I figured that was the field I wanted to go into so I could have a car like that.

Two things changed my mind about this career choice. The first was organic chemistry, and the second was my interest in debating.

When I graduated from high school I won a scholarship from Kappa Alpha Psi for their oratorical contest. I won a two-hundred dollar scholarship to any college I wanted to attend, so I went to Morehouse.

After my first year at Morehouse I became very interested in debating and became a member of the debating team, then captain of the debating team, and then president of the debating society. Doing the research to get ready for debates intrigued me. I enjoyed looking up stuff, preparing arguments based on what I had read about historical events, and so forth. I became pretty good at it.

One evening I went into one of the classrooms, cleaned off two sections of the Blackboard, and wrote "law" at the top of one and "dentistry" at the top of the other. I methodically wrote down what I considered to be the advantages and disadvantages with respect to each of those professions. Then I sat back, considered everything, and decided dentistry was not for me, law was a better choice. But actually my decision was made before I went into that classroom that evening, when I saw my grades in organic chemistry.

Getting into law school at the time was a difficult process. There weren't any law schools in the Deep South that you could enter, because the law schools at the state universities didn't accept Blacks. The nearest law school you could enter was Howard University in Washington. But I decided I wanted to go to Harvard. I wrote to Harvard for a catalog, but when I saw that the tuition was five-hundred dollars a year I knew I couldn't begin to raise that kind of money. I had to work waiting tables during the summertime and also during the school term in order to stay in college. Talking about five-hundred dollars just for tuition was out of the question.

As I was deciding what to do about law school, a picture appeared in the *New York Times* of the recently constructed legal research building at the University of Michigan along with a story of a Michigan graduate who had made a lot of money on Wall Street in corporate law. This man had endowed the Law School, and some of his money went to build the legal research building. I sent for a catalog, saw that their tuition was one-hundred fifty dollars a year for out-of-state students, and figured I would be able to make that amount. I sent in my application and I was accepted.

The year before I came to Michigan there were five Blacks in the law school and all five of those Blacks had flunked out. There were just two Blacks accepted in 1931 when I entered. The other chap was from Fisk, and he didn't quite make it. As a result, for the rest of my time in law school I was the only Black in my class.

I was generally well accepted by my professors and fellow students at the Law School. I can't think of any acts of discrimination against me, but obviously you didn't enjoy the same camaraderie and friendliness that you had experienced in college. You would walk through the courtyard and here comes your professor who teaches domestic relations and knows you are a student in his class, but he finds some reason to look in the opposite direction just as he approaches you. That happened to me with one professor several times. On the other hand, I had other professors who went out of their way to be friendly if I initiated the conversation.

There was one advantage to being Black. The library had some rooms reserved for group discussions and studying. If I got over to the library in time I could go into one of those rooms and have complete privacy, because nobody else would come in and study with me.

My class had about 300 students, and it was divided into two sections. So every session I was the only Black, surrounded by 140 plus white students. When the teacher calls on you, you feel that you're the only Black and that 149 pairs of white people's eyes are looking at you, asking, Is it true what I hear about Blacks? That was and should be an inducement to study even harder. When I prepared for class I didn't just study the principal case. You could ask me about any case in the footnotes and I would have read all of them and would probably have even briefed one or two.

When I was in my senior year the dean announced that all seniors who thought they were entitled to a recommendation from him should come in and speak with him. I went to talk to the dean, but when he asked me where I wanted the recommendation sent, I couldn't answer him. There wasn't a Black law firm that I knew of anywhere in the country that was sufficiently prominent and prosperous enough in 1934 to take on young Black lawyers as associates, clerks, or whatever.

The dean told me it was unfortunate that I had not graduated the previous year, because he had had a request from Washington to recommend some Black Michigan graduates to serve on the legal staff of Roosevelt's New Deal administration. The Dean told me he couldn't help me get a Justice Department job without a specific request from the administration. Because he was a Republican and Roosevelt was a Democrat, he had no influence. He did say he thought I should be able to teach law, and I thought that as dean he could have offered me a position at the University of Michigan. But it would be almost fifty years after my graduation before Michigan took on its first Black faculty member.

The dean said he knew Charles Houston, who was then the dean at Howard Law School, and he sent a letter of recommendation down there. Houston wrote back expressing thanks for the recommendation and praised my record, but said he had just filled the vacancy with a brilliant graduate from the Harvard Law School whose name was William Hastings. Hastings and I used to laugh about this.

What finally happened was this: I went back to the dean and told him I wanted to go into private practice in West Virginia. I asked him if I could borrow some money from the University, because, frankly, I had no money to go into practice. He said he had never heard of the school making a loan to a student, but he asked me to prepare a budget and he'd see what he could do.

So I made out a budget for one year and included things like bus fare for myself and my wife to West Virginia, room rent for us, first month's office rent, and second-hand furniture, though I didn't even include money for law books or a secretary. The whole thing came to five-hundred dollars, and the dean arranged the loan from the university. It carried no interest and my payment rate was five dollars a month.

One of the reasons I wanted to go to West Virginia was that I had a problem with my conscience. Life in the North was altogether different from my life in the South, and like most southern boys who got a taste of what we said was freedom in the North, I wanted to stay there. At the same time I realized that I was from the Deep South, that there was a need down there for lawyers, and, thus, I should go back. So I decided on a border state. Plus, Black people in West Virginia voted, unlike in the Deep South. Consequently there were three Blacks in the state legislature and a Black was an assistant superintendent of a school system there.

When I got to West Virginia I discovered I would not be able to practice law due to state residency requirements. I would have to live in West Virginia for a year before I could even take their bar exam. Obviously I didn't have the money to stay in West Virginia for a year. I tried to get on the faculty of West Virginia State, but they were giving their positions to their graduates. So I went back to Jacksonville, took the Florida bar, passed it, and began practicing law in Florida my first year out of school. I think I was probably the sixth Black to pass the bar in Jacksonville.

My practice was, obviously, limited to a Black clientele. I got a position with the most prominent Black lawyer in Florida, Rusty McGill. Really, I was just a glorified clerk with a salary of ten dollars a week. That's how much I earned fresh out of the University of Michigan Law School. But I had an office, access to a stenographer, and a pretty good law library. My whole practice at the time, if you could call it a practice, consisted of divorces, a few property matters, and serving as counsel to a couple of Black insurance companies.

While working with McGill I did work on a few celebrated civil rights cases that ended with the U.S. Supreme Court changing the law. One case was *Chambers v. Florida*, which involved police misconduct and the legality of confessions. McGill's office was called in after the defendants had been convicted and the time for appeal had passed. Our first job was to figure out how to get this case back to the Florida supreme court in preparation for asking the United States

Supreme Court to review it, because we knew we weren't going to win in Florida. I was given the job of figuring this out, and I toiled over the law books until I discovered something that I hadn't heard of before, the "writ of coram nobis," which allows for appeal if the court rendered a judgment that it would not have rendered had a particular question of fact been known to the court during the trial. So we prepared an appeal based on the issue of the coerced confession and took it to the Florida supreme court, which turned us down. We appealed to the U.S. Supreme Court. I wasn't involved in that appeal, but the U.S. Supreme Court upheld our position.

I didn't want to stay in Florida because I didn't see much of a future there in terms of making a decent living, doing community work, or broadening my acceptance in legal circles—certainly not in politics. I was by then making fifteen dollars a week and my father wouldn't lend me the money to move, so I got a job waiting tables in Saratoga, New York, during the summer.

A former high school classmate who went with me to Morehouse waited tables in Saratoga and needed a divorce. We made a deal that I would do his divorce for free if he got me a position in Saratoga. He said, "You mean to tell me you are a graduate from the University of Michigan Law School, you practice law, and you want to go up there and wait tables?" I said, "That's exactly what I'm going to do. You get me the job." He got me the job, I got him the divorce. I waited tables and saved up my tips.

With that money I moved to West Virginia, where I began practicing in Fairmount, which is in the northern part of the state, from 1935 to 1939. I was able to get a legal job with the federal government through the senior senator of West Virginia, Matthew Neary. His office was in the same building as my office, and he asked me to campaign for him since I was the only Black lawyer in the northern part of the state. I changed my voter registration from Republican to Democrat. He asked what I wanted in return for my support, and I told him, a job with the U.S. Justice Department. He told me it would be next to impossible to get a Justice Department job because every senator and congressman with a lawyer in the family had a relative in the Justice Department.

About three months after Senator Neary was overwhelmingly re-elected, I got a telegram from the Department of Labor's Wage and Hour Division telling me to come to Washington for an interview. So

I went to Washington for the interview and became the first Black lawyer employed by that division of the Department of Labor. My job was to enforce the federal wage and hour law. I did litigation, and I wrote and published a number of articles on the wage law. One of my articles on the Fair Labor Standards Act was published in the *University of Michigan Law Review*. I think I was probably the first Black author published in that review.

Whenever employers would come to Washington to plead their case with us to avoid litigation, a funny thing would happen. I shared an office with a white fellow. The employers would walk into the room and just know this Black guy wasn't attorney Crockett. They would always go over to the white guy and start talking, and he would say, "Oh, you want attorney Crockett over there."

By the time I was elected a judge I had plenty of civil experience but not much experience in criminal law. One of the few criminal cases that I had ever tried was that Communist Party case. I got my baptism, as far as criminal law was concerned, in that case. I learned more about criminal law, criminal procedure, and criminal practice from that one case than in any law school course in criminal law. That case went on for nine months and involved just about everything that can be imagined in criminal procedure.

When I went on the criminal court bench I knew something about criminal law, but nothing about the routine operation of a criminal court. The business of plea bargaining and all that, I didn't have any experience in it.

From my first day on the bench I saw practices that I thought were repugnant. At the time the recorder's court in Detroit had a reputation as a court that was literally controlled by the police department. Whatever the policeman said, that was it. Police officers walked through the court swaggering, sitting wherever they wanted, putting their feet up on the railings, and laughing whenever they wanted. It was disgraceful, really.

One of the first things I did when I became a judge was to make it known to the police department that, as far as they were concerned, when they came to my court they were just like any other witness. I told them they were to sit where the other witnesses sat, not in the jury box as had been the practice. The police didn't like that. I started off my judicial career on the wrong foot.

In cases of police brutality, for example, generally it was the practice to take the policeman's version of what happened, not what the defendants said. I had a case in which the defendant had been beaten. You could see the scars on his head and so forth. He entered a plea of guilty. It wasn't a case where he was forced to plead guilty, but it was a case where the police had done a pretty good job of beating him while he was in police custody.

So when it came down to sentencing I said I would like to know a little more about the defendant's claim about being beaten while in police custody. I asked for a member of the bar to volunteer to represent him, to take testimony on his claim. This had never been done before. The testimony convinced me that he had been beaten, not only while in custody but while he was handcuffed. The beating occurred in the back of the police car on the way to prison. I said it was the judgment of this court that the state was only entitled to one bite of the apple. The state had its bite when the policeman beat this man and was not going to get another bite by having him put in jail. I put the man on probation. Of course, there was an outcry from the police and in newspaper editorials.

Rendering decisions like this made me the target of criticism. The criticism became routine. Every day when I came home my wife would ask me, "Now what did you do today?" She would ask this because she knew that as soon as she turned on the evening news there would be something on about Judge Crockett's courtroom.

If anything, the controversy created by a lot of my decisions in the courtroom made me a better judge. It made me more independent in my thinking. A judge sometimes has to stand alone. A judge hears all of the testimony and is in the best position to make the tough decisions. The media do the criticizing, but usually the media are not there for the whole trial to hear all of the testimony. So, much of the media criticism of a given disposition is not based on having all of the relevant facts.

I'm probably one of the few judges in the country who has gotten criticism from a president, governors, legislators, and the media. During the 1967 riots in Detroit I was criticized by the president, or at least criticized by the White House, because I refused to abuse the bail process. People were being purposely held in jail on high bails. This was wrong, and I won't go along with it.

I had only been on the recorder's court a matter of months when the Detroit riot broke out. The police were arresting Blacks wholesale. It was decided that the recorder's court would be in session around the clock to process all the people being arrested. They didn't have enough jail facilities, so they were incarcerating people in the buses they were brought in on. They had buses lined up all around the courthouse, filled with prisoners. They had these rent-a-johns that they put on the sidewalk so that if a people on the bus needed to go to the bathroom, policemen could escort them off the bus over to the john and then right back on the bus until they were called for court.

Most of the charges were misdemeanors or very low-level felonies. In calmer times the bond in most of these cases would have been a personal bond—being released on a small amount of money, based on the promise that you will return for court. Unfortunately, most of my colleagues were setting high bonds because the prosecution and the newspapers were demanding us to "get these people off the streets." You don't get them off the streets by giving them a personal bond but by giving them a bond they can't make so they have to go to jail, and that way you get them off the streets.

In the rush to get people off the streets these high bails were imposed in an assembly-line fashion with no individual inquiry to determine if the bail was reasonable or justified. There were people with long residence records who had regular jobs and no previous police record who were put in maximum security prisons on high bails.

There was a high-level conference about how to handle the riot. The governor came down, the police commissioner was there, and so was a White House representative. President Johnson had sent an assistant secretary of state to the city. At this meeting these officials advocated setting high bails so as not to let these people back on the streets. I took the position that it would be unconstitutional to use high bails to keep people locked up. I said that under the law we are required to set bail according to the gravity of the offense and the likelihood that the defendant would or would not show up for trial. I told them that those were the only two legal considerations for bail, not some desire to keep people off the streets. I told them I was going to continue setting bail based on those two considerations.

Well, of course, I was severely criticized for that position but I stuck with it. After the riot a report issued by the University of Michigan

Law School criticized the city's high bail practice. The report said Detroit judges had abandoned their judicial responsibilities by acting as extensions of the administrative branch, to help quell the riots.

About a year or so after the riots I was attacked by the governor, both houses of the Michigan legislature, and the chief justice. Again, this was for rulings that were based on the letter of the law. This time there was an effort to remove me from the bench. It became a really big thing. This was the New Bethel Church incident I talked about earlier.

An organization called the Republic of New Africa had scheduled a national convention in Detroit at the New Bethel Baptist Church. This was in early 1969. The Republic of New Africa was a Black separatist organization that wanted to have an independent Black nation in the South. The Republic, or RNA, had a uniformed corps that carried long guns. Carrying rifles and shotguns in public was not prohibited under Michigan law. Michigan law only prohibited the carrying of concealed guns. Anyway, this convention was in its final stages on a Saturday night, at about 10 P.M. The church had been the subject of constant patrols by the Detroit police department. Somehow an altercation ensued in front of the church, involving two police officers in a squad car and two or more members of the uniformed corps, and as a result one police officer was killed and another officer seriously wounded.

An SOS went out and carloads of police converged on the church. A lot of people were still inside the church. The police literally shot their way into the church, without seeing who they were shooting at. They arrested a total of 140 people and brought them down to the police garage because they didn't have any other adequate lock-up facilities for that many people. Most of these people, women and children included, were just attending the convention. Many were not even members of this group. They were all locked up around 11 P.M. Saturday night.

At about six o'clock the next morning there is a knock at my door and it is the pastor of New Bethel Church and a member of the Michigan Legislature. They told me what had happened the night before at the church. They also told me there were crowds of Blacks already assembling around police headquarters and that they feared another disturbance like the Detroit riot.

It just so happened that I was scheduled to be on the bench that day. We had a regular court session at noon on Sundays to relieve the pressure on the jails. I put on my clothes and left early because I didn't think it was advisable for the police to keep those people locked up until noon.

I went down to police headquarters. I asked the police commissioner for the list of people who had been arrested at the church, and he said it wasn't ready yet. I told him that under the law, when a person is arrested, that person must be brought before a magistrate without unnecessary delay. I told the commissioner that I was going to convene a session of recorder's court in the police headquarters immediately and that I would like for him to make a room available. I told him I wanted to start processing people and fixing bail. I asked him to notify the prosecutor.

The prosecutor got there around 8 A.M., and when we started, the prosecutor objected very adamantly both to my conducting a session of recorder's court at the police headquarters and my ordering the release of these people, some on personal bond of one-hundred dollars. I didn't release people from outside of the city, but I explained to them that a regular session of court would be held at noon and that their cases would be considered at that time.

Well, the prosecutor interfered with my orders and ordered the police not to bring any more prisoners before me, and the police obeyed the prosecutor instead of me. I told the prosecutor to appear before me at that noon session of court. I was going to charge him with contempt of court for interfering with my order.

With that I left and went back to my house and prepared a writ of habeas corpus report of what I had done at police headquarters, and then at noon I convened a regular session of the court. I certified my report, put it on the record, and proceeded to a hearing on the habeas corpus.

At that time the prosecutor announced that they had decided to release, with the court's permission, all of the defendants, except ten. The prosecutor said they had performed nitrate tests and found what they considered to be evidence that these ten defendants had been in close proximity to gunfire. The prosecutor wanted to hold these defendants based on the tests. I inquired whether these defendants had benefit of counsel before the tests were made, and the prosecutor said no. I inquired as to when they had been arrested and how long they were in custody. The prosecutor indicated they had been in custody since 11 o'clock the night before. I asked if they had had the opportunity to talk to anyone since they were taken into custody. The answer was that they had been held incommunicado.

I said that under the circumstances I didn't think the prosecutors were justified in making the paraffin tests and therefore I wouldn't even consider the results. There's also another factor about these tests. I'm told that naphtha, the naphtha you get from ordinary soap, will leave a film on your hands which under your so-called paraffin test is indistinguishable from the residue left by gunfire. Under these circumstances I ordered the release of those ten. I told the prosecutor they could not be held unless there were outstanding warrants against them. Three of them had outstanding warrants, traffic and other minor warrants, so they were detained.

Now this was just the beginning of the New Bethel Church case. The newspapers came out with big headlines: JUDGE CROCKETT HAS INTERRUPTED THE ADMINISTRATION OF JUSTICE and similar statements. Both houses of the state legislature were in session and both of them suspended their routine business in order to pass resolutions calling for my impeachment. The governor went on statewide television to announce that he was asking the state Judicial Council to inquire into my fitness to continue on the bench. This council was the agency that handled matters involving judicial discipline. Even J. Edgar Hoover of the FBI went before a congressional committee and said something about me releasing trigger-happy Black militants. The organization of police officers put a picket line around the courthouse where I was holding court, and then the Blacks in the community put up another picket line in opposition to the police officers' picket line.

At the time of the competing picket lines the presiding judge came to me and said he had been downstairs to ask the protesters to disperse. The Black pickets said they would only disperse if Judge Crockett asked them to; otherwise they were going to stay. So the presiding judge wanted to know if I would go downstairs to speak with them. I said no. I told him that as far as I knew, picketing the courthouse was not illegal. Picketing a courthouse was a matter of freedom of speech, unless of course you had a court rule based upon a finding that picketing interferes with the administration of justice because of the noise or something like that, but I had no recollection that we had such a rule. I told the judge that if such a rule were passed, well, that would be another matter.

So the presiding judge immediately canvassed all of the judges, and all of us agreed that there should be a court rule. The rule was drafted and approved. Then he went downstairs and read the court rule to the picketers and told them to disperse. They wanted to know if Judge Crockett had agreed to the court rule and he told them yes, and that's when they agreed to disperse.

Well, it was touch and go for a long while. There were bumper stickers all over the state saying SOCK IT TO CROCKETT and bumper stickers saying SUPPORT JUDGE CROCKETT. The police officers' associations were taking space in the newspapers condemning Judge Crockett and so forth.

Finally there was this civic/corporate organization called New Detroit, and they formed this top-level legal committee to investigate the legal basis for my actions in the New Bethel Church case. They came out with a report that indicated I had complied with Michigan law in every respect. Then there were three prominent members of the Bar Association who examined this matter. These three were the then president of the American Bar Association, who was a Detroit lawyer, the president of the state bar, and the president of the city bar. They issued a statement saying that they had not found any incidence in which I had violated the law.

Most laymen wondered whether it was legitimate to hold court anyplace other than in the courthouse. The answer is that you certainly can hold court, even when you don't have a clerk or a bailiff or a stenographer. Michigan law provided that when court was in session for the purpose of habeas corpus hearings, wherever you find a judge, that is where court can be held. It's as simple as that. This law made it a misdemeanor offense for a judge to decline to issue a habeas writ for a person who is incarcerated. But that law about habeas hearings was not generally known in Michigan. Many lawyers didn't even know it. There were those on my bench who thought, "Well, Crockett has really done it this time." But they didn't know the law either. That's why I say that one function of being a judge is to teach people the law, and a judge does that in his or her rulings.

I didn't resign from the bench. I elected not to seek reelection. I had served two six-year terms. My wife and I had decided to retire, so I did not run for reelection. She had become ill with cancer, and the cancer had been diagnosed as terminal.

I went back to private practice, and a few years after that I decided to run for Congress. To tell you a little secret, some of my reasons for running for Congress were personal. The woman I wanted to marry lived in Washington and she said she would marry me but she wouldn't move to Detroit.

There is a vast difference in being a judge and being a legislator. Legislating is a group activity. It is not like making up your mind what justice is and doing it. In the legislature you have to go around and get support from your fellow legislators in order to pull together a majority decision. In judging, the decisions are made by one person, the judge.

When I came to Congress I wasn't so much concerned about passing new legislation as I was about doing whatever I could to make sure that current legislation is understood, recognized, and applied. But, of course, I shared with my congressional colleagues the fruits of my experiences in private legal practice and on the bench, in deliberations on new legislation.

One of the things I learned from being a lawyer, a judge, and a member of Congress is that we have too much legislation in this country. I believed that even before I went to Congress. Every time something new shows up we think we should pass a law on it. If we would take the time to look back we would find we already have laws to cover just about everything we've got. We've got the laws. The question is how are they being applied and who is applying them.

HENRY BRAMWELL

"The judge is the linchpin of law and order."

Whether he is attending the annual convention of the American Bar Association or having lunch with a friend, retired judge Henry Bramwell is fond of wearing a three-piece business suit with an African Kente-cloth tie. Bramwell is a proud conservative Republican who sees no ideological conflict in praising both the landmark civil rights rulings of the liberal Warren Court and the civil rights critic and U.S. Supreme Court Justice Clarence Thomas. Bramwell has publicly traded barbs with fellow Black jurists who opposed Thomas's elevation to the nation's highest court, and he has publicly blasted one of Thomas's key benefactors, President Ronald Reagan, for Reagan's pitiful record of appointing Blacks to the federal judiciary.

A short man with a pleasant disposition, Bramwell keeps an autographed photo of Justice Thomas on display in the living room of his Brooklyn home, just a few miles from the Bedford-Stuyvesant neighborhood, where he was born. When President Ford appointed him to the U.S. District Court for the Eastern District of New York in December 1974 he became the first African American federal judge ever to serve in Brooklyn.

Bramwell is hard-nosed about crime, particularly crime in the Black community. Crime is killing the Black community, according to Bramwell, who is highly critical of Black leaders for failing to more forcefully address the crime problem.

Bramwell was interviewed at his home near the Brooklyn Bridge in September 1992.

I am a conservative and a Republican. But being a conservative Republican didn't stop me from writing a letter to President Reagan in 1987 in which I told him he should place another Black in my position when I retired at the end of September that year. Reagan had appointed very few Blacks to the federal bench. He had been in office for six years by then and had made hundreds of judicial appointments during his term. I'd say my letter to President Reagan was somewhat critical. I felt Reagan could have and should have appointed more Blacks to the federal courts and told him so. I was a Republican, but I didn't agonize one bit about being critical of a sitting Republican president.

I had been appointed by a Republican president, Gerald Ford. That was in 1975. Ford was in office for less than three years and I think he appointed four Blacks. Reagan was a Republican also. By the time I wrote my letter Reagan had been in office longer than Ford, yet he had appointed something like five Blacks out of three hundred appointments to the federal district and appeals courts around the country.

I was a federal judge in Brooklyn, which is in the Eastern District of the federal district court in New York. I was the only Black judge in the Eastern District. The Eastern District includes Brooklyn, Queens, Staten Island, and Nassau and Suffolk counties. There were no Black federal magistrates in the Eastern District at the time, and there were no Black federal bankruptcy judges in the district.

By the time I retired at the end of September in 1987 there was only one Black U.S. district judge in New York City. Twelve years before that there had been five active Black district court judges as well as one active Black federal judge on the Court of International trade in New York City. Gradually these judges took senior status, and they were not replaced by Black judges.

I didn't get any feedback at all from the White House about my letter. I made the letter public, and it was carried in the press.

You have to remember the problem with the lack of Black appointments to the federal bench is not just with the White House. U.S. senators make recommendations to the White House for judgeships in their states.

After I wrote the president I got word that my senator, Alfonse D'Amato, was putting a white man in my slot, which he eventually did. I got very angry, very angry. I wrote him a letter. I sent a letter to

New York's other senator, Daniel Patrick Moynihan, also. I told both of the senators they had not done a good job in appointing Blacks to the federal bench. I told them their behavior on judicial nominations indicated a callous disregard of the Blacks of New York City.

Moynihan had appointed Mary Johnson Lowe, a Black woman. She took senior status and he put in a Puerto Rican woman. Moynihan is a Democrat, and senators from the president's political party really have the most say in judicial nominations. That's why D'Amato was so significant. He was a Republican like Reagan. He got the most appointments, and he appointed his own people. Maybe he was so busy appointing his own people that he didn't have time for anybody else.

I didn't get any feedback from D'Amato or anybody about my letters. My fellow judges didn't say anything either. They wouldn't talk against him to me. The only reaction I got from those letters was from the press. If anybody had told me I could put two articles back to back in the *New York Times* I never would have believed it.

I don't think President Reagan or President Bush were biased against Blacks in their judicial appointments. A lot of Blacks think they were.

Reagan and Bush were just trying to remold the federal judiciary with conservatives. They wanted judges in there who reflected *their* approach to conservative thinking. For example, when Bush was going to replace Justice Marshall on the Supreme Court one of the names mentioned as a replacement was Amalya Kearse, a Black federal appeals judge here in New York. She's a Republican, but the Republicans won't appoint her because she's too liberal. They wanted a conservative thinker like Clarence Thomas.

Bush had hundreds of Blacks in his administration. He had Colin Powell as head of the military and that fellow Sullivan as head of Health and Human Services. So, I don't think I'd say there was a bias, a racial bias. Reagan didn't appoint Blacks to big jobs the way Bush has.

Reagan and Bush put in a lot of conservative judges. The impact of those appointments on the Black community isn't too apparent to me at this point. I don't think they will especially pick out Blacks or Black litigants to do anything special to them. I don't think these judges will hurt the Black community to any extent. I don't see that happening. The impact these judges have will be on the entire society.

President Carter appointed a lot of Blacks to the federal judiciary. I think he appointed more to the federal bench than any other president. Carter appointed a lot of Blacks to the federal courts of appeal.

I don't think we will get very many Black judicial appointments from President Clinton. Clinton went after the white middle-class vote during his campaign, and I think he will continue to direct his attention to pleasing the white middle class because that's where the marbles are. He isn't going to pay too much attention to Blacks, because he feels they are going to vote for him anyway.

I feel it is important to have Blacks in the federal judiciary. Black judges can articulate the problems of the Black community. Black federal judges are required as mentors and leaders. Black federal judges are also needed to combat the prejudice, discrimination, and racism that is deeply rooted in our society. I make this statement fully acknowledging there are Black racists as well as white racists. Black federal judges can have a positive, equalizing effect on the Black community. Black people go into a court, they see a Black judge, and immediately they feel up to par.

One of my projects when I was on the bench was bringing Black high school classes into my courtroom. Each year I would bring in a dozen classes. I would bring them into court on the day I had my criminal sentencing and let them sit there and watch the sentencing. After the sentencing was over I would discuss it with the class. I would also take the classes into my chambers, show them around, and let them talk with the clerks and the secretary. This was an important learning experience for them.

My judicial philosophy is conservative with a strong approach to law and order. Most Black judges are liberal. There are Black judges who say they are conservative, but they are probably on the moderate end of the conservative spectrum.

What is the difference between liberal and conservative? A liberal approach is a "free lunch." A conservative approach is there is no free lunch. A liberal approach says the government is responsible to give you the things that you need and would like to have. A conservative approach says you have got to work for what you get. No work, you don't get anything. The conservative approach focuses more on the work ethic, and the liberal approach focuses more on what the government's responsibility is to you.

In my way of thinking the work ethic is so important. I feel this is the direction that Blacks should be going in. I guess this emphasis on the work ethic is what interested me in being a conservative, because being a conservative was not in my basic thinking prior to my starting out in the law. Being a conservative is something I picked up along the way. I started out in life as a Democrat.

Being a conservative is not popular in the Black community. That's why many of the Black judges didn't like Clarence Thomas when he was nominated for the U.S. Supreme Court. He is a strict conservative.

I like Clarence Thomas, Justice Thomas. I didn't think Leon Higginbotham's open letter to Justice Thomas was appropriate. I wrote him a letter and told him so. His letter smacked of Black racism, Black-on-Black racism. He only attacked Thomas because Thomas is Black. Who anointed Higginbotham a judge of the character and qualifications of other Black judges?

I like Justice Thomas's conservative approach to law and order. I am a law and order man myself. I believe the judge is the linchpin of law and order. Justice Thomas believes in a stricter enforcement of legal procedures against criminals. I believe stricter enforcement of criminal laws is needed to balance out the Black community.

In the Black community today there are serious, serious problems when it comes to crime. I think the figures show that approximately one in four Black youths is in some way tied up in the criminal process, and this really is a serious situation.

Crime is a serious problem for the Black community, and Black leaders, Black politicians and other influential Blacks within the community have not fully addressed this problem of crime. They permit crime to stand basically unchallenged, and some Black criminals even come out as heroes. This should not be.

The leadership in the Black community should be in some way directing the people in their community so that crime is not such a big problem. If the Black community can correct this crime problem then I think that a lot of the problems the Black community faces today will be lessened, because the Black community will be more acceptable. Now, with the amount of crime in the Black community, everybody looks at it and says, "Well, everybody is a criminal over there. I don't want them in my backyard." This is the problem.

The nature of crime is much more violent and more vicious now than when I was young. The nature of crime has changed because not enough emphasis is put on enforcement in the criminal justice system. Actually, the criminal justice system is gradually falling apart. It is not really keeping crime contained. Something must be done in order to contain crime and contain criminals.

If the criminal were made to adhere to the system, or if he himself could find in the system something that would give his life meaning in some way, then he wouldn't be as apt to become a repeat criminal. I think it has been correctly noted that many criminals like incarceration because it is a better life than they have on the streets. Actually, jail should be for punishment, but evidently that is not the case. It is not working out.

There are those who think we should have alternatives to incarceration. I don't know that there is an alternative to incarceration. I believe the seriousness with which you address the criminal problems will give a commensurate result. Criminals have to know they will go to jail.

I do not think crime among Blacks is a consequence of some kind of genetic predisposition. The crime problem in the Black community can be corrected. But it is more than a social phenomenon that can be solved by throwing money at it or by getting somebody a job. Don't get me wrong. Money and jobs help. To my way of thinking, in order to correct crime, it has to be corrected within the family structure. Today, there are not the strong family structures in the Black community that are required to correct this type of problem.

When I was growing up in the Bedford-Stuyvesant section of Brooklyn there were father-mother family structures. The family structure has deteriorated just as communities have physically deteriorated. Back when I was growing up you didn't have abandonment in families and you didn't have the abandonment of buildings that you have today. The family structure was much better for everybody then.

Another thing that must be addressed is the work ethic. There is a work ethic in the Black community, but it must be strengthened. There is too much of the liberal approach—you know, people saying, "Listen, we are entitled to this, and you have got to give us this and you got to give us that." Black people have to work for what they want. They have to do the things necessary to advance themselves rather than expect somebody to come in and say, "Here it is. I'm giving it to you." If you are unskilled you have to work a job paying a subminimum wage. You can't choose not to work at all just because you think that you should be making twenty dollars an hour even though you have no skills. You have to work the subminimum wage job. Too many young Blacks have a different concept of what the value of their work is, rather than going ahead and just working this out.

Actually, most of what needs to be done to correct crime in the Black community and improve the community itself must be drawn from the strengths within the community. This is a problem because the community's strength is not put into doing the necessary things.

The average criminal who came before me when I was a judge was not Black. This was because the top operators in crime are not Black, and, usually, especially in the federal courts, you get the top operators. Historically in Black communities, organized crime ran the illegal operations. Those were the Italians. They ran everything. The bigger fellows in the drug war in Harlem now are the Dominicans. I guess there are some Hispanics other than Dominicans who are in this business, but, at any rate, Blacks are not the top operators.

But I do think you see a higher proportion of Blacks in the federal criminal justice system than there should be. There are disparities in the federal system and the state court systems, too. There is discrimination of a subtle sort. It's subtle, but things tend to balance themselves out, for the most part. But there are disparities. There is no question about that. Each person has his own prejudices and his own view of right and wrong and good and bad.

What should be done about these disparities? Make more federal judges, and make sure many of these new judges are Black. That would help a lot, because the new Black judges would have an equalizing effect on the system. There is no question in my mind that an increase in the number of Black federal judges would help a lot.

On the other hand, there are a lot of Black judges in the state systems, and I know there are still problems there. The State of New York issued a report last year that said the state judicial system was infected with racism. There have been a number of Blacks who have served as administrative judges in this city. They should have been able to do more about this problem. If you are in there, nothing should be wrong in terms of racial equality.

* * *

I know there is a belief that being conservative is somehow being antiBlack, but that is based on misunderstandings.

The history of racism shows that it was and is a product of the southern Democratic Party, from the Civil War to much of the present time. The tree of racism was built and supported by the Eastlands and Bilbos of Mississippi, the Talmadges of Georgia, Huey Long of Louisiana, George Wallace of Alabama, and Strom Thurmond of South Carolina. They were the Democratic Party members who supported and built racism. At the present time, Democratic Party members speak of David Duke as a symbol of racism, but Democrats choose to ignore the many traditional racists in their party and what they did for the growth of racism. They are now "reformed" racists. Strom Thurmond, for instance, supported the nomination of Clarence Thomas and is just as reformed as any of the others. For Democrats, Black and white, to ignore the history of racism is political double-talk on their part. Whether you are a conservative or a liberal, when it comes to the issue of racism, I do not feel there is any automatic difference. The one is no more anti-Black than the other.

Most people won't admit this, but liberal and conservative judges both practice judicial activism. Each side has a certain amount of activism and a certain amount of constraint. Of course, in the liberal philosophy the activism is greater, I think. It is greater in the liberal philosophy because they seek to innovate, initiate, create, and do things that didn't exist before.

Although I am a conservative I don't criticize the Warren Court the way other conservatives do. Many conservatives like to say the Warren Court did things that shouldn't have been done by a court. They say legislatures should make those kinds of changes in the civil rights area, not the Supreme Court. But I don't think the justices were wrong in what they did in advancing civil rights.

I mean, liberal approaches were needed in order to get the Black community out of a lot of the problems that had been caused by decades of segregation that was legal, perfectly legal in this country. I see absolutely nothing wrong with what was done by the Warren Court on behalf of the Black community. The Black community in America would never have gotten to the position that it's in now if it hadn't been for some of the liberal changes. We would never have broken the barriers of segregation. Whether you agree with what was done or not, something had to be done, and doing something is better than doing nothing. The justices did what they thought and felt was best, and it didn't hurt anybody.

When I was growing up I was aware of what the NAACP was doing around the country in the civil rights movement to combat segregation. I used to read the Black newspapers. When I was at the Tuskegee airfield during World War II, I would always buy Black newspapers. The other guys at the field used to laugh at me and say, "Well, he's got the 'dispatch.' " Reading these papers helped me keep abreast of the advances that were being made.

Being aware of what was being done in the civil rights movement helped my life. As I progressed in life part of my progress was my understanding of what was acceptable. I could see that certain things were acceptable, and that helped me in dealing with other people by knowing who they are and the nature of their conduct and their experiences. This all came from an understanding of the civil rights movement, no question about it.

I remember when the first Black female judge in the country was appointed. Her name was Jane Bolin. She was appointed to the family court in New York City, in 1939, I think. A number of people in the Black community were proud of this, but it didn't have a lot of impact in the Black community because she wasn't that well known. She was not what I would call a community mixer. She was a very bright person and an outstanding person, but she wasn't politically active to any extent.

There were a few Black lawyers in my neighborhood when I was growing up, but not too many. There were a few other professionals in the community, such as doctors. One of the most common jobs for Blacks at that time was working for the post office. The people who worked for the post office were sort of the elite of Black society. They were the ones that had the better houses, lived better, and had better social lives. My father was a janitor and my mother was a housewife. They were both from Jamaica.

I decided to become a lawyer during World War II. America had a Black army and a white army during World War II. When I was coming back on the boat from Europe I got into a discussion with a white lawyer I had met, and he encouraged me to go to law school. I felt being a lawyer would be a good career, something that could be lucrative and afford me a good living.

I was in law school a month after I got back from the war. I was able to get admitted to law school without having an undergraduate degree. I went to Brooklyn Law School. Most of my class came directly out of World War II. We did three years' work in two years.

One of my strong points in law school was I was a good mixer. I could go among all groups, the Jewish group, the Italian group, or whatever. I would sit down with them and I knew everything that was going on. Mixing with all people taught me things. I could see what other people were doing and how I should conduct myself. I never had any problems in law school with the students or the professors. Brooklyn Law School has a reputation for being liberal like that.

I went into private practice my first year out of law school, and I almost went out of my mind doing nothing. But after that first year I had no problem making money. That first year, it was very lean times. What really supported me that first year was the government's 52–20 Club for World War II veterans. Under that program, if you were in business the government guaranteed you a hundred dollars a month.

When I was first admitted to the bar I joined the Brooklyn Bar Association. When I joined it there were maybe one or two other Blacks in it. The reason for that was Blacks were not encouraged to join or sought after to be members of the bar association. The bar association didn't want them there and actually kept them out. I made it a point to become a member. Three months after I became a lawyer I was a member of the bar association. I'm still a member. I'm not on the board of trustees, but I'm one of the sought-after individuals, and for that I am very happy.

When I first started in practice no big firm in New York would have me. They wouldn't even consider you if you were Black. So, I moved into an office in downtown Brooklyn with these other fellows who were Jewish. I was looking for desk space in a law office, and one of them had advertised that they had a desk to rent. Christians would never have permitted me the access these fellows gave me. Christians would never have accepted me. They were Jews, and they looked on people as people. I am still very close to them. Whenever they have a wedding or a bar mitvah, they don't leave me out.

Most of the Black attorneys who were in Bedford-Stuyvesant thought I was wrong to start out in the downtown area of Brooklyn. They told me I should have started out in the community first, built a practice, and then moved if I still wanted to. They told me the way I was doing it was not the way it was done, but I chose to move out of the community and to build, and I'd say that within two or three years I was making a good living.

My clientele was primarily Black. At that time I did a lot of real estate work, and as I went along I got work from the white community when they had problems that involved Blacks. One of my first big clients was the Black bus drivers' union in New York City. I did work for the union and I represented individual members, but not to any great extent.

I had always been active in politics from the time I was a young man. One of my brothers, Arthur, was active in the Democratic Party in Bedford-Stuyvesant. At that time most Blacks were Republican but were changing to Democrat because of all the things that Roosevelt had done.

I had been practicing law for about five years before the leader of the Republican Party in Bedford-Stuyvesant came to see me. He was a white man named William Webb. He was having a fight with a group of Blacks who were trying to take his party post. He asked me to work with him. His coleader was a Black woman, and he eventually lost his leadership. But we worked and helped get Eisenhower elected.

After the election and Eisenhower was in, Webb asked me if I would like to work in Brooklyn's tax department. He was a tax commissioner and he said he would put me on the payroll. I told him he probably wanted to pay me fifty dollars a week and I could make forty or fifty dollars a week in private practice, with no headaches and nobody telling me what to do. I told him I didn't want the job.

I went back to Webb a few months later and told him that there was one job I did want. I told him I wanted to work in the United States Attorney's office. He said, "You want it," and I said, "Yep." He said, "Well, you're number one for it," and then he went ahead and got me the job.

I wanted that job for the title. I knew if I got that title it would be a boost for me in anything I did for the rest of my life. I realized that. I started on the civil law side of the office, and after about four years I went into the criminal division. When I was on the civil side I organized the files in the office. There were something like eight hundred files. I organized them so that if you picked up a file and you read it, it made sense. I did a lot of cases on the civil side involving the federal housing department.

I wanted to move into the criminal division because you were in court all the time and the cases were more important. In criminal cases every case is serious and every case has got a certain aura about it that makes it important: you are dealing with the life of an individual. No matter what case I had I knew it was big because it was big for the person on the other end of that line.

I found out that prosecutors are really gung ho. They'll do anything to get a conviction. This is not only done to a person on the basis of race. They'd do that to anybody.

I once had an immigration case. It involved a real estate broker from Bedford-Stuyvesant and some Haitian woman who happened somehow to be involved with him. He pleaded guilty, and after he pleaded guilty he came to me and made out an affidavit to the effect that she had nothing to do with this. I told my boss I had this affidavit and I wanted to throw out the case against the woman. I said the woman had nothing to do with it.

Well, my boss didn't want me to drop the case. He thought that perhaps there was something to the case and I wasn't being fully candid with him about it. I told him I was going to lunch and that if he wanted he could go into my office and take any case he wanted and I wouldn't get mad. He took that case and assigned it to someone else.

I knew that case wouldn't go anywhere, because I had the affidavit from the main defendant. This new guy on the case was real gung ho to make this thing stick. He hadn't been in the office long. At one point he came to me and asked if he could destroy the affidavit. I said no, you can't. I told him he had better not destroy that affidavit and the affidavit had better be in the file.

This guy went ahead with the case anyway. When it came to trial I went and sat there. There was an Italian judge on the case. This guy finished the government's case and the judge says to him, "Mr. So-and-so, I want you to take each of the four counts of the indictment and tell me how you've made out a case against that woman." And as the prosecutor finished his argument on each count, the judge said, "Dismissed." I just sat there and laughed.

There were only a few Blacks in the U.S. Attorney's office when I worked there from 1953 to 1961. I think I was the first Black to work in the U.S. Attorney's office for the Eastern District of New York. I was treated pretty well. But one of the few times I have ever been disrespected since I became a lawyer occurred while I was working for the U.S. Attorney. I had a problem with the FBI.

At that time, when an assistant had a case and needed to go somewhere to investigate it, it was customary for an FBI agent to drive you there. All of the FBI agents had their own individual cars, which were supplied to them by the government. I had a case, a social security check case, out on Long Island, and I had to visit the scene. I called the FBI and I got this southern FBI agent. I asked him to bring his car so we could go out on this case. This became one hell of a mess.

My boss says to me, "The FBI sent word to tell Bramwell that if he needs a chauffeur, he'll have to chauffeur himself." I told my boss the son of a bitch was wrong, that they worked for us, and if that was the way they wanted to play with this thing I'd throw the damn case out. The FBI had the transportation, we didn't. This was their case. We were getting rid of work for them. I didn't go out to Long Island. I gave the case to someone else.

I stayed in the U.S. Attorney's office throughout the entire Eisenhower administration, and then I decided to leave. By the time Kennedy came in as president I had broken in a lot of assistants while I was in the office, and I had gotten to the point where I wasn't going to break in any more new people. I went back into private practice

Not long after I went back to private practice the county Republican leader called me and said he had a job for me. He said he had a job for me in the New York State Rent Commission as an associate attorney, which was the highest level of attorney they had at the commission. I told him I didn't want the job. He said he'd like for me to take the job as a favor to him, and I told him if it was a favor to him, I took the job yesterday. I took the job. After that you couldn't tell him nothing about me.

I was cochairman of the enforcement section at the commission. I kept that job. I stayed there from 1961 to 1963 when my position was eliminated in a budget cut. I went back to private practice.

Two years later, when Rockefeller was governor, there was a statewide addition of 125 judgeships. One of those judgeships was slated for me. It was a political thing through the Republican Party. At the time there was a judge, a Black judge, in Manhattan named Francis Rivers. He retired, his job was moved to Brooklyn, and I got it.

I was supposed to go into criminal court but the county party leader called me and said I would be assigned to civil court, which was much,

much nicer. I was a state judge right here in Brooklyn for six years. It was a good job. I became the administrative judge for about a year and a half. I was an acting supreme court judge for about a year. We did a lot of work. It was from this job that I went to the federal judgeship.

During the time I was in civil court we brought the court calendars up to date. The calendars were seven years behind when I began. I handled mostly negligence matters and other matters, such as real estate cases.

On many weekends I would have to go into the criminal court. I had been a prosecutor and I understood the criminal process, so it was easy for me. I often sat with Bruce Wright in Manhattan. He was in criminal court then.

I wanted to become a judge because of the prestige. I liked the prestige and the acceptance. Your acceptance in the community is far greater as a judge. I had never envisioned myself on the bench. When I was a practicing lawyer I never believed that I would get a judgeship, a state judgeship, and certainly not a federal judgeship. In no way in the world would I have believed that I would become a federal judge.

One of the men who was in the U.S. Attorney's office with me actually assisted me in getting the federal judgeship. We became friends when he and I were assistant U.S. Attorneys. When he left the U.S. Attorney's office he became the regional administrator in New York for the federal Securities and Exchange Commission. Then he went into private practice on Wall Street. He was chairman of Senator Javits' judicial selection committee.

I liked being a state court judge, but the great court was the federal court. That is the court where a judge has a lot of control and a lot of power. Power is using your position to compel people to do certain things or to have certain things done because you want them done. As a federal judge you get all kinds of cases from all over the world. I had a case involving the Russian airline, Aeroflot. I had a case involving robot technology, trademark cases, cases involving claims from prisoners, all kinds of cases.

In the early eighties I issued orders, four orders I think, giving the FBI authority to install electronic eavesdropping devices in the home of Big Paul Castellano. He was one of the godfather's of organized crime. I just issued the orders; I didn't try the cases brought against Castellano.

* * *

There have been tremendous changes in the law during my time on the bench. One of those changes is mandatory sentencing.

Mandatory sentencing was brought about in order to equalize sentencing, because there were some judges who would send everybody home no matter what the crime was. This was done to prevent judges from undersentencing and oversentencing. Mandatory sentencing works because it is a control not only on the prosecutor but on the court, and it is a control on the defendant because the sentences are based on a particular defendant's history.

Mandatory sentencing gives everybody input into what is done. If the judge goes under the sentencing guidelines the prosecutor can appeal. If the judge goes over the sentencing guidelines the defendant can appeal.

I don't see anything wrong with mandatory sentencing. It has its place, and I am sure it works well. Of course, I liked it the other way, before mandatory sentencing, because the judge had more latitude in sentencing.

Another change, of course, is that during the past twelve years Reagan and Bush have just about packed the U.S. Supreme Court. For the remainder of this century, I would say, the Supreme Court is going to be conservative. But whether that is good or bad depends on whether you see the glass half full or half empty.

CHARLES Z. SMITH

"I have received death threats unrelated to the cases I decide."

Shortly after Charles Smith was appointed to Seattle's municipal court in 1965 two diverse groups sent representatives to the courtroom of the first Black judge in Washington State to determine if he was biased. The American Legion had heard Smith was unfair to whites. The NAACP had heard Smith was unfair to Blacks. Both groups were wrong. Race-based favoritism was not a part of the judicial decision making of this son of a Cuban father and African American mother.

A native of Florida who graduated from Temple University before attending the University of Washington Law School, Smith's legal career has included being a prosecutor and a law professor, and he has a string of impressive judicial firsts: first Black judge in Washington State, first Black superior court judge, and first Black justice on Washington's supreme court. But the glow of these firsts has been dimmed by discrimination and death threats. An articulate man with fine features and a dignified manner, Smith has been subjected to the second degree when trying to pay by check in a supermarket. He maintains an extraordinary level of security at his supreme court chambers and at home as a result of death threats unrelated to his judicial dispositions. He acknowledges that he may be a little too security conscious, but says he'd rather be safe than sorry—or dead.

Justice Charles Z. Smith was interviewed in his spacious office at the Temple of Justice on the grounds of the capitol complex in Olympia, Washington, in January 1993.

I was the first nonwhite person in the history of the state of Washington to become a judge. This occurred in 1965, when I was appointed to municipal court for the city of Seattle. Two years later I was appointed to the superior court, which is the court of general jurisdiction for King County. Seattle is located in King County. Again I was the first nonwhite person to become a superior court judge in the history of the state of Washington. In 1988 I became the first and only person of color to serve on the Supreme Court of the State of Washington.

There are people who think, Aha, he has risen up the great political ladder and is at the pinnacle. He has it made. Well, right now, I can walk into a grocery store and write a check for seventeen dollars and be treated differently because I am a person of color.

That happened to me two years ago. I was trying to write a check for some groceries, and the clerk called the manager over to have me display every credit card I had in my pocket. I was well dressed. I speak well. I know I am a dignified person. But here was this clerk in a grocery store so traumatized either by my appearance, my voice, or the fact that I was nonwhite. While this was happening there were grungy, shabbily dressed persons, who were white, writing checks for hundreds of dollars over the amount of their purchases. I was writing a check for the exact amount of my purchase, seventeen dollars.

I tell this story to say that if people like me think we have it made, we are deluding ourselves. Our society is structured on the white acceptance model. This is not a racist statement. It is a statement of reality. It doesn't make any difference what one's credentials are, what one's title is, what one's status is, or what one's education is. If a person is not white he or she is going to be treated differently, because society is based on acceptance of whites, not nonwhites. There are people in this building now, right now, who refer to me as "the nigger." If a person of color comes into this building, many will automatically assume that person is coming to see me.

This is the great Pacific Northwest, the cradle of pseudoliberalism. This is the place where everybody loves everybody and treats everybody fairly and equally. It is a good theory, but as a practical matter it simply does not pan out.

I have a double whammy. My mother is African American. I consider myself Black. My father was Cuban, and the Latinos consider me a Latino. There are people who are baffled by the fact that I am a

Black person who is also Latino. They simply cannot understand this, so they get very traumatized. One of my colleagues on the court is very, very upset. He simply cannot understand that I can be Latino and Black at the same time. Things like that bother other people, but it doesn't bother me. I am a better person because of these experiences.

The difference between the experience of persons of color and persons not of color is that we persons of color have the advantage of having to turn negative experiences into positive experiences. We have a more mature outlook on life; we understand the importance of being fair to other persons because we don't want other persons to have the negative experience that we have had.

I would like to think that my experience as a person of color serves the role of a supreme court justice, by making me more sensitive, more aware of the need for treating all persons as decent human beings.

It is amusing sometimes, the expectations people have about judges who are not white. I remember one experience I had when I was on the municipal court, which is the people's court. I had heard that the NAACP had a meeting during which it was reported that I was rougher on Black people than I was on white people. They sent some court observers to watch me in court. At the same time the American Legion had heard that I was rougher on whites than I was on Blacks, so they sent observers to sit in my court to find out how I conducted myself.

It was funny to me because I know how level I am in dealing with people. Race and ethnicity play absolutely no part in my decision making. The only time either would play a part would be in criminal cases, at the dispositional level, when I would consider lack of education, lack of job security, lack of home security, and so on. But this is not favoritism based on race.

I was sensitive to persons of any group who had personal problems, because I come from the grass roots—I didn't just spring out of a law school and spring into a court. I was not naive. I had been around and, so, people could not pull a fast one over on me by telling me a story that I would believe hook, line, and sinker.

I think that gradually the newspapers reported this battle between the whites and Blacks, each arguing that I was treating the other more fairly. Even now I laugh about it.

I have never felt any kind of pressure or expectations as a person of color on the court. I think this is partly because I have been part of the leadership for court reform without reference to race or ethnicity at a local level and a national level. The way I conducted my court became a model for other judges. My way of doing things was better, I think because my experience was wider. I had a better understanding of people in the real world. I had a better understanding of how the court system ought to be.

I have attended seminars and programs around the country, so I am aware of court systems outside the narrow confines of our community. For a long time, unfortunately, most of the judges in this state had hardly ever been outside the county where they resided, so they had absolutely no idea what was going on in the rest of the world.

When the Kerner Commission report came out in 1968, I could not get my fellow judges in King County to read it. Only three out of the twenty-one judges on my court at the time even read the report. And again this is not to discredit any of those really nice people, but they were part of the system. They were judges, rendering decisions that affected people's lives, and they thought that the Kerner report was something for me.

Of the three other judges who were willing to read the report, one was Asian, one Jewish (the only Jew on the court), and one an older judge who I considered one of my mentors. The others simply would not read it. As far as they were concerned it was a piece of garbage and wasn't worth the time it would take to read it. They weren't even concerned.

Times have changed. Now, of the forty-nine judges on that particular court, I would say that forty-five of them would gladly read the report. We are talking about generational changes. We are talking about changes in communication, changes in travel, and changes in opportunity for interchange. We are now internationally oriented. We no longer think in parochial terms of the world existing in this county and this county alone. There is a world beyond your county, your state, and your nation. I think more and more judges are becoming a part of that worldly perspective. The older ones among us, especially those of us who are not white, are in the forefront in recognizing that the world exists somewhere outside our own communities.

My operating theory is that systems in the private sector and the public sector should reflect a cross section of the population. For all too many years systems, especially the courts and particularly the appellate courts, have been all white and male. This is not white-male bashing. This is a recognition of the reality of it.

We have one woman on our court who is the second woman on the Washington supreme court. She replaced a woman who left to go to the federal bench. In the recent election, to the surprise of many people, a young woman won a contested election, so next week we will have a second woman on our court. It's not a big deal. Minnesota has seven justices on its supreme court and four of them are women. I have always maintained that parity should be achieved in terms of gender as well as race. If 51 percent of the population is women, then 51 percent of an institution ought to be women. Under that theory five of our nine justices, rather than two of nine, ought to be women.

Women have been neglected in the judiciary for years, but things are changing. Today there are more women judges, but not women of color. There are approximately five hundred judges nationwide who are women of color. Pennsylvania and New York are perhaps in the forefront in terms of the number of judges who are women of color. Pennsylvania has a number of Black female judges yet only one Asian female judge and one Hispanic.

There are just about ten African American females in a federal judiciary of nearly nine hundred. President Carter did the best in appointing women of color to the federal judiciary. He set a standard for what can be done. President Clinton does not seem to be following a pattern of appointing persons of color to the federal judiciary. Mr. Clinton needs to spend some time looking at the face of the judiciary. He talked a lot about the face of government reflecting the face of America. He's done a good job appointing African Americans to government but he has neglected Asians and Latinos.

I would like to see a person who is pure Latino sitting on the supreme court of Washington. I count myself as a Black on this court. The Latinos consider me a Latino on the court, but I think that is double counting. I know some young judges and young lawyers whose parents are both Latino. They ought to be on this court. We should not limit the court to one person of color. There are other Blacks who are competent to be on this court. We have no Asians in the appellate system and no Latinos.

Within the state of Washington we have 450 judges. Of those, 21 are persons of color. I am one of the 21, and I am on the supreme court. There are none in the intermediate appellate court, not one person of color in the intermediate appellate court, which has a total of 17 judges. There is one Latino on the municipal court in Tacoma. One Native American sits on the superior court in Tacoma. All the other nonwhite judges are in Seattle, either on the Seattle municipal court or the King County superior court. In the eastern part of the state there is not a single person of color on the bench. Even in Yakima County, where 35 percent of the population is Latino, there has never been a nonwhite judge.

There is one exception to this nonwhite judicial presence in eastern Washington. In Spokane there is an ethnic Japanese court commissioner in the court of appeals. Court commissioners are employees of the court. They are hired by judges and function as judges. At the court of appeals level, commissioners make decisions and even write opinions, but their decisions are appealable to the judges who hired them. At the supreme court level we have a court commissioner who makes decisions, prepares and signs orders, but who cannot write opinions. This commissioner's decisions are appealable to the full court. The lower courts have commissioners also. There are no court commissioners of color in eastern Washington, with that one exception. They are all centered in western Washington.

One of my goals, one of my professional as well as my personal goals, is to get at least one Latino in eastern Washington and at least one other person of color on the bench.

In this state, you are either appointed or elected to the bench. You won't get appointed to fill vacancies on the bench unless you pass the muster of some evaluating committee. For the past four terms the governors took the position that they would not appoint someone for a vacancy unless the person had the approval of the bar association. Many minority lawyers are not familiar with the political process that determines who becomes a judge or they feel the process is unfair. You don't have too many persons of color who seek a judgeship, because of a fear of rejection.

I have lectured to minority lawyers across the country who aspire to become judges about how the process works, what the politics are, what the positives are, what the negatives are, and what it takes to be qualified as a practical matter or under the state constitutions. In Washington state, all you have to do to be qualified is to be a lawyer and a member of the bar in good standing. Those are all the requirements that you have to meet. Other requirements have been engrafted, some of them political. I point out to these lawyers that you do not necessarily sell yourself to the devil in getting the imprimatur of whatever group presumes to approve or disapprove of potential judges. You are presenting yourself as a professional who is going to render public service. And I tell them they can convince the people who count, the voters.

Sometimes I think we are victims of our own perceptions. Some persons of color feel the bar rating process is stacked against them. One major criticism voiced during the public hearings on bias in the court system conducted by the State of Washington Minority and Justice Task Force was that the Judicial Selection Committee of the Seattle–King County Bar Association was stacked with white males from major law firms who did not consider public-service law as important as corporate law and who did not understand women or minorities. The leadership of the bar took exception to the criticism. But the criticism at the time was based upon the truth, and it was based upon the perceptions of ethnic minorities who either had appeared before the committee or chose not to appear before the committee because of what they had heard.

Outside of King County, the rating of judicial candidates is done by bar polls. I have a Latino friend who wanted to be appointed to the superior court. The bar pool was conducted and she came out on top. The leadership of this county's bar decided that a mistake had been made in the process, so they would do it over again. They did another poll and she came out on the bottom. That kind of thing is a real problem. That was pure and simple manipulation of the process. I don't think you have that kind of problem in Seattle.

While bar association ratings are important for appointments, often they are not important in elections. I have a former student who is an older person, not a person of color, who was rated "unqualified" by the Seattle–King County bar. She won the election by 67 percent of the vote. Every newspaper in town endorsed her opponent, who was a former president of the Seattle–King County bar, but she won. So all this is to say that in this state, ultimately, judges are elected by the people, and so it doesn't really make a great deal of difference whether some bar committee says that you are qualified or unqualified or whether some newspaper says you are unqualified. It is what the people think that matters.

* * *

I never wanted to be a judge, I never expected to be a judge, and yet I have been a judge at three different levels in the state of Washington. I never wanted to be a first anything, except my wife's first husband. The opportunities that I have had I never sought. I became a superior court judge and supreme court judge by being at the right place at the right time.

I have enjoyed the work. I enjoy what I do now, but I am not here because it was my ambition to be on the supreme court. I am here because when the governor called me and asked me if I would accept an appointment, I said, "Make me an offer." He made me an offer and I said OK. I had turned down an appointment to the supreme court in 1981 by another governor who was a personal friend of mine. Not very many people know that.

There is a running joke, even now, about my being the only person in the court system who was appointed to one court by a Republican governor and to another court by a Democratic governor. Way back in the "Dark Ages," when I was permitted to be in politics, I was a Republican. I was appointed to the municipal court by a Democratic governor. I was appointed to the superior court by Dan Evans, who was the governor and a Republican. It was a Republican governor who asked me if I would accept an appointment to the supreme court in 1981, and I said no. Several years later, in 1988, when a Democratic governor, Booth Gardner, whom I didn't know, asked me to join the court, I decided, almost with a shrug of the shoulders, why not? A lot of Democrats were upset with Booth Gardner for appointing me, whom they referred to as a Republican.

Joining the supreme court isn't as smooth as joining a fraternity of your close personal friends, but it's not the worst place in the world to be. I have been in worse places than this. Everybody on the court was a personal friend. We were either law school classmates or we worked together over the years. They were all very friendly persons. The practical aspect of a court of nine justices, all of whom have egos and all of whom have histories, is being politically aware of what is developing and understanding motivation.

Being a person of color means that you have extraordinary stresses that persons not of color don't have. These are the things we don't talk about. These are the things we don't write about. Certainly I am not trying to malign my wonderful court and my wonderful state of

Washington by publicly disclosing the experiences that I have had based solely on the fact that I am not white.

I chose not to put my name on my office door because I get death threats. These threats have been unrelated to the cases I have decided. The first threat I received came the same week a federal judge in Atlanta was killed by a pipe bomb. Someone called the office and said, "Tell Judge Smith his Christmas present is coming early. Don't open any doors. Don't open any cabinets. I'm sorry for the staff." Now this is on December 19, 1989, and that is merely typical of the kinds of things that happen. In fact, the reason they have locks on the elevators in this building is because of threats to me.

I maintain a level of personal security on my own. I have very elaborate security systems at my house in Seattle and very elaborate security systems at my house here in Olympia. My automobiles are wired for contact, and all of these precautions are things that ordinary persons don't need to be concerned with.

These threats are not necessarily attendant to being a supreme court justice, but to being a supreme court justice who is not white. You never know when it is a prank or when it is real. You never know whether there is anything behind it. So, what you do is live your life without taking any chances.

I have a cellular telephone. I stay in touch with my family. If I am on my way home I'll call my wife and say I expect to be home at about eleven o'clock. This is extraordinary security, but I used to be an investigative lawyer. I was at the U.S. Justice Department. I know that things can happen to people. I know that when you are inadvertent you are likely to have something terrible happen to you, so I won't go in a dark parking lot. It is a way of life. It permeates everything you do. I wish that I did not have to be security conscious, but I am. I will not allow myself to become a victim.

I am more paranoid about security than my family is. My wife is rather casual about security. She gets annoyed by my requests to activate the security system at home during the day. I'm paranoid, but I'm alive today. The NAACP office in Tacoma was firebombed this year. There are people out there stupid enough to do something to me.

I went to law school pretty much by the flip of a coin. I never intended to finish law school. I never wanted to be a lawyer.

I was born in Florida and spent my early years in the state. My father [John R. Smith] was a Cuban refugee from the Spanish-American War and my mother [Eva Lovesmith] was an African American from North Carolina. My parents had eight children. I was fourteen when my parents separated, but by that time I was living with the family of Dr. William H. Gray Jr., who was the president of Florida A&M University. After serving in the Army I moved to Pennsylvania, where I graduated from Temple University. My foster father, Rev. Gray, the father of former congressman William H. Gray III, had decided that I could go to medical school. I soon learned that I could not stand the sight of blood, so he gave me some alternatives. I wanted to be a social worker. He decided I should go to law school. So it was partly because of that pressure that I decided to go to law school, to get him off my back. At the time, my mother had moved to the state of Washington, so I decided to try the University of Washington.

I was admitted to the University of Washington Law School merely by walking in and showing them a copy of my transcript. Admittedly, admission standards were not as stringent in 1952, as they are now, but as a college graduate with a 3.97 average, I could get admitted. I was challenged by law school and found that I really enjoyed it, so I stuck with it until I graduated. I graduated in 1955, took the Washington bar exam, and that was the beginning of my legal career.

I came here to the state supreme court as a law clerk in 1955. I was the second person of color to be a law clerk for the court. An Asian of Chinese ancestry had preceded me by three years. I became a law clerk partly because no law firm in Washington would even give me an interview. One of my law school professors arranged for me to come to the supreme court for an interview, and one of the justices hired me. Becoming a law clerk became another unplanned springboard in my career. Even now, people identify me with Justice Matthew W. Hill because I was a law clerk for him in 1955.

After clerking for the supreme court I went into the prosecuting attorney's office of King County. I was very good. I am always good at what I do, and I'm not modest. I tried two-hundred felony cases and I was the "hotshot of the office." I thoroughly enjoyed it.

I tried significant criminal cases, one of which was the case against Dave Beck, who was then the president of the International Brotherhood of Teamsters. This was a state case against Beck, as opposed to a federal case, but in the course of that activity I got to know Bob

Kennedy, who was then with the old Senate "rackets" committee. When Jack Kennedy was elected president and appointed his brother as attorney general, Bob Kennedy called me and asked if I would come to work with him. I ended up working as a special assistant to Attorney General Robert Kennedy, conducting grand jury investigations around the country.

Ultimately, I prosecuted Jimmy Hoffa for mail fraud and wire fraud in Chicago. In many ways my career was built in large measure on the downfall of the presidents of the International Brotherhood of Teamsters although I am not anti-union. In fact, my greatest political support in the state of Washington is from the Teamsters union.

I was in Washington, D.C., for four years. Then I came back to Seattle and was appointed to the Seattle Municipal Criminal Court. That was 1965, and I was the first nonwhite ever to serve as a judge in the state of Washington. At the time, you had only two courts in the city of Seattle: the traffic court and the criminal court.

In the municipal court I was the only criminal court judge, so I had 68 percent of all arrests made by the Seattle Police Department. This was about three-hundred cases a day. There was constant movement in the court, and, believe it or not, I enjoyed that. I would not take a recess except for lunch. I'd start at 9 A.M. and go to 1 P.M., come back after lunch and stay the rest of the afternoon. My staff was rotating because they could not take the pressure. I would start back after lunch and go until I finished the list, because if I didn't finish I would have a backlog. I enjoyed the municipal court because I was totally in control of the system as the only criminal court judge for the city of Seattle handling only city misdemeanor violations.

After two years on the municipal court I was appointed to the Superior Court of King County. When I went on the superior court I was a junior judge out of twenty-one judges on that court. Now the superior court has forty-nine judges, and I would go crazy being in a court of forty-nine judges. In a court where there is more than one judge, there is a tendency toward group decisions, and that's where you lose your control. If I compare the municipal court, where I was autonomous, to the superior court, where I was one of twenty-one judges, the municipal court was more enjoyable.

I created some innovations in the criminal justice system when I was a trial judge. *Time* magazine called my innovations "oddball dispositions" in criminal cases. Now it is an accepted thing to have community service instead of prison. When I started community service I had to monitor my probations personally, because the probation officers did not understand the process. So I would have hearings out of the ordinary period of my court day, which was from 9:30 to 4, so I would have probation review hearings at 8:30 and at 4:30. My court reporters and clerks just went crazy because they were overloaded.

One of the "oddball dispositions" in the *Time* article involved a case where I required an elderly man who had received proceeds from prostitution to set up a scholarship fund for prostitutes. He had allowed a prostitute to live in his apartment. An undercover policeman came to the apartment, paid twenty dollars for sex, and the elderly man took the money. This was his third case, so I could have easily imposed jail time, but I tried an alternative, the scholarship fund. He had inherited money from his father. The sentence worked well. When his money was depleted, another woman in the community put money into her will for the scholarship fund because she thought it was a good idea.

In another case I didn't send a forger to prison. I found out the forger couldn't read or write. A friend had gotten this man to cash a forged check for him. Instead of prison, I required him to enroll in a literacy program.

Time called these sentences "oddball." I call them innovative. What was my alternative? Send a sixty-five-year-old man to prison for twenty years? Send an illiterate man to prison for fifteen years so that when he gets out he is still illiterate and can still be conned? I didn't do this in a vacuum. I had presentence reports, so I knew about the individuals and their circumstances. I used my discretion to tailor the punishment to the individual.

This was before the Sentencing Reform Act here in the state, which requires mandatories and limits a judge's options in sentencing. The act took away the judge's prerogative to give probation. They are finding out that the act is not as good as it was supposed to be. It is not a panacea. I think a judge should have discretion in sentencing.

As with the municipal court I was the first nonwhite to serve on a superior court in the state. I stayed on the court for six years. I experienced burnout and decided I had to get out. Although I had been elected five times without opposition while serving on the municipal and superior courts, I decided to let my term run out, and I left the court in 1973.

I was overloaded and I didn't realize it. At the end of six years I finally came to the realization that I was overworking. I also came to the realization that I was fighting against an intractable system. At the time, there was a turn-of-the-century approach to the court system for civil and criminal cases. There was a great deal of resistance to change from some of the older, established judges in the system.

Sitting in my office on a Saturday, I made my decision to leave the bench. This happened to be the day judges were taking a photograph to announce to the newspapers that they were running for reelection. They called to remind me that I was to sit in on the reelection photograph, and I said, "I won't join you, because I am not going to file for reelection." It just happened like that.

Many people could not understand. When I left the court in 1973, it was unheard of that anyone would give up a judicial position, which is, in effect, a lifetime appointment. Very few judges were defeated in elections. The people could not understand why I was not so gratefully honored to be the only Black person on the court. My considerations for leaving were a combination of many things, but the fact that I never sought to become a judge is, I think, what made the difference in deciding to leave. I stayed until my term expired and left.

Shortly after I left the court I had my choice of law firms to go to, unlike when I graduated from law school. I also had the opportunity to go to the University of Washington Law School to teach. I decided to go to the Law School. I was an associate dean of the Law School and a professor of law, tenured, fully tenured. I am still technically on the faculty there. I was at the Law School for thirteen years, and then I took an early retirement in 1986. I decided to try my hand at private practice. I had never been in private practice.

A few years after I was in private practice a vacancy came up at the supreme court, and the governor persuaded me that I owed it to the people to make myself available. I never sought anything at any level at any time. Somehow or other the doors open and somebody would throw me in, so I ended up getting appointed here to the supreme court in 1988 to fill the two-year balance of a term. I was then elected unopposed to a six-year term.

I am a person of absolute integrity. I think that as an elected public official I have an obligation to serve the people who elected me, and so whatever I do is in consonance with serving the public with integrity and intelligence. That's what I think all public officials should do, particularly judges and even more particularly justices on the supreme court.

If a person loses sight of his or her integrity and humanity that person will not be successful in any endeavor, particularly not the practice of law. The practice of law is an honorable profession where integrity is just as important as ability. The person who wishes to function effectively in the practice of law at any level must have integrity and sensitivity.

Lawyers and judges are under attack all over the country. We must demonstrate in our personal and professional conduct that this is a profession worthy of respect. A great deal of our responsibility is to comport ourselves in such a way in what we do personally and professionally that we convince the public that our judicial system is in good hands.

There is a significant difference between the superior court and the supreme court. The biggest difference is the lack of contact with people. When I was on the superior court, the trial court, I had an opportunity to go on the court of appeals. I turned it down because I didn't want to be cloistered. I enjoy interaction with people. I enjoy witnesses, parties to cases, and juries. I did not want to cloister myself at the time, and thus my resistance to the appellate court system, either at the intermediate appellate court or the supreme court level.

Here on the supreme court the only time I come in contact with human beings other than my colleagues on the court is when lawyers argue cases or when people come to my office. Here, I am very much like a researcher in a law school. We are essentially researchers and writers and are not dealing with human beings on a day-to-day basis. That is the part of the job I enjoy the least, and this is not to say I don't enjoy what I am doing.

I spend all my time reading briefs, listening to oral arguments, writing opinions, and reviewing other people's opinions. I work a twenty-hour day most of the time, which includes travel time between the office and other things I'm involved in. If I were younger, I think I would be very unhappy here at the appellate court level. But I think my being here is consistent with my level of achievement in the profession. I was admitted to the bar in 1955. It is now 1993, nearly forty years later. I have no intention of leaving this court before my term is out.

The fascinating part of the supreme court experience is analyzing a case and working with my law clerks to prepare the research necessary to come to a conclusion and make a recommendation to my colleagues.

I find that the formal around-the-table conference process is the most valuable avenue of communication. I think I would resent lobbying a position. When I vote I have reached a firm conclusion based upon what I have read, what I have heard, and what I have reasoned. It would take a great deal for me to flip positions because someone has crafted their language a certain way in a draft opinion.

I would characterize myself more as a conciliatory personality than as philosophically conservative or liberal. I think I am liberal, but my children think I'm conservative.

I don't think that intellectually I can be put in anyone's pigeon hole. I tend to get aboard what people might consider to be liberal policies. That, however, has nothing to do with trying to fit myself into a conservative or liberal category. I give my personal commitment to things that I happen to believe in. If that makes me a liberal, then I'm liberal. On the other hand, because I'm so cautious, if cautious makes me conservative, then I'm a conservative.

Sometimes I say, with tongue in cheek, that I have gotten these firsts—first judge, first person of color in this or that—because I have always been the safe person. I have never worn a dashiki. I don't have enough hair to wear an Afro. I speak well. I've never cursed anyone out. My credentials are good. I am a retired lieutenant colonel from the Marine Corps, and you don't get any more conservative than the Marine Corps. So people look at the credentials and they say, "He is safe."

There are people who are willing to take a chance on me, when they wouldn't be willing to take a chance on my brother, because all the indicia of acceptability and middle-class orientation and conservatism are there. I am neither conservative nor middle-class, but I am a safe quantity. A law professor at the University of Washington, former superior court judge, an officer in the Marine Corps. Groups will say, "We are looking for one and he meets our criteria," so somebody calls and says, "Say, we would like you to do this." And, of course, my ego tells me to leap in, so I say yes. And that's how it happens. I'm sure it also has a little to do with my generation and age. There was a time when there were only a limited number of names that were available and accessible as a known quantity. I'm joking somewhat about being "safe," but there is a bit of reality to it.

I was the first nonwhite person ever to serve on the American Bar Association's Standing Committee on the Federal Judiciary. This committee passes on the qualifications of persons seriously being considered for appointment to the federal courts, and has nothing to do with the initial selection. By the time the nominees come before the committee the persons have already been screened and selected for appointment, subject to the recommendation of the committee. The people who come before the committee have already passed political muster, are about to be appointed, and will be appointed, in the main.

I went on the committee around 1974 or 1975. I was then at the University of Washington. At that time we had one person of color on the committee and one woman. The woman ultimately became the chairperson of the committee.

My appointment to the committee was a combination of many things. I had a national reputation, whether earned or not earned. People knew who I was, and so somebody got the germ of an idea about the committee representing a cross section of the population. Somebody said, "Why don't you ask Charley Smith?" That's the way things happen. Joining the committee was not something that I sought out.

The committee finds a nominee either exceptionally well qualified, well qualified, qualified, not qualified, or unqualified by reason of age. The American Bar committee believed that people over the age of fifty-five should not be considered for lifetime appointments to the federal court. On one occasion a very significant, well-known, national figure was being considered for appointment to one of the courts of appeals, and our committee found that person "not qualified by reason of age." There was absolutely no question about whether the person would have been an outstanding addition to the bench.

At the time I was on the committee we did not consider anything about a nominee's cultural awareness, recognition of the status of women, or background regarding intergroup relations. My contribution to the committee process was saying, "Wait a minute. We are going about this the wrong way. There are other factors that we need to look into to determine whether this person, this nominee, would be a good lifetime appointee to the federal court. What about this nominee's record on the treatment of women? What about this nominee's understanding of racial and ethnic and linguistic minorities?" So the committee, through a process of evolution, engrafted onto its inquiry process what was broadly considered to be an examination of sensitivity. I don't claim to be the author of that new approach. I think that it was just the evolutionary process of improving the procedure for examination.

There was absolutely no resistance among committee members to incorporating these new elements into the examination process. I think that reflects the intelligence level of lawyers. Most lawyers have an undergraduate degree or more and a law degree, which means they have spent at least seven years sitting in a classroom, reading materials about the world as it is presented in the classroom. Then they have practiced law and have emerged into leadership in the American Bar Association, so they are not naive and they have had wide experiences. So when somebody joins their group and says, "We ought to take a look at this," there is open acceptance, absolutely no resistance.

I went off the committee in 1979. I regret getting off the committee, because, of all the American Bar activities I have been and still am involved in, that was by far the most fulfilling for me. I went off the committee because I was being considered for an appointment to the United States Court of Appeals and there was a conflict of interest between my being on the committee and making myself available for the court of appeals. I didn't get the appointment. Even now people are always asking me if I'm interested in the federal court. Well, I'm over fifty-five, and the selection process disrupts your life. I have no need for it. I don't seek prestige. I have gained whatever prestige I ever wanted or needed, and I'm not looking for an additional accomplishment to put on my résumé. My greater concern is to have more time to spend with my grandchildren and enjoy it.

Another one of those "Hey, let's ask Charley Smith" deals led to my becoming chair of the Minority Justice Task Force here in Washington state. This task force examined the impact of race and ethnic bias in the court system of our state. It was created in 1987. A woman state senator decided to tack on to the court administrator's budget that year a requirement that a task force be set up to investigate gender bias in the courts. An African American senator said that if there was going to be a gender-bias investigation there should also be an investigation of race bias. So the appropriations bill came out with a provision requiring the state supreme court to set up a task force to determine the existence of gender bias and race bias in the courts. The then chief justice of the supreme court wisely decided to bifurcate the investigation, by having a separate gender-bias task force and a separate minority-justice task force.

I was in private practice at the time. The chief justice and the court administrator came to me and persuaded me that I was needed for the chairmanship, that I was the only person who could do it. I told them I would serve as chairperson for the task force on the condition that I select the task force's members and staff and that staff personnel report directly to me and not to the court administrator. They agreed. I think they agreed to my conditions because I am above board all of the time.

The task force conducted public hearings around the state, as did task forces in New York and the other states that have undertaken this type of examination. During these hearings we heard all kinds of experiences: lawyers of color talked about this common experience of being mistaken for defendants in criminal cases, and lawyers not of color bore witness to the fact that their clients who were of color were treated with less respect than white clients.

We issued our report in 1990. I think the most significant finding was the lack of inclusion of a cross section of the population in the staffing of the courts. If you walk into practically any court in the state of Washington, everybody will be white—you won't see Latinos, you won't see Asians, you won't see African Americans, with the exception of the courts in the City of Seattle.

The next finding of import is the paucity of persons of color serving as judges in the court system, a problem I pointed out earlier. Out of 450 judges in this state, only 21 are persons of color. I know all of them—half of them were my law school students—and there is something wrong with that. I should not know every nonwhite judge in the state. Of course, I know most of the judges regardless of their color, but it should not be that all the persons of color in the court system are either my law school classmates or my former students. We need to do something about that.

The third item of the report that I think is significant is the absence of qualified language interpreters. Each of the race-bias commissions and task forces around the country has found the absence of interpreters to be a most serious problem. In this state our principal second language is Spanish, then Vietnamese and the other Indochinese languages, and then Chinese, Japanese, and Korean. This finding led to the appointment of another task force, on language interpreters. We established a system for training qualified, competent language interpreters. We started with Spanish, then Vietnamese, and now we are adding other languages.

One of the things we did early on in the task-force process was come up with training programs for judges and court personnel to teach them about what we at one time called "intergroup relations" but now call "cultural awareness, diversity and inclusiveness." If fact, we are having a meeting tomorrow to approve a contract for a consulting firm that is going to do cultural-awareness training programs for judges and court personnel, and the only problem is that all judges in this state are constitutional judges and are autonomous. Since they are autonomous, not even justices of the supreme court can direct them to attend any session. The judges' attendance and participation will be purely voluntary.

When our task force conducted its cultural-awareness training seminars in different parts of the state, with the exception of our being invited to judges' conferences to put on presentations, I am aware of only one court of appeals judge and one supreme court justice having attended.

We found court-system personnel who were not serious about the process. We had professional researchers, and in the eastern end of the state when our questionnaires were returned the box for "Asian" was checked on virtually all of them. We knew better. The researchers called and said, "Has a mistake been made?" The response was, "Ha, Ha. We are all Asian—Caucasian." They thought it was a joke. Then one group of questionnaires came back with everybody checked off as Native Americans. We called and someone said, "Ha, Ha. Can't you take a joke. We are all native Americans. We were born in America." So that set our research back by two months and cost us $3,500 to $4,500 because we had to do the questionnaires over again. That was the tenor of the response to our call for cultural awareness. All we were trying to do was get an idea of who worked in the court system.

On my own court we have nine justices. Three and a half justices returned the questionnaires. I was one of them. That was the attitude on this court three years ago. Right now, I think I'd get a 100 percent return from the court if we asked about the ethnic composition of its staff.

There is a need for more staff diversity on this court. Take law clerks, for example. We each have two law clerks. There was one Black woman law clerk when I came here in 1988. Then, the only nonwhite law clerks who were hired were hired by me. Fortunately, times have changed. I have a Latino law clerk now. I have had an Asian clerk. I have had one Black woman law clerk, and I intend now to always have an ethnic minority as one of my two law clerks, if not both of them.

I don't care whether I get the reputation of being an ethnic minority who hires only ethnic minorities. It worked the other way for so long. I am not embarrassed or ashamed about hiring minority law clerks. Call it being counted. I don't mind being counted as long as the system changes.

One of my colleagues had a young woman who is of Korean ancestry. We now have three ethnic-minority law clerks out of eighteen law clerks in the building. I know that two of my colleagues who have hired ethnic minorities deliberately sought to identify, recruit, encourage, and change the composition of their staff. This is the kind of attitude that we would like to foster. It is a very natural thing to do.

During the "season" for hiring law clerks I get ten applications a day. I go through them to see if there is anything outstanding about each person. I look at the basic qualifications, the grade performance, and the references. I also look to see what their service activities are, and whether they identify themselves with an ethnic-minority interest. Sometimes names can be misleading.

One applicant was insulted when I wrote him a letter asking him if he would mind telling me the history of his name. From the application he appeared to be Latino and Japanese. He wrote back saying he refused to give the history of his own name, but he did say his middle name was actually his wife's maiden name. Needless to say, that person is no longer on my list. If someone is applying to me for a job and I am interested in knowing something about the history of their name, if they want to work for me, they will tell. Most persons of color are proud of their ancestry. If I wrote to somebody applying for a job, I would be proud of my poor Cuban father and my poor Black mother.

What we were trying to do with the task force, and now the commission, is to create an atmosphere in the court system in this state where it is natural to look up and see that the judge can be anybody: a woman or a man a person of color or a white person; and the staff can be women, men, persons of all colors. We need to have this atmosphere so that when people come into court they will not be alienated. They will see that the court system is conducted by persons who represent a cross section of the population. That is what all of the task forces around the country are trying to do: create a new atmosphere where things will change and where the composition of our courts will reflect the real world.

One month before we issued the task force report in December 1990, the task force officially came to an end. It was then a matter for the supreme court to create a commission, which would be a permanent group as opposed to a limited task force.

Internally on this court, there was a lot of resistance to creating a commission. All kinds of devices were used to convince the others among us that we had no business being in the business of monitoring judicial activity. I literally had to battle for our existence, even though the national Conference of Chief Justices had passed a resolution in 1988 urging the states to create such task forces or commissions.

One justice took the position that the task force commission was my personal project. I said, "No, this is not my personal project. This is a court project." I said, "I don't really care whether you create a commission. You will be the ones who will have to answer to the people of the state of Washington, who want the commission." Another member of our court had been out campaigning for reelection and had met with some of the ethnic-minority bar associations. This member found out from these bar associations how significant the task force was, and this person decided to make a motion before the court to create a commission. It was created. Now we have a commission. Its duration is five years.

I was asked to continue as chairperson, which I gladly did.

The biggest problem the commission has is the budget. Our budget was cut by $200,000. We requested $643,000. This is part of the court's budget. We are dealing with fiscal management in the bureaucracy of a state that at least publicly says it is operating one and a half billion dollars in the red. You have to accept the fact that you can't get everything you ask for from the legislature. Fortunately, our commission has support from the legislature—much greater support from the legislature than it has from the court system . . . but I don't want to be unfair to my colleagues in the system.

I do think that my colleagues on this court are now firmly of the opinion that the commission's activity is worthwhile, and the negative responses to our commission are working themselves out as justices retire or are defeated in elections. I believe that again this year the commission's work will have the complete and firm support of my colleagues. The court is solidly behind the commission's activity, and the commission is now considered to be a major aspect of the court's work. This support may be related to the fact that we get national attention for our work.

I happen to be the chairperson of the National Consortium of Task Forces and Commissions on Race Bias in the Courts. New York created its task force at the same time our commission was created. Michigan had created one two years earlier. New Jersey had a commission that was begun in 1981. The four of us got together and formed a consortium. Then, following through on the Conference of Chief Justices resolution, we have promoted the development of other task forces and commissions. There are now sixteen such commissions in the United States, and the state of Washington is in the forefront because we have gone further than most other states.

All of this has come to the attention of the members of my court. We had our national consortium meeting in Seattle on May 3, 1992. All of the members of my court attended, except for one who got stuck east of the mountains and couldn't get a flight out. All of the members who attended the meeting found out how significant this activity is on a national level. And they found out that it isn't back-room activity to promote an individual like me or to promote the interests of one selfish interest group. They found out that it is a national movement for inclusion and recognition of the need to treat everybody more fairly in the court system.

I think our state will continue to be a flagship in the movement for activities of this nature, and we in public office like to see some measure of success. Every time I am asked to go somewhere around the country to talk about these issues I give credit to my court for having taken the leadership. All of this is appropriate, and that is the way the system works.

The issue of race and bias in the judicial system has suddenly become popular. Every time you turn around there is a new conference on the subject. The more it becomes a popular subject, the louder is the unanswered question, "Why not before now?"

I think Florida should be praised. The task force there did their work in three years. They documented a range of problems and their report was accepted by the courts and the legislature. Increasing the number of judges of color was one of the task force's recommendations. There were twenty-seven openings on courts around the state, and the governor appointed twenty-five African Americans and two Latinos. It is reliably acknowledged that but for the task force and its powerful recommendation, the governor would not have known of the paucity of nonwhite judges.

You know, I still have media people shoving microphones in my face, asking me whether I think I can be fair to white people who come before me. This question, of course, reflects institutional guilt. The person who asked the question is white and recognizes that whites have not always treated Blacks fairly. Therefore a Black judge must necessarily not be able to treat white people fairly.

I remember one question I was asked when I was appointed to the supreme court in 1988. A young television reporter came up to me and said, "Aren't you excited about being the first nonwhite person appointed to the supreme court?"

I said, "No, absolutely not. I am not excited."

The dude was taken aback by that response.

I said, "I'll be excited when there are five women on this court. I'll be excited when my daughter—if my daughter who is a lawyer wants to be a judge—is appointed to the supreme court. I'll be excited when my granddaughter—if my granddaughter who is two years old becomes a lawyer and wants to become a judge—is appointed to the supreme court."

Part IV

THE FUTURE

ABIGAIL R. ROGERS

"Being a woman judge causes people more uneasiness . . . than my being Black."

Abigail Rogers vividly remembers family visits to the courthouse in her hometown of Columbia, South Carolina, when she was a small child during the early sixties. She had to watch the proceedings from the balcony because Blacks were barred from the floor of the courtroom. Three decades after those childhood visits to the segregated courthouse Rogers became the first Black female judge in the history of the Palmetto state when she was elected to the family court on July 1, 1991.

An energetic woman who jogs regularly with her husband, Rogers waged a six-year campaign to secure her judicial election in the state legislature. She deliberately sought family court for two reasons: she felt she could make a real contribution in that court, particularly with children, and she felt that legislators would more readily accept a Black female in family court than in the general-jurisdiction circuit court. While she was able to win the respect of legislators, she has discovered, much to her dismay, that Black youths regularly disrespect her, whether she is speaking in a classroom or presiding in court. She has had to cite a number of youths for contempt, for talking back to her in court.

Rogers attended the University of South Carolina in Columbia for undergraduate and law degrees. She worked as both a prosecutor and public defender in preparation for her goal of becoming a jurist.

Judge Abigail R. Rogers was interviewed at her home in Columbia in November 1992.

I heard a case last year that caused me pain, real emotional anguish. This case was appalling. It never should have been in court. The prosecutor's office in Greenville was bringing a case against this Black girl who was thirteen or fourteen, whose cousin had cocaine and money in a bag and gave it to her to keep. She turned it in to the principal. She turned the drugs in to the principal, and the principal expelled her and her cousin. Both of them end up in court for the drugs. She was an A and B student, no C's or D's ever. She never missed a day in school, was never tardy, was involved in everything. Here we are fighting to keep kids in school and they were putting this good kid out of school because she had turned in some drugs.

What I did in that case became headline news. It really created havoc in Greenville County.

At trial I heard the prosecutor's case against the cousin. He pled guilty, of course. He said that he gave the drugs and money to his cousin. The girl was represented by a white lawyer. Her mother was the cleaning woman in the lawyer's house. The girl and her mother were from the projects. They were poor. The lawyer was a retired state senator. I didn't know any of this background at the time. It came out later. That lawyer put up a fight for this girl like you wouldn't believe.

The prosecutor's whole case was that she had the drugs, she brought them to the principal, and she turned them in. The principal testified that she had turned the drugs in. During cross-examination her lawyer brought out that her grades were excellent. She was a good girl. She had been expelled solely because she had turned in drugs given to her by the cousin. It also came out during cross-examination that the school had not followed the proper procedures when they expelled her. The superintendent had not been notified, nor the school board. This was against school policy.

I was sitting there listening to this and I just couldn't believe what I was hearing. I could not believe that such things happen. This was a good kid who did the right thing. They were putting her out of school and charging her with possessing drugs.

There were some other things about this case that were just amazing. This child had been out of school for months. She knew she would be left back because she was missing so many school days, so her mama took her to her teacher's home at night to get her homework assignments so she wouldn't fail. The principal stopped the teacher from doing that for the girl. I couldn't believe it. I told myself, "I must be dreaming. This is straight out of *Roots*."

So, after the prosecution finished its case I said, "I know I have only been on the bench a couple of months, but am I missing something here?" I simply asked the prosecutor, "Where was the intent of this girl to commit a crime? Tell me?" He sits there and says that the mere fact that she had the drugs was a crime.

So I granted a directed verdict of not guilty. The defense didn't even have to put on their case. Then I told the school officials—this will give you an idea of how new and naive I was—I told them, "How dare you do that! I understand you are out there trying to get drugs out of the school system, but you threw out the baby with the bath water. You threw out a good student." I told them, "Put that student back in school."

The next day the headline said SCHOOL THROWS OUT BABY WITH BATH WATER, JUDGE CRITICIZES SCHOOL SYSTEM. My comments started an uproar in Greenville. The editorials were saying, "Black female judge coming in here and telling us what to do!" That's how they referred to me: "Afro American judge coming in telling the school district what to do. She's out of her league. She can't do this." They couldn't believe that the courts are where you come to settle disputes. Their position was, "How dare she come down here and tell us what to do!"

The school refused to let the girl back in. They would not let the girl back in school after I ordered them to. They said I was without jurisdiction.

I left Greenville on a Friday. Family court judges in South Carolina ride the circuit. We travel all around the state. We have statewide jurisdiction. Well, the next day, Saturday, the girl's lawyer has a heart attack and dies. So the girl is without a lawyer, and she can't get back in school.

The girl's parents called me at my office in Richmond, but I was at home in Columbia. I called some judges in Greenville and said, "Somebody up there, please help these people." The judges said it wasn't their case. And there I sat. I couldn't do a thing. I didn't know what to do. I felt bad. So the girl stayed out of school.

The girl's parents had no money. Their attorney had represented them for free. They called all the Black lawyers in town and asked them to take the case for free.

I just came back from Greenville recently, and while I was there a Black lawyer told me they had gotten her back into school. They had to straight out sue the school district and subpoena the board of trustees and the superintendent to let them testify about the procedures they used to put the girl out. We all knew they hadn't used proper procedures. They put her back in. I thought I had seen it all.

The girl is back in school making straight A's. I asked the lawyer if the girl realized what all went on, and he said she didn't realize it.

The prosecutors in that case should have exercised better discretion. I don't know how the case ever got into court.

I need to be on the bench longer. I have only been on the bench a year and four months, but I suspect the longer I'm on the bench, the better I will be able to see how things work in different areas of the state. That case just amazed me.

I know now not to make comments from the bench. Senior judges can sit there and make comments all day. I can't. One of my mentors, a senior judge, said, "Abigail, will you stop criticizing people? Don't you know the press is everywhere you go?" A couple of mentors told me not to make comments. I said, "You don't understand!" They said they did understand but I should just give my decision and not say anything.

I was elected on July 1, 1991. I'm the only Black female judge in the entire judiciary in South Carolina. There is no other Black woman. There are a few Black female magistrates and a few on municipal courts, but those are local positions. Getting to the state level, in line for the state supreme court, well, I'm the first. I'm the first Black woman judge in South Carolina and the first Black woman judge in family court.

I campaigned for my judgeship for six years. Everybody laughs about that now. They say, "That child campaigned!" I literally had to go to the state legislature and campaign for all of their votes. Only the members of the state house and senate can vote. The governor doesn't even have a vote. The governor only has input if a judge dies in office or gets removed. Then the governor appoints someone until the next legislative session. The public doesn't vote directly for judges. It's an insulated election. South Carolina keeps its judges away from the public.

For six years I plotted and I planned and I studied each legislator, because I knew that it was almost going to take the impossible to get them to vote for a Black woman when a Black woman had never been a state court judge of that level. You don't have a Black woman on the federal court in South Carolina. You never had a Black woman on the state court. You can always go back and find out that there was a Black man on our state supreme court after the Civil War, but you can't do that for a Black woman. There was none.

I studied each legislator. I researched each one of them. I researched their backgrounds. I had picture books with each legislator's photograph and bio. I read about them. I knew where they were. If I ever saw them in public, I would introduce myself and tell them I wanted to be a judge. They would laugh at me, but after a while I had said it so often they almost began to believe me.

I didn't get elected the first time I sought a judgeship. When I found out the legislators weren't too receptive I had to figure out a way to get them to vote for me. I positioned myself to get on family court. I knew that they would see me more in a family court than circuit court; plus, that's where I wanted to go. I knew I had to get them to feel comfortable with me.

The first time I ran for office I just met the minimum required by state law. State law says you must be in trial practice for five years. I was practicing in the prosecutor's office at the time.

That first time, I went to the Black bar association because I thought I needed their endorsement for the judgeship I knew was opening up. The bar association had this massive meeting saying that the judgeship was opening up and they wanted people who were interested. Well, I went down there and they thought I was awfully young. I guess I was about twenty-eight at the time. They also thought I was crazy. They didn't endorse me.

I got four votes. Those were the votes of the three girls who rode with me to the meeting, and my own. There were just four votes. My friends had laughed at me before the meeting, saying they thought I was being utterly ridiculous. They were saying, number one, why would the bar endorse a Black woman? And, number two, if the bar were to endorse a Black woman, why would it be me? They said I was too young and I wasn't married. I was just *out.* My friends were correct. In essence, that's what the bar association told me.

But I knew the legislators had to vote anyway. So I went to the legislators. Being born and raised in South Carolina, in Columbia, and my father being a county councilman, I made friends. I went to the Black legislators and told them I wanted to be a judge. They said there was nothing wrong with wanting to be a judge, but they said my timing was off. One of them told me I could go around and talk to other members of the legislature but they wouldn't vote for me, and I was as likely to make enemies as I was to make friends. I went to the legislators and tried to see if they would be receptive to me. I found out they were not receptive. I didn't get the opening. I'm not sure if I was even considered.

After this experience, when I found out the legislators weren't receptive, that's when I started studying them. That's when I started trying to figure out a way to get them to vote for me for the next judicial opening. I started doing this on faith, because you don't know when the next opening is coming. I just started campaigning.

I was positive another opening would come. I started getting active with the Black bar association and the South Carolina Bar Association. Through the South Carolina bar I heard white people talking about the possibility of an opening. I said, OK, that means I am going to have to tighten up now. An opening did come up because a whole new judicial circuit was created. The guy the Black bar had endorsed about five years back moved up, so there was an opening. I said, This time I think I am ready.

I started working on getting someone in the legislature to say they would support me if an opening did come up. And that's what I did. To do it I spent thousands of dollars, because I was constantly mailing people letters, using postage, making long-distance telephone calls, and driving all across the state visiting people. I was working for the state then, and I knew I didn't want the state to think that I was using their time and money.

I got elected. I had opposition, but I felt that seat was mine because I had worked for it.

When this second opening came up I didn't go to the Black bar seeking its endorsement. I said to myself, Why should I go back to the Black bar and subject myself to that awful experience again? But I went back to a meeting a few weeks before the election and said I was in the race and I would appreciate their endorsement. I didn't go in there saying I would need their endorsement to become a judge. I said I would appreciate the endorsement, but if you don't give it to me I am still going to run. I didn't get it. They had their own people they wanted to endorse. They still thought I wasn't ready. They could have been operating on the same feeling as some legislators: She's just a woman, and all those sorts of things.

Being a woman judge causes people more uneasiness on the family court bench than my being Black. People warned me about that. When I was first sworn in the women judges said that people would get more upset when they walked in the courtroom and saw a woman than if they walked in and saw a Black man on the bench. And that is true. That is true. I've gotten that reaction from both lawyers and litigants. It's about equal.

In divorce cases, for example, some male litigants think that a woman judge is going to rule with the woman. Women judges say that is ridiculous because, if that were so, before women got on the bench all women would have felt that they didn't stand a chance in court because only men were judges. And women will come in and think, She's a woman, so she's going to rule with me. That's not necessarily so either.

It's just that we bring our backgrounds with us, and I'm the only one on the family court bench who grew up as a Black woman in a Black neighborhood in Columbia. There's nobody else who brings that background to the bench.

When I was elected I expected that other judges would discriminate against me. It is the opposite. I've had no problems with judges. I remember the first family court dinner meeting I went to. We talked about traveling around and the problems we encounter on the bench. The judges gave me suggestions about how to settle things and resolve things. I've gotten together with judges on the circuit courts and the supreme court, and they just treat me wonderfully. They are very nice. I can call anybody, anytime. I'm just surprised.

But when it comes to just being a Black on the bench, me being a Black judge, there are things that I can talk about with other Black judges that I cannot say to white judges. There is now another Black judge on family court, and when he and I talk we find that he feels the way I feel in a lot of situations. One day I had only Black kids as defendants in my courtroom, and I thought that was a shame. He'd say that's a shame, too.

I wanted to start in family court, for two reasons. One, I thought it would be a good starting point for my judicial career. I would like to serve on the state supreme court someday. And number two, I think I can make a contribution here. So many Black kids end up in family court. You have a purpose everywhere you go. I believe in God and in prayer, so I feel that each of us was put on this earth to perform a duty. I am so lucky to have found my niche in a job that I love.

My first day in court I was so excited. I still feel the same way every time I try a case. I remember that first day. Everything in court is so formal, but I didn't know that. So I put on my robe, ran through my courtroom's back door onto the bench and started asking where my litigants and their attorneys were, because I was ready to start session. My court personnel, the security guards and the clerks and everybody, told me to go back into the robing room. They said, "This is how it works: We call the case, get everyone ready, and then we call you in." I was so excited I just wanted to get started.

We ride the circuit, which I love to do because each town is so different. It is fun as all get out.

Down in Lexington there is another judge named Rogers. He is a white male. Most people down there don't realize there is also a Black woman who is a judge. This adds confusion because, when I'm in town, there are two Judge Rogerses. We get a kick out of it.

I was sitting in the courtroom one day in Lexington, looking at my schedule, and this lawyer walks in and says, "Excuse me, would you mind getting my exhibits marked before the judge gets in? I need to have the exhibits marked because he likes to move things right fast." So I just told this lawyer I wasn't marking anything. I told him I wasn't the person to mark exhibits. He says, "Oh, I didn't know. I was just waiting for the judge." Now you see, he just assumed I couldn't be the judge. I get those kinds of comments a lot.

I get a better reaction from people in rural areas than I do in urban areas. In rural areas the people are so thankful. They act as though Queen Elizabeth has arrived. They make me feel exactly how happy they are to have me. They feed me to death. They just pamper me. Everybody wants to talk.

There is this very small town up there in the corner of South Carolina, right before you get to North Carolina, named Walhalla. It's just like you picture it in your mind. Those people will come by the courthouse just to talk to me, bring me food from their homes and baked goods. They bring their children by. One time there was a group of them waiting in the parking lot for me when I arrived. They said they heard I was coming, they heard I was Black, and they just wanted to come down and see me. I feel wonderful getting this type of reaction. It makes me feel good just knowing that other people feel proud to have a Black female judge. Now, my security staff doesn't like this. They say I'm out there with the people too much. I am just so flattered.

But, I'll tell you who is not impressed with my being a judge: young Black kids. Now when I was growing up, if you met a Black judge, or met anybody who had achieved something, you just thanked them for letting you be in their presence. No, not these Black kids today. Black kids don't respect me. When I take the time to go into their classrooms their attitude is, "So what?" They don't even respect me in my court. I have to hold them in contempt for talking back to me in court.

I think these young Black kids today don't respect anyone because they are not hungry. To use the words that the motivational speaker Les Brown uses in his speeches, we just wanted to be somebody when we were young. These kids today don't have a sense, a taste for something better in their lives. The civil rights movement is foreign to them. It might as well have been World War II to them. These kids don't see that to be Black and to achieve was at one time not the norm but the exception. Something is missing from their view on where things were and where they are today. Their parents must not be doing something.

I was brought up in the South, where you had not only parents but a community and a church that came in and took care of you. When you did something wrong in church, that church group would get you. Or if you did something wrong in the community, then the community group would get you. You had so much of a support system in place that when my mom and dad were unable to pick us up from school, neighbors took us home and went over our homework with us.

These kids today don't have that, which is very apparent. That's nationwide. It's not just here in Columbia. They don't have a sense of community, of achievement, of hard work. They end up coming into the family court because they have no respect for authority, for people, or for other people's things.

You know what really hurts when you hold a kid in contempt, when you put him in jail, in one of those kiddy prisons? The thing that hurts is looking at the parents. You see the pain and suffering in the parents' faces when you have to send their kid away. I often bring the kids up and say, "Now, you take a look at your mom and dad. You see what you are doing to them?" I tell them they think they're going to a party, but they are killing their parents by being sent away.

Typically, the parents say, "I don't know what happened to my child." The parents will say, "I didn't know my child was into that." While these parents are wearing designer clothes and trying to make payments, say, on a BMW or a big house, these kids are getting into things that the parents are not even aware of until their child ends up in court. The parents are about as shocked with their children as I am.

It's not just lower-class children that are out here doing things that are wrong. I get all classes in family court. Yes, I get the Rolls-Royce set. I get white and Black. I get more Black than I do white, but it is spread throughout the economic ladder. And that's bad.

Kids everywhere, of all classes, are just out of the box. They are incorrigible. It's more than just youthful rebelliousness.

In one case that really got to me I had to send a good kid to the Department of Youth Services. He was a good kid. He was not a troublemaker. But I had to send him to jail. This kid was a straight-A student, and he took his daddy's loaded gun to school to threaten some boys to leave him alone. A straight-A student. Can you believe that?

So what do you do with a kid who takes a loaded gun to school to threaten somebody? You have to send him to the Department of Youth Services, because you just don't take a loaded gun to school. This boy didn't see that the gun could go off and could kill somebody. He just said the boys were bothering him. I have no doubt that they were bothering him. My fear is that this kid will not be able to recover. That is my fear, but I had to send him to the Department of Youth Services. I had to send him there.

There is a movement afoot now in South Carolina not to put kids in the Department of Youth Services because it's not as focused on rehabilitation as it should be. I wish there was a place we could put them where they would truly be rehabilitated.

I took a day off last year and went and visited all of the youth jails in our state. It was disheartening, discouraging, and downright sad. I think it is a valuable experience for a jurist to visit these places. Jurists need to see where they are sending these kids. Now when I get ready to send them somewhere, I have this picture in my mind where they are going. I think more judges should go into these correctional facilities, visit the service agency, and see them for themselves.

These kids need to be rehabilitated. They need discipline. My husband is a first sergeant in the army, and he is very regimented. He does everything in a very disciplinary, regimented style. That's what I think we need with a lot of the kids who end up in family court. You've got to bring back that discipline in the homes and in the schools. My husband wants to go into the school system because he says the school systems need more men, more Black men, particularly at the elementary level.

I saw a show recently on *Sixty Minutes* about kids and gangs. Two of the kids featured on the show were in prison, and they were doing well. The commentator said that this was the only regimentation these two kids had ever had. Prison was the only kind of discipline they had ever had, and they were doing well in prison. That made me so sad. I was sad that some kids have to go to prison to get some kind of discipline.

There are people who are trying to develop alternatives on how best to handle the kids that come into the system. I'm not on the committee studying this, but Justice Toal, who is the only woman on our supreme court, told me they were trying to find alternative means of rehabilitating kids without locking them up.

I think this can be done in a community-based setting. I think that it can be done, and I think that if the parents understood and worked with the kids, that would help tremendously. I know this means investing a lot of time. I'm not a parent, but I tutor kids every Thursday, poor kids at a church. These are kids from the neighborhood who have a problem with homework. It is a real sacrifice of my time going in and going over it again and again with the kids who don't understand. I have got to stay there until they get it, and that means staying there from six to eight-thirty, which kills me. I say, Lord, if I had children at my house and I had to work all day, then go home to them every night and keep up with them on the weekends, I think I'd die.

It's a tremendous sacrifice dealing with kids. I can easily see why some parents don't want to make that sacrifice. They want their own time or they want to hang out and be into their own things. But it's their kids. They have to spend a lot of time with them.

I think that if you can get the parents involved and there is some community involvement, some structure, some church groups, some recreation, some soccer practices, football, whatever—I think it will work. We can work with these kids in a community setting, and we can work with them so they don't end up in family court. We need changes, too, in the larger system, in society. It's not just the criminal justice system. It's the family, the church, the community, the extended family.

Being a judge is something I've wanted to do probably all my life. I knew when I was very young that I wanted to be a lawyer.

I was raised right here in Columbia. I was able to read at a very early age because I had to know which water fountains to use. This was South Carolina, and they had separate fountains for whites and colored people. You had to be able to read to know which bathrooms to use.

My father and mother took us on tours everywhere when we were young. They were trying to expose us to everything. My parents were school teachers. When it was time for us to go to the courthouse, of course we had to go through the back door and sit in the balcony. My dad took my brother and me to the balcony, and we watched the proceedings. I was probably four or five at the time. Everyone in the court was white. The judge was white. The lawyers were white. The defendants and plaintiffs were white. The jury was white. I was so fascinated by the fact that the lawyer was representing people, just like on TV. I also knew then that Black people were still second-class citizens.

I went up to my dad one day, after he had explained to me what a lawyer was, and I said I wished I could be like the lawyers down there. He said, "Well, you can." My parents were very spiritual. What they were saying to me at that time was, if that's what you want to do, then that's what you do.

Even as a child I had a sense that women weren't lawyers. And I definitely had a sense that Black women, colored women, weren't lawyers. I grew up a confused child because my parents were telling me I could do anything and everything and there were no limitations, but I wasn't dumb. I saw that Blacks were suppressed and we weren't doing everything.

But I still said to myself, Well, you know, Dad and Mom said that if you believe in God and you work real hard, you'll get done what you need to get done, and that's how I have always approached things. I've always felt that if I work very hard and if I pray, then I will achieve, and that's what I did. I went through school telling everybody I was going to be a lawyer.

I went to the University of South Carolina here in Columbia. When I graduated I told my dad that I wanted to go to Georgetown for law school. He asked me where I was planning to practice law, and I said here in Columbia. And he said, knowing the South, I'd be better off going to law school at USC because the whole state revolves around USC's law school.

That was some wise advice because most of the lawyers you find in this area are from the University of South Carolina Law School. That is the only law school in the state. When I got ready to run for a judgeship the legislators who were lawyers were from USC Law School, the judges on the bench were from USC Law School, and my recommendations came from USC Law School. My father was absolutely right. I had wanted to get up north to law school and then come back. But it's harder to come back and fit in.

There were about twenty-five Black students in the law school when I entered. Seven graduated. I was in a class of about 282 students. Almost two hundred students in my class graduated, yet only seven of us who graduated were Black. They used to tell us that the attrition rate was very high at USC. It was high. I haven't been keeping up with it, but I suspect that it is a little better now at the Law School because there is a recognition that Black students were getting hit pretty hard.

It was a struggle in law school, but everything I have done has been a struggle. That struggle prepared me for the struggle to get on the bench. I studied really hard in law school and worked really hard. I am not a naturally bright student, so I worked extremely hard. It was so competitive the first year, just like the first year in any law school. The strongest survive, was the attitude. I've got mine, you get yours.

After the first year everything relaxed. By the second year everybody realized that we needed each other. A few of my professors warmed up after the first year. A few even became my mentors. That first year I cannot recall one professor who was receptive to the other Black students or me. But all law students were programmed to think that law professors are not very helpful or very encouraging.

While I was in law school I clerked for one of the judges on the court of appeals. Then I clerked at the public defender's office for two years, and when I passed the bar I went to the district attorney's office. In the DA's office I worked for the Highway Patrol. From there I went to the judgeship.

When I was with the public defender's office I really wanted to be a public defender. You know how idealists think they are going to save America. But I saw where the real power is and that you may need to position yourself somewhere else to save America. I learned that in the public defender's office. I learned that the real power was coming from the bench. That's when I decided I wanted to be a judge.

After deciding to be a judge, I knew I needed to see what happened in the district attorney's office. That's where I learned how cops look at people, and how juries think. I was in the public defender's office for about two years, and I stayed in the district attorney's office a little over four years. But all along I was plotting to get a judgeship.

The public defender's office taught me that I would have to get to the bench. My father and mother taught my brother and me to be very public-service oriented. That's why I have never gone into private practice. I never wanted to go into private practice. I never wanted to work for money. I wanted to do public service.

Family court in South Carolina handles juvenile matters, divorces, domestic matters, and adoptions. We also handle domestic abuse. Most of the people involved in domestic abuse cases are Black. Almost all of them are Black. I don't know why this is. Do they think that the court should solve their problems? I just don't know. Most of these cases involve the poor.

I would suspect that those with money know better than to bring their troubles into court unless they are going straight through a divorce. I get cases where they say, "He hit me," or "He stole my car," or "He won't let me see the children," or "He stole the children." So I say, "Are you gonna get a divorce?" They say no, they don't want a divorce. They just want their car back or just want their children back. They say, "He don't have no money." I said once, "Money or no money, it's time to divorce."

Most of the divorces involve white people. I have to divide the money. They have a lot of property and a lot of money. There are houses at the beach, in Bermuda, and in New York, there's a Rolls-Royce in storage, and there are coin collections and stamp collections. Black people basically do not have these types of assets. They don't have to divide anything.

I get a lot of satisfaction out of adoption cases. Whenever parents or adults adopt kids through the Department of Social Services, I get a good feeling from that. It's good to see Black foster parents who go in search of kids who need extra help and say they'll take them on. It's good to see people—any people—volunteering to be guardians.

I have approved interracial adoptions, adoptions in which white couples adopted Black kids. That's a controversial area. It was a lot for me to take in the first time I handled an interracial adoption case. I looked down there, saw this white couple and this baby, and I flipped through my notes and saw this was an African American baby—oh, my heart failed.

But then I began to read the file, and the social worker was Black and she took the stand and said, "We have so many Black babies and anytime somebody will take a child and give it a home, we are in favor of it." They brought in psychologists, they brought in church members. I questioned those people. I questioned them about raising a Black child, giving the child a sense of Malcolm X and Martin Luther King, and the parents' response was that they had read all about them. They said they planned for the child to know the heritage of his people. I said, "Why a Black baby?" And they said they were from this Christian sect that wanted to do something for children and make it count. They had heard there was an oversupply of Black kids available for adoption in Columbia.

I said to myself, Maybe it is best that I give them a baby. I went and told one of the white judges that it was hard for me to approve that adoption. He said, "I think it was great. I would have come down there and shaken their hands, because any time you can find a family for a child, then you have done something." That kid will end up learning as much about Black history as I did growing up, because his parents will teach him. Besides, there are a lot of Black families that don't teach Black history.

I also get satisfaction from cases in which the kids seem really to have learned their lesson from the Department of Youth Services. Then you don't hear from them anymore. A lot of the kids I send to the Department of Youth Services, I see come back again and again. But every now and then there is one kid who will say, "You will never see me, Judge Rogers, ever again," and I don't see them. Now, that is the best feeling.

TIMOTHY K. LEWIS

"I will not let my appointments become a defense for the indefensible."

Third Circuit Court Judge Timothy Lewis was the youngest member of the federal judiciary when he was appointed in 1991, at the age of thirty-six, to the federal district court bench in Pittsburgh. Lewis maintained that age distinction when he was appointed to the appeals court bench eighteen months later.

Lewis was one of only two Black jurists among President Bush's more than thirty appointments to the federal appeals bench. The paucity of Black judges selected for the federal bench is a source of widespread criticism of both Bush and his predecessor, Ronald Reagan. While publicly commending Bush for appointing him, Lewis has also publicly criticized Bush and Reagan for including so few Blacks in their nearly one thousand federal judicial appointments.

A former county and federal prosecutor who graduated from Duquesne Law School, Lewis entered the law with the intention of becoming a criminal defense lawyer. Lewis is a native of Pittsburgh, Pennsylvania, and his family roots in the area date from the early nineteenth century. Like some of his ancestors who were active in the Underground Railroad and other struggles against societal deprivations, Lewis is dedicated to making the concept of equal justice under the law a reality for all.

Judge Lewis was interviewed in his Pittsburgh chambers in January 1993.

The politics behind federal judicial appointments is really fascinating. I'm sure my being a registered Republican was a benefit. But I was never really active in partisan politics, as a Republican or a Democrat.

I registered as a Republican following the defeat of President Jimmy Carter. I had switched my registration because there was a lot of talk in Pittsburgh and around the country about how the Republican Party wanted more Black participation. A few of us thought this might provide a good opportunity to make some positive changes. Things never quite worked out as we wished. Plus, I became a prosecutor a short time later and could not participate in partisan politics.

I have been through two judicial confirmations in about eighteen months: one for the federal district court and the other for the court of appeals. I did not aspire to become a judge. I was asked to apply for the vacancy on the federal district court in 1990. I did so. The process began, and I became a federal judge.

The first time I went through the confirmation process it was difficult because I had not experienced so much paper pushing and application completing in my life. It took a great deal of time. Yet it was a very educational experience for me and, of course, well worth it.

The second process for the appeals court was much more difficult, for a number of reasons. Once again I really had no aspiration to go on the court of appeals. I did not apply for the position. I did not ask for the position. I was contacted by the Bush administration and asked if I would be interested in going to Washington to be interviewed for the court of appeals. I was quite happy and quite satisfied in my new position as a district court judge. Things were going well and I was enjoying myself, so I had serious reservations about giving up such a fine position for a position that I really didn't know whether I would enjoy as much.

Ultimately I decided that I had a responsibility to many people who had done a great deal before me and I owed it to them to seriously pursue the court of appeals position. I felt a responsibility to people like the late Judge Hastie, who was the nation's first Black federal appeals judge, Judge Leon Higginbotham, and my mentor in the legal profession, Wendell Freeland. I decided to pursue the offer, and fortunately it worked out under rather unusual circumstances.

Last year was a presidential election year and the confirmation process during an election year is unusual and fraught with difficulties. I was confirmed to the Third Circuit Court of Appeals under some very unusual and difficult circumstances. The most distressing of these circumstances occurred during an interview with the Department of Justice.

During the two confirmations, I had been very pleased that just about everybody who interviewed me at the Department of Justice was truly professional and as a matter of fact, went out of their way to try to help me in this process and were extremely gracious. Yet there was one person who interviewed me, whom I will not identify, that convinced me that the process might be different for Blacks than for whites, and I was quite disappointed to see that. I was asked my views, for example, on racial segregation, housing desegregation, school desegregation, affirmative action, and the problems of the inner city. Now, as a sitting federal judge, I was taken aback that anyone—especially a lawyer at the U.S. Department of Justice—would ask me questions like that during an interview for a position on the court of appeals. Fortunately that was an isolated incident. Everybody else whom I spoke with at the Department of Justice was wonderful and went out of their way to be fair and very balanced. But I was surprised at that situation, and I thought that it was inappropriate.

Over the past twelve years very few Blacks have been appointed by the administrations that have been in power. This low number of appointments by Presidents Reagan and Bush was not good enough. Reagan and Bush didn't do enough, particularly in appointments to the courts of appeal.

Last October there was a historic gathering in Chicago, when for the first time all of the Black members of the federal judiciary got together, all sixty or so of us. It was uplifting and it was important, but when we went home and back to work we were either the only Black or one of but a handful. Some of my colleagues and I are acutely aware of the dearth of representation of Blacks on the federal bench.

I am grateful to President Bush for my two appointments. I have publicly commended him for my appointments. But I have also publicly criticized both Bush and Reagan for their record on Black judicial appointments, which clearly is not worthy of commendation.

I will not let my appointment to the court of appeals become a defense for the indefensible. I am the only Black person who was appointed to a court of appeals in the past four years who is still there. In the history of the United States there have been but sixteen such appointments since Judge William Hastie was appointed by President Truman to the Third Circuit in 1949.

While there have been more, there have still not been enough appointments of Blacks to the district courts since Judge James Parsons of the Northern District of Illinois was appointed by President Kennedy in 1961. The United States Courts of Appeals, as Judge Higginbotham has accurately noted, serve as the courts of last resort for more than 99 percent of federal litigants. Very few of the cases appealed to the U.S. Supreme Court are accepted for review. The courts of appeals are the courts for the vast majority of the litigants. So how can anyone not notice that something is wrong when there are only seven active Black judges serving on those courts?

The vast majority of our state court systems, particularly at the appellate level, are no better when you consider the disparity between the number of appointed and elected Black judges throughout this country and the number of white judges. I recently read in the newsletter of the Joint Center for Political Studies that while there are a total of 526 Black state court judges in the United States, the number of Black judges serving on state courts of last resort is just eight.

There are only eight Blacks serving on state supreme courts, the courts of last resort for their respective state court system. But as pathetic as that number is, for the past twelve years the appointment of Blacks to the federal bench, which does not require a statewide campaign and access to funds and reliance upon the whims and the vagaries of the electorate, has been at a comparative standstill. There are many excuses offered, none particularly impressive, for the low level of Black federal appointments under Reagan and Bush. I heard that there weren't enough Blacks of the proper political persuasion, that there weren't enough Blacks with the appropriate background and qualifications, and on and on.

Of course we need people of experience, judgment, honor, and, above all, integrity of the highest order. Yet there are Blacks who easily fit that bill. There are many, many African American lawyers and judges who are competent, capable, ready, and willing to serve this country as members of its federal judiciary. They have been ignored, and that is not a good thing for this country. It is my hope that this situation will improve, and I think it is very important that a greater emphasis be placed on finding these people. They are not hiding. They are not difficult to find.

The sad truth is that in the years since Judge Hastie was appointed in 1949, with the exception of the years 1976 through 1980, when Jimmy Carter was president, there has been a palpable lack of concern among too many of the people who are in a position to do something about it. Carter appointed more Black federal appeals and district judges than any president in history, probably combined. Judge Stephen Reinhardt of the Ninth Circuit was not wrong when, in referring to the courts of appeals, he called them "a symbol of white power."

I want to be clear here. I do not wish to appear ungrateful for the fact that I was appointed to two federal benches in the short span of one and a half years, particularly in light of the fact that I was, at the time of both appointments, the youngest federal judge in the country. I am extremely grateful for both appointments and consider myself fortunate to be where I am today. But I know exactly how and why I got here. And I believe I know what to do now that I am here. I also know what I do not want to do. I do not want to become lonely.

I was the youngest federal judge in the United States when I was appointed to the district court bench in 1991. I was also the youngest federal judge ever appointed here in western Pennsylvania. Receiving an appointment to the federal bench at a young age was difficult in some respects and it was irrelevant in most others.

The fact that I am thirty-eight now as opposed to fifty-eight really doesn't mean anything to me. My age was and is irrelevant. I have the same work load that everybody else has, and I try to do my job the same as everybody else does. I suppose there was a natural tendency for many to question whether or not I was ready to serve as a judge because of my young age.

I recognize that most people have a certain image of a judge and that it includes a bit more gray hair than I have been able to accumulate up to now and a little bit more experience than I had before I went on the district court. I was aware of that and only that. My awareness of those images, I suppose, added to the sense of importance I placed on meeting my standards of excellence. I suppose I should add another invisible force that drives me: the image of Blacks not being good enough. That image is preposterous, and I want to prove it so every day.

Becoming a judge was never a goal I had set for my life. My goal in life was meeting my own personal standards of excellence. All I wanted to be was the best possible lawyer.

I knew from the time I was seven or eight years old that the law was going to be my choice. From as early as I can remember my father implored me that I should only consider the three professional endeavors that, based on his life experiences, offered the best potential for equality and excellence and success while enabling me to return something of value—even if just of symbolic value—to my community and to my country. I was thus limited to a career in either medicine, dentistry, or law. He told my brother, my sister, and me that those were the only three options available to us.

My father told me that and admonished me that way because he was convinced that those were the only three areas of pursuit that Blacks could use to overcome racism and segregation in this country and at the same time make a meaningful contribution not only to their community but to the country. This conviction of my father's grew out of his experiences growing up in Pittsburgh, which was a segregated upbringing, and the experiences he had with segregation in the army, where he was beaten in the South.

My father was beaten by army MPs when he was stationed at Fort Rucker in Alabama during World War II. He had the temerity to object when a store clerk in town refused to fix the stem on his watch because "niggers weren't allowed" into this particular shop. My father questioned why the clerk wouldn't fix his watch when he was wearing the uniform of the United States Army and it was wartime. The clerk told him he must be one of them northern niggers who didn't know his place down there in Alabama. One irony was my father felt relieved when two passing MPs were called into the shop. The MPs listened as both my father and the clerk explained their sides, and then they grabbed my father, took him outside, beat him up, threw him in a jeep, and took him back to base, where he was thrown in jail.

I don't know what it was exactly that caused me to decide at such an early age to study law instead of studying dentistry as my father had. It might have been the fact that there were always lawyers around my house. There were people like Wendell Freeland, who was very active in the civil rights movement. He had a commanding presence at our dining-room table. And there was Henry Smith, who went on to become a common pleas court judge in Pittsburgh. These men inspired me. For whatever reason, I knew at any early age that I was going to become a lawyer, and there was never any question about it from that point on.

Mr. Freeland became my mentor. Even at an early age we would debate things and discuss things. When I was just a kid Wendell Freeland allowed me to sit around his office, listening to him and learning from him. I watched him put together important civil rights cases. He was the senior vice president of the National Urban League at a time of difficulty and turmoil. It was Wendell Freeland who first introduced me to the classics and to the works of men like John Marshall, John Harlan, Langston Hughes, E. B. White, and Richard Kluger. I came to understand that the pursuit of the knowledge of man and man's knowledge of himself is relevant to the practice of law, that we derive an understanding of issues not just through tangling with the applicable law but through a knowledge of ourselves and our world and of mankind which transcends the law. This does not control how I rule as a judge, but it should and does affect the way I think. Part of my enthusiasm for being on the court of appeals derives from the opportunity it affords me to seize the intellectual challenges and to define and continue to refine a judicial philosophy. But Wendell had planted these seeds before I even knew what the *Federal Reporter* was.

Prior to becoming a district court judge it was fortunate that I had served as a federal prosecutor for so many years. As a result of trying cases in federal court for all those years I was familiar with the federal rules of evidence, the federal rules of criminal procedure, and most of the procedures of the court itself. I had not, however, had any civil experience before I became a federal judge, and I knew that I would have a lot of work to do in that respect; but it was a challenge to me, and it was a challenge that I embraced as I embrace all challenges. It was a challenge that I met with great enthusiasm. It was not intimidating. I was confident that I would perform the job well.

The transition period from bar to bench for me was made a bit easier by virtue of my decisions as far as my staff was concerned. I hired two law clerks, for example, who had been practicing for a number of years rather than hiring people right out of law school. The clerks I hired had a lot of civil experience, which I did not have, and that helped me a great deal. One of the clerks I hired also had been a federal court law clerk before, and that was very helpful to me.

But most of all I knew, as I have always known, that there is absolutely nothing that one cannot do if one puts one's mind to it and works extremely hard. It doesn't matter how old you are. It doesn't matter what your background is. Nothing matters as long as you are willing and able to commit and to work; then there is nothing that one cannot accomplish. That goes back, again, to what my father taught me, what he overcame. I learned those lessons my father taught me at a very early age, and I see their value today.

I don't think I would be sitting here today as a member of the Third Circuit Court of Appeals if it had not been for the efforts, the beliefs, and the accomplishments of my ancestors. The history of my father's family and the way it influenced my father and was then passed on to me is an important part of my being here.

My father was born poor and didn't really have much to look forward to in his life. He was born right before the depression. By then the family had lost whatever it had been able to accumulate through the generations. There was a lot of deprivation, discrimination, and racial segregation, and my father's only sense of direction came from knowing what his ancestors had been able to accomplish under extremely difficult circumstances during the 1800s. This legacy of accomplishment provided my father a source of inspiration and motivation.

My father's family has been in the Pittsburgh area since the 1830s. One of the patriarchs of my father's family was Louis Woodson, who founded the first Black church in Pittsburgh, the First Bethel AME Church. Louis was the son of Thomas Woodson, who moved his family here to Pittsburgh back in the early 1830s. Thomas Woodson had been born a slave in Virginia but was able to purchase his freedom at a young age. He then moved to Ohio and finally here to Pittsburgh.

Louis Woodson also became a very important advocate in Pennsylvania for the abolitionist movement. Woodson, along with a number of other Black ministers, founded a few stations in Pittsburgh and western Pennsylvania for the Underground Railroad. The Underground Railroad helped slaves escape to the north and into Canada.

Louis Woodson was sort of an activist of his time. He wrote a number of pieces about the abolitionist movement. These articles and essays are, by the way, very eloquent, very beautifully written. I have a number of them. Many of them were written under the pen name of Augustine, and they were sent to newspaper editors throughout the northeast, trying to help gather support for the abolitionist cause.

Louis Woodson not only believed strongly in a very firm, disciplined approach to life generally but in education. Even back then, in the 1800s, he saw to it that all his children were educated. He was one of the cofounders of Wilberforce University in Ohio and was throughout his life very committed to education. He helped educate Martin Delaney, who lived in Pittsburgh for a period of time. Delaney studied under my great, great, great, great grandfather—I believe I counted enough "great grands" in there—and went on to become a very important African American leader in the second half of the 1800s. Delaney is considered by many to be the father of Black Nationalism. I am very proud of my family legacy, and it has always been a very important part of my own self-perspective.

My father often told me that when he was growing up he felt he was destined to go on and do something, no matter what obstacles were placed in his way. He was forced to go to a segregated school. He was not permitted to go to the high school of his choice because the school had already met its quota for Black students. My father was sent to trade school to become an auto mechanic. Then, through the G.I. Bill, he was later able to go to college. He made it through college and dental school in forty-eight months. As a matter of fact, he never graduated from college, but they didn't learn that until right before he was graduating from dental school. By then it was too late, so they had to let him go through with graduation. What fueled his motivation and what made it possible for him to do what he did was his knowledge of what members of his family had been able to do in even more difficult times.

There was far less emphasis placed on family histories and legacies when I was growing up than there is now. I really acquired my sense of direction during the 1960s, and that was not a time when we looked too far back for motivation or for inspiration. All one had to do then was turn on the television or have a conversation with a neighbor to get motivation. But I always knew that Louis Woodson and others were part of my family history and that this was a part of the history of Black Americans that went well beyond my family. I also knew that this history of Black Americans was not a part of our history books and that too few people, white and Black, were aware of this history. But it meant something to me. And I think that it helped give me a sense of inner strength that made it more likely that I would be able to do something with my life.

Even before I went to law school my goal was to become a criminal defense lawyer. I had studied the great defense lawyer Clarence Darrow. I had read his biography by Irving Stone. I believe I had watched my dear friend Wendell Freeland in court. He was a fine criminal defense lawyer. At some point I also had an interest in becoming involved in a group that Julian Bond had put together, the Southern Poverty Law Center. I was thinking of moving out of Pittsburgh and going down South and devoting some time to that Center.

But when I was in law school I had an opportunity to spend some time working as an intern at the district attorney's office for Allegheny County, and I became convinced that the best way for me to hone my skills as a criminal defense attorney was to spend some time working at a district attorney's office. I went to the DA's office upon graduation from law school, and my idea was that I would spend a couple of years doing that and then take my acquired knowledge and skills over to the other side and become an effective advocate for the poor, the powerless, and the penniless.

In spite of my plans, two years into my work as an assistant district attorney, I received an offer to go to work as an assistant United States Attorney. At that time there had been only a handful of Blacks, perhaps four, who had ever worked in the U.S. Attorney's office in Pittsburgh. I felt then as I do today: one does not turn down the opportunity to help pioneer and to help serve as a pioneer. I could not turn down the opportunity to get some experience as an assistant U.S. Attorney. It just turned out that I stayed much longer than I had planned. I think I stayed there for about eight and a half years. I had no intention of ever being a career prosecutor. It just turned out that way, and I still have not realized my ultimate goal of serving as a criminal defense attorney. Who knows? Maybe at some point I will, but not right now.

I learned a lot about the nature of crime as a prosecutor. So much of the nature of crime is circumstantial, and by that I mean it is rooted in a person's life circumstances at that particular moment. It should not be a surprise to anyone that most crime in this country is committed by people who don't have means, economic means. People who are poor have to find an alternative means of acquiring much of anything. Now this is certainly not an excuse for the commission of crime. But we have very deep-rooted, cyclical problems in this society and nothing much is being done to treat them. The problems that give rise to crime are joblessness, poverty, a lack of empowerment, and a lack of direction.

I suppose the predominant lesson I learned as a prosecutor was this:

often the reasons for the commission of a particular crime go well beyond the apparent facts of the case. Of course, there are some people who simply enjoy committing crime. There are some people just looking to do bad things. They enjoy harming other people. They enjoy stealing from other people. There are just some people out there who really are sick and who get a kick out of crime. But I'd have to say that, by and large, our crime problem is linked very closely to the economic difficulties that this country faces.

The criminal justice system is not necessarily a part of the crime problem. I think there are many, many reasons for the crime rate in this country that go beyond the system itself. I recently read an article put out by the Joint Center for Political and Economic Studies on Black single-parent families and the difficulties young Black males have today. There is a correlation between the extremely high jobless rate among young Black males and the crime problem in the Black community. Crime, like many of our other problems, has a lot to do with the direction that this country is taking in terms of economic conditions and the various social policies that directly affect people's lives.

The dynamics that drive crime among the poor are different from those behind white-collar crime. White-collar offenses are fueled primarily by greed, not so much by need as by greed. There are circumstances in which people feel that, for whatever reason, they have run a huge debt or have come across hard times and think that they need more when in fact, if they just worked a little bit harder, they would not. Anyway, these people have been prompted to create elaborate schemes to defraud others. But by and large it is greed that gives rise to a desire to bilk people out of huge sums of money, whether it is a bank, a group of investors, or whatever the case might be.

White-collar crime is not the predominant crime in this country, although clearly white-collar crime is the most costly in terms of dollar amounts taken. However, we spend more public tax dollars combating street crime. The state court systems are clogged with the predominant type of crime—street crime. The federal courts handle more of the white-collar crime.

We as a society, and our legal system, treat white-collar crime and street crime differently in many respects. First of all, I think that the penalties for first-time offenders in white-collar crimes are far more lenient than they are for the typical first-time perpetrator of street crime. Society may have good reasons for the disparity in sentencing schemes in that regard. It may be that society, expressing itself through state legislatures and through the national legislature, simply feels there is a greater threat, a greater danger from street crime than from white-collar crime.

I think that juries look at white-collar criminals a little bit differently. I think the sentences that are meted out tend to be comparatively lenient, and I think that the nature of the offenses themselves is sometimes more difficult to establish and more akin to a civil case and a civil investigation than a criminal case. The civil nature of white-collar crime in turn makes it more difficult for the juries to understand and more difficult for judges to comprehend. Street crime and white-collar crime are considered to have different characteristics, and as a result there are some disparities in response and treatment.

There are instances in which the criminal justice system has failed African Americans in ways that it has not failed white Americans. When you talk about the criminal justice system you are not just talking about what happens in court. The criminal justice system includes police officers, prosecutors, defense lawyers, judges, and juries.

Anyone who observed the Rodney King trial in Los Angeles last year would have to seriously question the system. I was not in the jury room and I respect the decisions of juries too much to state that their decision was wrong, but I would have to question—seriously question—whether or not the fact that the police officers in that case were white and the alleged victim was Black had something to do with the verdict. There was a predominately white jury in Simi Valley.

Every day in this country someone makes a decision that an objective observer could look at and deem racist, whether it was a decision to arrest, a decision to prosecute, a decision to convict, or a decision about sentencing. Our justice system has by no means been purged entirely of racism, and I have personally seen examples of it, as has any Black and as has any white person who has spent a considerable amount of time working with the system. The system tries to be fair, but it is not without prejudices and racism, the same as society.

I do not believe that racism is a predominant, prevalent factor in our criminal justice system. It is there. I know it is there. I also know that most judges, white and Black, try very hard to be fair. My experiences as a prosecutor and judge have shown me that judges try to put aside their personal predilections and judge cases fairly. I believe most juries try hard to be fair and to perform their very difficult task in a way that would exclude any hint of racism. But when you are talking about an institution, which racism is, that in turn has permeated every institution in this country in one way or another, one certainly cannot conclude that our system of justice is devoid of racism any more than one could conclude that the political system or the corporate system is devoid of racism. We have not come to that point yet. That is why we have so many civil rights cases pending today.

I recall when I was an assistant district attorney there was a controversy about prosecutors deliberately striking Blacks from serving on juries in which the defendant was Black, and I have participated in jury selection as both an assistant district attorney and as an assistant United States Attorney where white defense lawyers have deliberately struck prospective Black jurors because I was prosecuting the case. They believed I would have some greater ability to communicate with Black jurors which would be an advantage to the prosecution. I have seen this form of racism in jury selection work both ways on both sides, and it is a part of the institutional racism that I was referring to.

Whenever I have been involved in cases, either as a prosecutor or as a judge, in which I have seen an action that may have had racial overtones, I have stepped in, either openly or privately, to see to it that the issue of racism is addressed.

I have privately spoken with defense attorneys who I felt were striking Black jurors from the panel for purely racial reasons. I've done this on a number of occasions when the defense attorney for a white defendant would strike Black jurors out of fear that since I was Black the Black jurors would not be fair to his client. This was an example of abuse of the system along racial lines. It was an insult to me and an insult to the potential jurors.

I do not think the average American citizen has an adequate understanding of the judicial system and how it works. I don't think we have performed our responsibility in that respect, although I am not really convinced that it is necessarily the responsibility of the judicial system to educate the public. There is much that goes on during the course of a trial and during the entire course of processing the accused through the criminal justice system that the public does not understand. That's everything from jury selection to the judge's charge, which is the instructions the jury is given to apply to the facts of the case. Understanding the various parts of the process is important because it permits people to make much more informed assessments of whether or not the system as a whole has performed its job. While this understanding begins in the schools, I also feel the media has a responsibility to concentrate less on sensationalizing and more on educating. I think that would help the public a great deal.

I agree with people who, like law professor Derrick Bell, feel that the law has not met our expectations as a vehicle for overcoming racism. The law can only do so much to fulfill the commitment to equality under the law as articulated in the U.S. Constitution. It is my belief that racism can only be eradicated through unrelenting education to dispel the underlying ignorance that is its cause. The law can help. We see this on the legislative level. In the past few years the national legislature has reacted to U.S. Supreme Court decisions that have rolled back civil rights gains. The 1991 Civil Rights Restoration Law is an example of how legislatures can act. The law has served and will always serve a key purpose, but there must be people out in the community and in the corporate world speaking the gospel of the need to eliminate racism.

Today's emphasis on racial problems is not necessarily all bad, because there can be some positive effects in terms of heightening awareness of the resurgence of racism. The question of how to get rid of racism remains, and many, like Professor Bell, feel racism is an evil that can't be gotten rid of. I'm not quite that pessimistic. Blacks holding key positions in government will bring down barriers. When you see Blacks leading the U.S. Commerce Department, like Ron Brown, who is doing an excellent job, and Blacks leading the military, like Colin Powell, you can no longer say that Blacks can't do the job.

Like Judge Higginbotham I also believe that our society needs more emphasis on pluralism and diversity. Pluralism and diversity will have an impact. There is a need for diversity in every important institution in American life, maybe more so in the judiciary than in other institutions. This diversity is not for the sake of diversity but for the sake of pluralism.

I do not believe that the judiciary or the country would be helped by the appointment of judges strictly for the sake of diversity. I think that it is important to put more than just a face or a gender on the court. It is important to put somebody who brings with them a sense of themselves and a sense of whatever their race or their gender happens to be in the context of the court and the world. Pluralism is one of the basic tenets of a constitutional democracy. Diversity for the sake of diversity is an empty gesture. It smacks of tokenism. I believe that tokenism is abhorrent to fundamental notions of a constitutional democracy.

We need to have women on the bench, federal and state. We need to have Blacks. We need to have Hispanics. We need more than ever before to have more persons on the bench from groups that have been historically excluded from participation in the federal judiciary, so that our judiciary is improved, so that our country is improved. Anytime that more people from diverse backgrounds and experiences become a part of any system, the marketplace of ideas, the pluralism I described, is improved, because there is a wider range of perspectives, which ultimately improves fairness.

United States Supreme Court Justice Sandra Day O'Connor spoke to that issue when she wrote a tribute to Justice Marshall. In that article Justice O'Connor wrote about Justice Marshall's contributions in conference, when cases before the Supreme Court are discussed. She spoke of his eloquent discussions of his background as a civil rights lawyer traveling the southern backroads, trying cases under difficult circumstances and settings. O'Connor stated how Marshall's perspective taught her certain things that were very important for her to understand as a Supreme Court justice. That is an example of the importance of having diversity.

We will continue to see, I hope, an increase in the level of African American representation on the bench as more and more Black law students graduate from law schools and do well in various areas of the law. As these graduates go on to teach at some of the better law schools, as many of these graduates work in some of the better firms, or work as district attorneys as I did or as public defenders getting hands-on experience in trying cases, they will establish the track record of experience necessary for judicial service.

But I think the real key is that no matter what young Black lawyers make, no matter where they work, it is critical at all times for them to keep in mind a standard of excellence that must be met under all circumstances. If that is the focus, everything else should take care of itself. Things will become more equal if that standard is met constantly. And there is one other area that I think should be emphasized. While it is critical that we maintain a sense of heritage about ourselves as Black people and Black lawyers, it is also critical that as professionals our performance and our perspective of ourselves transcend race.

A young lawyer is a lawyer, not a Black lawyer or a white lawyer. A young lawyer should be a lawyer first in terms of getting the job done. Then, when for reasons of pluralism and trying to improve the overall status it is necessary to work in certain areas, then the identity can change. But when it comes to appearing in court, when it comes to preparing pleadings, when it comes to writing a memorandum for a senior partner, when it comes to all of those things that are really tied in with the performance of a lawyer, a person should be a lawyer first and a Black lawyer second. I think that is a very important point that young people have to focus on.

I think younger judges add to the diversity that is needed on the bench. I'd like to think that younger judges might bring a fresh perspective. Perhaps, they just bring a sense of enthusiasm that is related to their youth.

It is only recently that those of us who came into our own during the 1960s have begun to assume positions of importance within the United States government and within other governmental institutions. We bring the background of those turbulent times to these positions. I think that our perspectives and the depth of our understanding have been influenced by that time. That influence is intangible, but it is nonetheless an identifiable part of our perspective. I think that anyone who has come through that emotionally, politically, intellectually, and socially tumultuous time and who has spent time not only reflecting on it but carrying those reflections forward into the 1980s and 1990s is more perceptive. So I think young judges bring that experience in a difficult period to our perspective.

The perspective of the sixties tempered by time ties into my basic sense of what a judge is supposed to be. In my view a judge is someone who should be engaged in a continuing effort to pursue the knowledge of man and man's knowledge of himself. I don't know if there is another time in our nation's history when that pursuit was furthered as it was in the 1960s, and those of us who came through that period really do bring a lot to the table today. So, to the extent that a wide-ranging sense of mankind is the most significant feature to judging—and I think it is—our education was intensified during that period, and that helps.

The law is certainly a vehicle for change, for social change. Laws are enacted by state legislatures and by our national legislatures. Judges are then given the very difficult responsibility of interpreting and applying those laws. I think that in the course of doing so, we judges must understand and remain conscious of not only our national history but our constitutional history. The decisions by the United States Supreme Court in the areas many people would view as areas impacting social change have done just that for the betterment of the country, the other branches of government, our constitutional democracy, and the court itself. I do think the law can be used and has been used effectively as a vehicle for social change. However, judges ought not be social engineers.

It is such an honor to serve on the same court that Judge William Hastie and Judge Leon Higginbotham served so long and so well. I have two strongly ambivalent feelings about serving on the same court as Hastie and Higginbotham. One is an almost indescribable sense of pride and humility. Judges Hastie and Higginbotham are giants in the legal profession. Their influence and their importance as judges transcend race, and in some sense even transcend the law. They have made contributions to our society and to our constitutional democracy that will not be seen for many, many years to come. They are just people who were extraordinary in their abilities, and they combined their abilities with a very strong sense of themselves and of this country and of the world. That combination is very difficult to come by.

The other strong feeling I have being on this court is how difficult if not impossible it will be for me to maintain the high standards of Judges Hastie and Higginbotham. I will certainly do my best, but I think my responsibility in that regard is just overwhelming. Yet if I can uphold the legacies of Judge Hastie and Judge Higginbotham in a respectable fashion, then I will feel that I have done well. If I can carry their legacies forward in a way that is worthy of pride, then I will be quite satisfied with my job.

The legacy of Hastie and Higginbotham is a legacy of striving for excellence in all phases of one's life. Theirs is a legacy of commitment to excellence to further the demanding standard that Dr. Du Bois and others advocated, which was an emphasis on the importance of showing that one is capable of doing anything and everything others are doing, and going beyond. I view the work of Hastie, Charles Houston, Higginbotham, Thurgood Marshall, and others as furthering the commitment of Du Bois.

This legacy involves recognition of one's work as a Black judge and its importance to the Black community and every litigant who appears before you. This legacy, I think, also involves a strong commitment to civil rights. Leon Higginbotham is an excellent example of a judge who has retained his commitment to civil rights. It is always important to understand that racism is alive and well in this country, and it is the responsibility of Black leaders to do all they can to make sure the situation of racism in the country changes. Black judges fall into the category of Black leaders.

I view my position on the court of appeals as no different than my position as a lawyer or as a district court judge. As Wendell Freeland said at my investiture for the Third Circuit, it is my task to teach the next course in Black excellence. I share that responsibility with a number of other people who are engaged in a number of other pursuits. I take that responsibility extremely seriously. In addition to my duties as a judge, I will be mindful of my responsibility to Black excellence at all times, and I will be thinking of Judges Hastie and Higginbotham as I try to do so.

Part V

CLOSING ARGUMENT

BRUCE M. WRIGHT

"Black judges should not be emotionally white."

There is a picture of the legendary nineteenth-century Black activist Frederick Douglass on the wall of the chambers of New York Supreme Court justice Bruce Wright. Wright is fond of noting that Douglass always challenged injustice, and in his last will and testament the fiery activist urged his fellow African Americans to "agitate, agitate, agitate."

Bruce Wright has accepted Douglass's charge literally and figuratively. A feisty septuagenarian, Wright has consistently challenged racist actions by white jurists, both as a lawyer and jurist, often going as far as filing formal disciplinary complaints. Following his appointment to New York City's criminal court in 1970 Wright's refusal to allow the police free reign of his courtroom made him a bitter enemy of the police union, which frequently filed formal complaints against him.

Wright's agitation reached the level of art form when, in 1987, he authored the scathing indictment of racism in the judicial system Black Robes, White Justice, *which included the names of fellow jurists whom he considered guilty of racist behavior.*

A graduate of Lincoln University and the New York Law School, Wright's passionate avocations include writing poetry and listening to jazz. As an attorney he represented many legendary jazzmen, including drummer Art Blakey.

Judge Wright was interviewed in his chambers at the New York County Courthouse in November 1992.

Racism in the courts is camouflaged by politeness. Racism is camouflaged by judges not saying, "Nigger, I'm going to give you the maximum." Racism is camouflaged by judges acting as though everything is OK, everything is equal, but making up their minds in advance. Racism is camouflaged by judges indulging their preconceptions based purely on racial things, like, for example, the way a Black man walks. There is a certain arrogant swagger to a lot of Black men. A good psychologist would call this swagger "compensatory arrogance"—the person literally has nothing material to be arrogant about, so he becomes arrogant about his manhood and mannerisms. Many white judges, however, believe this swagger is a sign of guilt.

Law and not justice is what is emphasized in America. The arena of justice is a confused and baffled world. Improving the quality of justice in our criminal courts depends upon judges and their understandings.

Most of the judges in America are white and male. The law is too pale and too male. Most of these judges have worn the badge of their privileged white skin with all kinds of arrogance. They have no idea of the insults that have been handed out to us and no idea how all the sensitive ones among us have suffered all kinds of emotional trauma. These insults, these injustices are things that make you angry. These things will make you so tense, you will be past tense, damn it.

I don't think we will ever achieve equal justice in this country as long as people perceive color and as long as color suggests what it does in the minds of the people who perceive it. One of my colleagues once wanted to show me what a great liberal he was. He said, "You know, Bruce, you are always talking about racism." He says, "We never see the color of the defendant when he stands before the bench." He told me he had "a little colored kid" before him a few days prior and didn't notice his color. Here he was trying to tell me how liberal he was and that he did not notice the color. This claim of not seeing color but clearly seeing color is fairly typical.

Color consciousness is deeply embedded in our culture. There seems to be almost a chemical reaction in people about skin color. I remember one day I was on the bench and I was feeling exhausted. In addition to my judicial duties I was teaching at three colleges. Well, I got tired on the bench and my staff thought I was having a heart attack. They rushed me to the hospital and I was put in a room with a white derelict. I was well dressed and the derelict had on mismatched clothes. I remember hearing the nurse say, "Hurry, Doctor. We have a judge in the room." When the doctor came into the room he immediately went to the white derelict. That color-conscious reaction effected an immediate cure in me. I took my exhaustion home.

One of my long-standing and persistent concerns has been the large number of white judges who are called upon daily to preside over the trials of Black defendants accused of crime. What magic abolishes color in their eyes? What magic gives these judges instant objectivity, the ability to analyze human foibles entirely divorced from historical racism? Whites, even liberal whites, are weaned on racism.

Yes, I'm concerned about racism in the courts. I'm concerned about the judge in Memphis who awarded a white man workman's compensation because the man said he couldn't work with Blacks. I'm concerned about the federal judge who said that only two or three of the fifty-six blows delivered to Rodney King were serious. I'm concerned about the judge in Los Angeles who gave a Korean woman probation for murdering a Black teenage girl in cold blood. All of these flawed judgments are the result of the privilege of the judges' white skin.

Another of my concerns is the pageant of the poor that come through our courts every day. Every day these urban peasants are judged by those who are ignorant of and indifferent to the debased reality they live. Seldom do judges have any personal familiarity with the realities that impact upon the lives of poor people. They know nothing about the realities that diminish the lives of the poor. What do these judges study in college or law school that might adequately prepare them to preside over the lives of these aliens to their lifestyles, these outsiders to their churches, these people they may even consider enemies?

Racism in the courts is a subject I have been making speeches on for a long time, long before I wrote the book, long before I became a judge. My book seems to have touched on some exposed nerves.

I have tried to reform the system and rehabilitate judges, but I understand my efforts to challenge racism are doomed to failure. I'm an Afro-Greek Sisyphus. I thought my book would help civilize my white colleagues and Black brethren who turned white overnight once they put on Black robes. But I discovered that civilizing the KKK or Aryans would be easier than civilizing my fellow judges. Judges feel they are a part of the domestic elite.

Not so long ago, a blue-ribbon task force studied the New York state court system and found it to be infested with racism. I wouldn't call this finding a vindication of my views, because the racism still exists. It is difficult to tell judges anything. They speak from a throne of arrogance. They tell people what to do. They don't believe racism exists within the court system.

Neither judges nor juries have to have affection for Blacks. What they have to have is objectivity and impartiality. The difficulty is bringing objectivity and impartiality to the process in this race-conscious nation. A jury clerk once showed me a legal pad that contained the jottings of the foreman of an all-white jury that was hearing a case against a Black defendant. The notations contained things like, "All niggers have guns" and "We should have Russian justice here—just shoot the bastards." There appeared to be a lament that the jury had to give "this nigger" a fair trial. Blacks have never sought favoritism or special treatment. All we want is fairness, for everybody to be treated the same.

The legal profession in America has done much to abate racism. In fact, what has been done to abate racism has been done largely by the legal profession. The problem with eliminating racism is the people in power are never fully cured. We need strong national leadership to eliminate racism, but that won't happen. The U.S. Supreme Court has been the instrument of segregation and suppression in this nation.

I've spoken out on the blatant racism in our courts because it was disgusting to see. It was sickening to see the preconceived notions of white judges who had never had any education concerning Black people and whose only experience with Blacks was generally with servants. These judges were filled with all kinds of stereotypical attitudes about us. You remember that fellow with one of the major league baseball teams—the Los Angeles Dodgers, I think—who said Blacks didn't have the brain power to manage a professional baseball team? This fellow was voicing what most people think, including many judges.

It is inescapable that white judges reach conclusions that reflect white community standards. There was a federal judge named Irving Ben Cooper, who sentenced these two defendants. One defendant was a white Wall Street stock broker convicted of making $250,000 from illegally selling stocks and perjuring himself before a federal grand jury. The other defendant was a Black truck driver convicted of stealing a television set from his truck—a TV that cost less than $100. From the bench, Cooper expressed his belief that the white defendant was unlikely to repeat his crime. He sentenced him to a year's probation with a ninety thousand dollar fine. The Black man was the sole supporter of a diabetic wife and daughter. Cooper sent him to prison for one year. Sending this Black man to prison may have satisfied some societal lust for vengeance, but it became society's folly. The Black man's wife was forced to go on welfare. For the white defendant, it would appear that crime did pay. It's simple math. He stole $250,000 and was forced to pay a ninety thousand dollar fine.

There are Black judges who are conservative, as conservative as some white judges. There are many Black judges who seem to be embarrassed when Blacks come before them. There are Black judges who see themselves as so remote in social distance from the Blacks who appear before them. They believe themselves to be charter members of the Black bourgeoisie. They are so white in their imitation of life and in their reactions to Black defendants that they are known as "Afro-Saxons." As soon as these Black judges put on the Black robes, they become emotionally white. But it's not surprising. We have Eurocentric educations. We learn white values. We've had a white education in this country.

Black judges should not be emotionally white. Black judges should know better, because they have had the Black experience and they have had the white experience. We have been discriminated against by white people. We have been arrested by them. We have worked the meanest, dirtiest jobs for them. They think of us in terms of criminals, waiters, and housekeepers—the lowest jobs that there are. Historically that has been our role in this country. We know more about white people than they know about us. It seems to me Blacks are better qualified to be judges in the kind of interracial society we have in this country, the "Afro-Saxons" notwithstanding.

Black judges rarely speak out on controversial subjects. They choose to maintain a low profile, wearing a mask of mute dignity. There are many so-called successful Blacks in America whose notions of conservatism reflect some of the same values as the most conservative whites. What some of us have learned is that it is better to kiss ass if you want to be successful—kowtow, bend your knee. We have seen that those who express what are generally called radical ideas and attitudes don't become mayors or legislators, and they certainly don't become judges.

The bane of Black progress in America is the burden of imagined respectability. However, historically, it has been the "respectable" white majority that has resisted change in racial and racist attitudes. Blacks who claim respectability and allow that mirage to keep them quiet, to keep them from being actors in the drama needed to change an oppressive society, are instruments of continued oppression.

There is a need for more Black judges. Historically the federal bench has almost universally been the preserve of white Protestants, white Christians. It was like a club. It's almost like the U.S. Senate—this is our thing for white people, the federal bench and the Senate.

Whether there is a conscious policy to keep Blacks off the bench or not doesn't matter, because the result is the same. We need not expect that when I step down in two years another Black judge will be my successor. It's just not in the cards.

The "ins" are always reluctant to step out of power. That is why we can't get more Black judges, Black administrators, and so on. Too many elected officials are afraid to appoint Blacks because they fear that will alienate white voters. Even Jack Kennedy, who is revered as the keeper of the flame along with Roosevelt, appointed some of the most racist judges you can imagine, especially in Mississippi, where it made the civil rights struggle even more difficult than it would otherwise have been.

One of the problems with really dealing with racism is people are unwilling to think beyond their own time. When President Roosevelt was confronted with a lawsuit to desegregate the nation's military he said, "What's wrong with segregation? It's always been with us!" There is a resistance to change. Change requires courage and there is too little courage in the political arena.

It's time that we really start integrating the bench, since we've had only white male judges for three hundred years. If we don't have Black judges and women judges on the bench, there is no point in fighting for integration, both racial and sexual. What is the point unless we can all participate and have a voice?

Racism and sexism are aberrations that must be challenged. It was the late Justice Thurgood Marshall who was brave enough to remind us during our patriotic orgasm of celebrating the bicentennial of the U.S. Constitution that the document was both racist and sexist.

We are entitled to the trappings of wealth if we succeed in life, but even if we don't we are entitled to a level playing field. White males are always arguing for a level playing field when the issue is affirmative action, but there never has been a level playing field. I don't think the current U.S. Supreme Court's conservative majority understands that things like set-asides are not for Blacks to get an advantage but to catch up.

There has never been nor is there now a level playing field for Blacks and women, but we as a society do not see this because we have been fed a history filled with lies and distortions. One of these distortions is that Blacks have always sought special breaks from the government when in fact the only thing we have sought is the same thing whites get—equality of opportunity, nothing more. Every day, scholastic perjury is committed in classrooms where students are taught, for example, that Columbus discovered America when in fact he never got close.

President George Bush said Clarence Thomas was the most qualified person to succeed Thurgood Marshall on the U.S. Supreme Court. He would be guilty of perjury if he had made that statement under oath. I would rather see a white liberal in that seat instead of Thomas. Absolutely. I think putting Ruth Ginsberg on the Court is good for women and those who do not subscribe to the views of Scalia and Thomas, but Ginsberg is not a screaming liberal, though she may have an interest in feminist issues.

The assertion that there are so few Black judges because there are so few qualified Black lawyers is ridiculous. One of former mayor Koch's top people used to say that. Black lawyers are as qualified as white lawyers. Now, that is another example of preconception about us, I suppose. Blacks go to law schools, pass the bar, and practice law just like whites. I don't know what they mean by a lack of qualifications unless there is some secret standard for being a judge that they haven't advertised yet. As I understand the standard, once you have been admitted to the bar for ten years you are eligible to run for a judgeship or to seek appointment.

I have testified against certain judges for their blatant racism. Yes I have. I have filed formal complaints against judges. And I resigned from the Harlem Lawyers Association when they wouldn't join me in protesting the conduct of one white judge. I believe the guy's name was George Carney.

This incident with Carney happened when I was practicing law. This particular judge had before him a white defendant to be sentenced, and the white defendant's white lawyer said, "Your Honor, place my client on probation. He can be rehabilitated."

The judge, looking through the presentence report, practically snarled in a courtroom full of Blacks and Latinos. "How is he going to be rehabilitated when he is living with a colored woman?" He said this not once but three times.

By the time he said it the third time, I realized that I, too, was living with what His Honor referred to as a "colored woman." My wife and I had parted that morning in a spirit of domestic *glasnost* and *perestroika* with a kiss, and I felt I should defend the honor of Black women.

I approached the bench with my hand up, announcing my membership in the bar, and I said, perhaps too sarcastically, "Your Honor, may I be heard on the question of the menace, jeopardy, and peril of living with what Your Honor calls a "colored woman"? Perhaps I have had a little more experience in this area than Your Honor, and I would be happy to offer you some survival techniques on living with a Black woman."

My mistake in confronting this judge was that I was angry and a little nasty in my tone. I was immediately surrounded by six white court officers, each with a loaded .38. Guns are guaranteed to temper the zeal of a coward such as myself, or even a brave man, knowing that those things are loaded. The judge did what I came to do when I became a judge. He called a recess and he left the bench.

I tried to have that judge removed from the bench. Eighty-five to 90 percent of the people who appear in New York City courts are Blacks and dark-skinned Latinos. I didn't think that a judge had the right to dispense justice with those kinds of attitudes toward Black women.

The president of the Harlem Lawyers Association asked me to draft a petition. He said, "We need to get this guy off the bench. Here he is presiding in the criminal court where 90 percent of the defendants are Black or dark Latinos. We can't have this."

I drafted the petition. The president called an emergency meeting of the association. The general sentiment expressed by the leaders of that association was, "Bruce is crazy. He is a radical. He may not be in politics, but we are not going to jeopardize our political careers by testifying against this man." They voted not to support me even though they lived with "colored women" themselves. I filed the complaint myself and I was the only witness against this guy.

Then the NAACP came into the picture and accepted the judge's apology. By the way, the apology was dictated by the judge's lawyer. The judge didn't seem to read it to me. He just put his initials on it. So he apologized. It was accepted by the NAACP. The judge said I was trying to crucify him. I said I had no interest in elevating him to the level of the deity. He was promoted shortly thereafter.

I once challenged a judge who told a Black defendant he wouldn't know the difference between a good lawyer and a watermelon. I challenged another judge who remarked about a nigger being in the woodpile. You have got to protest. You have to protest against the problems you see. Otherwise white society will think you love what it is doing to you, and they will think you will accept anything. What did Frederick Douglass tell us in his last will and testament? "Agitate, Agitate, Agitate." That is what he told us to do. If you don't do that you become complacent, smug, self-satisfied. You are in trouble then.

But there is a price to pay for protest, even in this land of free speech. If you speak out you are ostracized or penalized in some way. I have been penalized in many ways during my time on the bench. My life has been threatened numerous times by cowards acting under the cloak of anonymity, and I have been censured, vindictively, by authorities. I've learned that freedom of speech stops at the courthouse door. I've been hauled before discipline committees for speaking out. You would think the courthouse would be the place for free speech.

When I was assigned to criminal court, I was always assigned to night court on Christmas, New Year's, Thanksgiving, and Easter. I'd get all of the holidays, Veterans Day, you name it. Just being in night court was one of the ways of being penalized. Being assigned to work every holiday was further punishment.

When you are assigned to night court in the Bronx, a police car is supposed to transport you home at night because you often end up leaving court at two or three in the morning. Because the Bronx is considered such a war zone, it is customary to have police transport. But I never once was given police transport. I took the subway or a gypsy cab.

Even my mail has been tampered with. It has always been my habit to buy a series ticket to the U.S. Open Tennis Championship. One year my ticket disappeared, somehow, in the mail.

Once I was summarily transferred from the criminal court to the civil court at the special request of the Patrolmen's Benevolent Association (PBA), the union representing New York City police. The chief judge of the court of appeals lied about how the transfer happened. The administrative judge lied about how it happened. The former judge in whose chair I now sit lied about how it happened. It was finally through one of our spies at the Bar Association that we brought to heel the chief judge of the court of appeals, Charles Breitel. Breitel had been overheard in a conversation among other white men saying that he had transferred Wright. He had ordered Wright transferred. Nobody else did. Breitel thought no one would repeat what he said, because he was speaking among other white men. The administrative judge had testified that my transfer had resulted from my name being drawn from a hat containing the names of other judges. My name just happened to be picked from this hat. That was the testimony.

I commenced a federal legal action against the administrative judge, the DA, and the PBA. It was only after we sought to depose and examine the chief judge of the state court of appeals under oath before trial that he sent back the subpoena and the check we had sent for his transportation and ordered that I be sent back to the criminal court.

I have been censured any number of times before the state commission on judicial conduct because of complaints by the Patrolmen's Benevolent Association. Many of my problems with the police have arisen from my strange belief that everybody should be treated the same in court, including the police.

Most citizens of this country regard the police as the first line of protection against criminals. With so many of those who are arrested and charged with criminal conduct being Blacks and dark-skinned Hispanics, white society naturally sides with the police, regarding them as heroic guardians. Yet Blacks are outraged every time a white officer is acquitted of killing a Black. Such acquittals confirm the belief that no white officer will ever be convicted for shooting a Black, regardless of the evidence.

My slightest disagreements with police have been quickly reported to the newspapers and television stations by "Bruce Watchers" within the system—court officers, assistant district attorneys, and the like.

For example, I was in night court when a man was brought in for shooting a policeman. This man was charged with shooting the policeman, not killing him. The defendant had been shot through the jaw when he was captured. He couldn't even talk. His mouth was wired up. He found it difficult to even stand up. The courtroom was filled with police who felt that their presence would somehow ensure that I would impose a tremendous bail on the defendant.

Well, as we were preparing for this hearing, the police were in the courtroom talking and laughing and farting. Finally my clerk said to me, "Your Honor, do you want me to arrest these bastards for you?"

I said, "No, no. I'll take care of it."

I then pounded on the bench and said, "Let me tell you guys something. I don't expect you to respect me. I wouldn't ask you to do that. I wouldn't demand it. But you will respect this court. It is three hundred years old. You will respect this court. And if you want to talk to me outside—park your gun and talk to me man to man—that's another matter."

I also said, "By the way, Dr. Freud has written a little monograph about you policemen. He says that in a man's world it is a great glory to have a penis, but you guys have to have three: a night stick, the gun, and the other one." Well, that was reported to the authorities. I was accused of making intemperate remarks from the bench. I guess my sense of humor had taken over. One thing I've always thought I should have said to those officers that night was, "You know if you guys were arrested for streaking, the case would have to be dismissed for insufficient evidence."

I was charged with judicial misconduct another time. I was accused of corruption of justice for allegedly showing favor to a young white model. Apparently there is a belief that Black men are always susceptible to white women. The only time I had ever been in her home was when my wife and I went to see this woman's love, Yul Brenner, the movie star.

I have remained a judge in New York City by virtue of the united efforts of the Black community in Brooklyn, the Bronx, Queens, and Manhattan. Black people in this city have written letters to the administrative judge strongly supporting me. An administrative judge once had the nerve to stop me and say, "Wright, you are always complaining that you don't have any friends. Look at these letters," and he showed me letters that had been written by people who were illiterate.

The general theme of those letters was, "Leave that motherfucking judge alone or we will burn the motherfucking courthouse down."

I have had the support of poor Black people in this city. And I want you to know that it is deeply, deeply touching to me, the affection that they have shown me. One time when my people were campaigning for my reelection they went to the public housing projects, where people wouldn't open their doors. My campaigners would say, "I would like to give you some literature for Bruce Wright. He wants to be elected as blah-blah judge." The residents wouldn't open their doors. Finally, the campaigners had to say, "Look, we're representing Turn 'em Loose Bruce.' "

Well, when the people heard that—"Turn 'em Loose Bruce"—they would open doors and invite my people in for cake and coffee, and say that they were going to vote. You never know whether they did vote or not, but "Turn 'em Loose Bruce" is a term of affection in Harlem, the South Bronx, Bedford-Stuyvesant, and Jamaica, Queens. Black people have been extremely kind to me, and I know that I wouldn't be on the bench today without them. Most of these folks are just common people, urban peasants, of which I am one.

Many of my colleagues think I am crazy, a person who deliberately opposes the system, because I speak out. I have thus forfeited opportunities reserved for those Blacks who know their place and keep it. I've been told I could have easily been promoted if I would only have kept my place and stopped making critical statements about the judicial system and accusing it of being racist. I wasn't supposed to attack the police either. I was expected to express gratitude for my position and, of course, expected not to engage in public discussion of the defects in the criminal justice system.

I have been accused of being a Black man who hates the guts of all whites. Well, this is a curious comment since I had a white mother who was affectionate and devoted. I certainly loved her.

One of the saddest days in the life of my proud Irish mother was when Notre Dame, the most famous American Catholic university, refused to admit her son, exhibiting the same racism as Protestant Princeton.

I had been given a four-year scholarship to Princeton, but I was snatched away from registration when it was discovered I was "colored." The director of admissions had me hauled into his office. I thought he was going to commend me for rejecting Harvard. The director, Radcliffe Heermance, told me that under no circumstance could I attend Princeton, because a number of southerners attended the university and their attitudes must be respected. He told me to consider a school for my own kind. Yet he told me he liked Blacks and that his Black cook lived in his home.

This experience shattered my belief in America—my belief that you can be anything that you want.

My mother said she should have sent me to Notre Dame. She thought Notre Dame would welcome my coming, but Catholic Notre Dame was no better than Protestant Princeton. I was told by Father Reardon that Notre Dame rejected my application due to the "unfortunate circumstance" in which Blacks came to this country and because southern students at the school would not like my being there and they had to be respected.

I got to the bench purely by accident. I was appointed to the criminal court without ever having any ambitions whatsoever to be a judge. None.

I was perfectly happy in the practice of the law. My wife and I had practiced law together. My wife died, and I was quite depressed about that. Various politicians had been trying to get me to go into public service for a long time. So in 1967 when Mayor John Lindsay sent his talent-scouting team to my office, I yielded and became general counsel to the Human Resources Administration.

One day a few years later I was called to the mayor's office in City Hall. I thought I must have done something wrong. I must have committed some terrible, atrocious error. When I got to the mayor's office he asked me whether I would like to be a judge. My response was that I had no money to buy the office. The traditional notion was you had to have money to buy a judgeship.

The mayor blanched and said, "Of course you don't need any money." I said, "I'll think about it." I consulted my older sons, who were then teenagers, and they said, "Oh, yeah, Dad, it ought to be fun. Try it." So I accepted the mayor's offer. It was a moment of weakness in my character, you might say.

Two weeks after I was on the bench, a man named Tingling stopped me in Foley Square and said, "Bruce, how much did you pay? I was supposed to be next." That's what he said to me. He was astonished to learn that I had paid nothing and that I probably didn't have anything to pay.

I have never known exactly how much it has cost to purchase a judgeship. I do know that back in 1948 or '49 I heard a figure of one hundred thousand dollars. At the time, I was a prodigy of the first Black judge we ever had in this state, a man named James S. Watson. I happened to have been in Watson's home, in his study, when a delegation from Tammany Hall came in to talk to him. They looked to me suspiciously and asked if they could talk to the judge in private. They went into the next room and closed the sliding doors. When Watson came back, after they had gone, he had tears in his eyes. He finally took a drink of scotch and then he said to me, "Mayor O'Dwyer says it's time to have the city's first Negro supreme court justice, and they asked me, Bruce. But I don't have the hundred thousand dollars." That's what he said.

The position on the supreme court was offered to another Black gentleman, an assemblyman. I understand he didn't have the hundred thousand dollars either, but the mayor said, "Oh, hell, at least he's a Catholic." I would not have been surprised if there had been a run on conversions in Harlem among lawyers trying to better position themselves for consideration as judicial candidates.

One of my major motivations for writing the book *Black Robes, White Justice* was a cash advance from the publisher. The cash was one incentive. Another motivation was that Toni Morrison, the author, had asked me to write a book on what makes Bruce Wright Bruce Wright. At the time, I had been sketching some notes on how to civilize my judicial colleagues.

Prentice-Hall gave me a contract that said they would not pay me unless the manuscript was acceptable. They paid me, so I assumed it was acceptable. They had even sent me a proposed jacket design, asking for my approval. Then they had a change of administration at this publishing firm. I was told they would not publish the book because they were afraid they would be sued for libel by some of the individuals I named in the book. And so I waited six years for the statute of limitations to run out so they couldn't ask for their $13,000 back. I gave the book to another agent, and the agent finally landed it with another publisher, Lyle Stuart.

You know, not one white judge or one Black judge has ever mentioned that book to me? My white judicial colleagues don't speak to me. One fellow judge said, "Don't worry about getting the silent treatment. It's a fringe benefit."

I don't know what the white judges think of me but some Black judges think that I'm crazy. That is a valid thought, I suppose. Racism will make you crazy. We have a number of people in this country who, in my view, have been rendered absolutely insane by the racism in America.

What to do about crime and criminals is a question I have pondered often. It confounds me. It is clear the current approach is not working. Locking people away, warehousing people in these horrible prisons, has not provided satisfactory relief from crime. It simply has not worked.

The criminal justice system cannot deter crime. It never has and it never will.

I do not believe in jails. I have made that quite clear to the authorities in the time I have been on the bench. I do not send people to jail. That's how I got my nickname, "Turn 'em Loose Bruce."

Jails do not rehabilitate. They are dehumanizing. Jails will take you out of circulation for a while, but then you come back dehumanized and you are worse than ever. All you need to do is read the newspapers about people who are arrested and accused of certain crimes and you see that they had been convicted in the past and are out again.

Most prisons are carbon copies of the mean neighborhoods where most of the nonwhite prisoners come from. The prisoners are living in the same environment, just behind bars. How can we expect them to change? After the Attica riot one prisoner said there was no way prisoners were going to be rehabilitated because they'd never been "habilitated" in the first place.

Now if the prisons that we send poor Blacks and Latinos to were like the prisons that Nixon's Watergate gang was sent to, I'd sentence everybody to prison. The jails that oval-office gang went to had swimming pools, tennis courts, and wonderful libraries. You write books in those places, come out, and make a lot of money on talk shows.

We specialize in custody and ignore rehabilitation when it comes to the poor, Blacks, and Latinos. We have to give rehabilitation a try. I happen to think some people can be rehabilitated and we must try.

We must take the chance. For example, I've always felt that narcotics cases were better suited for hospital than jail. However, not very many people share my view.

I think we have to use all of the resources society has to address the causes of criminal behavior. As a society we rely on social workers and psychoanalysts, but we don't adequately utilize these professionals for prisoners.

One of the other things the powers that be didn't like about me when I was in criminal court was that I refused to fine prostitutes or send them to jail. A woman can do whatever she wishes with her body. A woman can have an abortion, so why can't she be a prostitute? They don't prosecute the johns who solicit the prostitutes the same way they prosecute the prostitutes. These periodic crackdowns on johns are just so much show. It's usually some poor fellow.

I am opposed to jails. They don't work. We often forget the fact, or just ignore the fact that many of those who are put in jail are falsely accused and falsely convicted. The law makes mistakes many times. The fact that the law makes mistakes seems to me to be the best argument against the death penalty in this country, especially because there are so many Blacks being given the death penalty.

Just last week the *New York Times* had a study on the death penalty and remarked that if you kill a white and you are Black, you are going to get the death penalty. Yet if you kill a Black, whether you are white or Black, it is not likely that you will go to the electric chair. It is a sad fact that all too often a Black is rewarded with a minimal rap on the wrist for harming another Black but is lashed harshly by the judicial system if he harms or deprives a white.

The death penalty doesn't deter murder. Most murders are committed by people who know each other. These murders are committed in a fit of passion or madness. Plus, people who can afford good representation don't go to the electric chair.

Judges play a big part in the process that is filling up our overcrowded jails with the poor and nonwhites. It's like an assembly line feeding right into the prisons. Many judges have a desire to be portrayed as tough in the tabloid press, so they hand out all these excessive sentences. I guess they want to be seen the same way as the politicians who appear in TV commercials standing in the jailhouse door, saying how tough on crime they are.

Politicians are always threatening to get tough on crime, but the more they threaten to stop crime and imprison criminals, the more crime we have. Most of the criminals today are the poor, the underclass. It seems to me that our society manufactures both the poor and its criminal element.

Much of what is defined as crime today is in many ways a violent, perverse reaction to generations of discrimination, deprivation, and exclusion. The hopeless desperation of poverty can provoke an attitude of "I got nothing to lose . . . why should I follow society's rules when they don't benefit me?"

When I tell my white colleagues that you cannot divorce the events of today from the historical context of racism, they claim that there are "advantages" for Blacks today. And they'll also say that whites do not commit crimes in the same proportion as Blacks—even poor whites. But Blacks have never lynched whites or barred them from their swimming pools, jobs, or neighborhoods. Blacks have not allowed racial vengeance to dictate their votes in jury verdicts. By pointing this out, I am not defending Black criminals or their crimes. I have never defended criminals or violent crime.

It doesn't require penetrating insight to see clearly how poverty provides a fertile ground for crime, even the violent crimes that seem to have no connection to poverty. Yet we as a nation have stopped trying to help the poor.

People used to ridicule the notion that poverty aids and abets crime. Now that idea is being reexamined. Poverty does incite crime. There are people in many cities who are destitute yet they see a great deal of wealth on the Park Avenues and the Madison Avenues. You would have fewer larcenies if there was a redistribution of the wealth. The tremendous imbalance between wealth and poverty in this country creates temptation in the have-nots. As Oscar Wilde used to say, "The only thing I couldn't resist is temptation!"

Racism in America is going to have to be dealt with if we as a nation are ever going to meaningfully deal with crime and the problems in the criminal justice system. That is my belief. Racism is ingrained in this country.

Some years ago when they were discussing having a new federal constitutional convention, where Blacks, women, and others could be present, the *New York Times* and CBS did a poll on what people would think about a federal constitutional convention. There was a surprising percentage of white people in this country who said, "Yes, we would like that, so long as the new constitution has a provision for racial discrimination."

A fellow once came up to me while I was having dinner with a friend, interrupted our conversation and said, "You know, if we ever have slavery in this country again, I would like to own you." Now, that is not a rare or unusual expression for white people. I have always felt that if whites were treated like Blacks, if whites were deprived of the fundamental rights guaranteed by the Constitution, they would have resorted to guerrilla warfare long, long ago.

Change in the justice system will have to come from judges. And for that change to work, judges have to be better educated. I think judges should be trained to be judges the way they are in certain countries, such as France. There is little chance of changing the system until society is prepared to better educate its judges before they go onto the bench.

Certainly judges should have sensitivity training. Judges should be trained in the subtleties of our multiracial society. These subtleties adversely influence the ideal of objectivity that all judges are supposed to ascribe to. Yes, judges have to have keen minds, and the ability to analyze and cut through the emotional arguments that are presented. But judges have to have an understanding of what our society is really like.

Judges or anyone wishing to practice law in our society should be required to study suppressed aspects of American history, like the legal subjugation of Blacks and other nonwhites. Judges have to understand the extent to which racist and transparently false premises have been transformed into policy. During the Great Depression, for example, police departments across this nation went from using .32-caliber revolvers to using .38-caliber guns because it was said that the smaller guns would not penetrate Black skin, particularly not the skin of Blacks addicted to cocaine. When it was asked how poor, destitute Blacks could afford cocaine, the question was ignored.

Yes, judges should study Black history. Just studying the lawsuits that Blacks have filed against racist practices in all sectors of our society would be an illuminating lesson for whites on the true meaning of democracy.

Learning these lessons might promote the even-handed justice that is now lacking in our judicial system. The current course of study is whitewashed, a fairy tale version, for the most part. With its exclusive focus on white history and white values this course of study only perpetuates the problems that preclude fairness. No judge should come to the bench as ignorant of Black circumstances as they now are.

No person should be put on the bench unless they pass a test on Black history and know the experiences of Blacks. Judging is a sociological calling as much as a legal one. The *Brown* school desegregation decision is an interesting and unprecedented mixture of law and sociology. Judges, prosecutors, and police need better educations in history and sociology before assuming their jobs.

I also think judges should have to pass psychological tests to see if racism taints their perceptions of fairness.

There are lots of things that have to be done, and generations are going to pass before you see any results—assuming for the sake of argument that those things are done. . .